Reflections on 100 Years of
Experimental Social Psychology

Reflections on 100 Years of Experimental Social Psychology

Edited by

Aroldo Rodrigues and
Robert V. Levine

BASIC
BOOKS

A Member of the Perseus Books Group

Copyright © 1999 by Basic Books, A Member of the Perseus Books Group

Published in 1999 in the United States of America by Basic Books, 10 East 53rd Street, New York, NY 10022

Library of Congress Cataloging-in-Publication Data
Reflections on 100 years of experimental social psychology / edited by Aroldo
   Rodrigues, Robert V. Levine.
      p.   cm.
   Collected contributions of a conference held in the Spring of 1997
at Yosemite National Park—Info. p.
   Includes bibliographical references and index.
   ISBN 0-8133-9086-9 (hardcover)
      1. Social psychology—History—Congresses.   2. Social psychology—
Biography.   I. Rodrigues, Aroldo.   II. Levine, Robert, 1945–   .
III. Title: Reflections on one hundred years of experimental social psychology.
HM251.R42   1999
302'.09—dc21   98-53162
                                                                                        CIP

The paper used in this publication meets the requirements of the American National Standard for Permanence of Paper for Printed Library Materials Z39.48-1984.

10   9   8   7   6   5   4   3   2   1

To Kurt Lewin, Fritz Heider, and Leon Festinger,
the leaders of the band

Contents

Preface

The beginning of modern experimental social psychology is most often traced to Norman Triplett's 1898 study of bicycle racers 100 years ago.[1] This book celebrates that century milestone by asking nine legends to look back upon the history of the field that they themselves have been so integral in creating.

Of course, the discipline of social psychology may be viewed as considerably older than 100 years. In his chapter on the history of the discipline in the second edition of *The Handbook of Social Psychology,* Gordon Allport argued that a case can be made that the founder of social psychology was Plato, or perhaps Aristotle, or at least one of the later political philosophers like Thomas Hobbes and Jeremy Bentham. Or, he suggests, we could look in more recent times for our founding father, perhaps to one of the great thinkers of the nineteenth century—such as Hegel, Comte, Lazarus, and Steinthal—who wrote about social psychological issues. But all of these early ancestors limited their social psychology to theory and philosophy. It is experimental social psychology whose beginnings are generally traced to Triplett's experiment.

Then again, to many of today's practitioners of the field, experimental social psychology is actually several decades younger than 100 years. As we shall see in the chapters that follow, the functional beginnings of modern experimental—or at least empirical—social psychology are most often located in the work of Kurt Lewin and his Research Center for Group Dynamics in the late 1930s and 1940s. Several of the contributors to this book worked with Lewin; all were closely associated with the next generation of his successors. Morton Deutsch captures the striking overlap between the modern era of the field and the careers of this book's contributors when he begins his chapter: "My life almost spans the existence of modern social psychology."

The relatively short span of experimental social psychology's history offers a unique opportunity for intimate reflection. The writer Tony Hiss once commented: "Our relationship with the places we know and meet up with—where you are right now; and where you've been earlier today; and wherever you'll be in another few hours—is a close bond, intricate in nature, and not abstract, not remote at all; it's enveloping, almost a continuum with all we are and think."[2] This sense of intimate connection to Triplett's experiment, and certainly to Lewin and his followers, is communicated throughout this book.

In 1996 Robert Cialdini, as president of the Society for Personality and Social Psychology, began a symposium on Lewin with the proclamation: "I would like to declare personality and social psychology a mature discipline." If Cialdini's claim is justified, the authors of the following nine chapters are certainly among those most responsible for leading us through our adolescence. This exceptional group of scholars have not only observed the course of our field but have been the crafters of its very history.

The present book grows out of a one and one-half day conference on the edge of Yosemite National Park, in March 1997, which brought this same group together to reflect on the history of the field. Experimental social psychology is a remarkably active discipline, with theory, research, and applications flowing at an ever increasing pace. With the notable exception of the so-called crisis in social psychology during the 1970s, however, social psychologists have rarely interrupted their frantic activity to ponder about the field, the course it has taken, the changes that have taken place, the roots from which it has grown, and the eventual corrections of course needed.

When the Yosemite conference was conceived, its objective was to gather together a sample of outstanding social psychologists, all with an unequivocal role in the development of the field. The core of the invited group was composed of some of the stars of the Lewinian generation: Len Berkowitz, Morton Deutsch, Hal Kelley, Hal Gerard, Al Pepitone, and Bert Raven. We added to this three eminent representatives of what Leon Festinger called the "third generation" of social psychologists: Elliot Aronson, Bob Zajonc, and Phil Zimbardo. Initially, Stan Schachter was to be a member of this group. But sadly, the illness that was to take his life months later caused him to cancel shortly before the conference began.

The "dream team," as they came to be called, were given a wide berth—to reflect freely upon the first century of the discipline. They were asked to comment on the development of experimental social psychology from whatever perspective—personal, historical, conceptual—they deemed most valuable. Each gave prepared presentations, which were accompanied by considerable discussion, both formal and informal. The conference was a remarkable event. Many of the speakers had not seen each other in years. To observe them together and hear their interchanges over that day was an electrifying experience for those fortunate enough to attend. The chapters in this book originated in these presentations and discussions.[3]

This book falls in the considerable shadow of Festinger's edited *Retrospections on Social Psychology,* published in 1980, a project for which four of the current contributors also wrote chapters. There are two significant differences between that book and this one. First, almost two decades—two active and eventful decades—have elapsed since the publication of Festinger's volume. If we opt to locate Lewin as the marker of the modern era of social psychology, then about one-third of our history has occurred since the Festinger *Retrospections* appeared. Second, the contributors to Festinger's book focused upon areas of research—

usually the authors' own specialties—within social psychology. As Festinger observed about the chapters in his volume, they were not intended to "represent an examination of all social psychology but, rather, a selection of what certain individuals think would show the field in its best light." The present contributions, in contrast, look back upon the development of the discipline itself. These reflections are both broader than those in Festinger's book and, in most cases, more personal.

Organization of the Book

The chapters that follow offer the richness of insiders' perspectives. Each is preceded by a brief abstract prepared by the editors. Some of the chapters take a more biographical approach; others focus more on a critical analysis of the discipline. All of them offer an extraordinary source of information, as well as critical analyses, trends detected, and anecdotes pertaining to 100 years of experimental social psychology. They are very loosely ordered from the more biographical to the more analytical—from the most personal reflections to the most conceptual. We have tried to arrange the more biographical chapters in terms of their historical roots, beginning with those going back furthest in time. On the anchors, this ordering was fairly easy to decide. We begin with Morton Deutsch's very personal autobiography of a career stretching back to Lewin's Research Center for Group Dynamics (RCGD) at the Massachusetts Institute of Technology (MIT), and even to Deutsch's meetings with Clark Hull before that. The final chapter contains Robert Zajonc's attempt to classify a century of social psychology according to researchers' views of the basic nature of the individual—specifically, the extent to which individuals are conceptualized as rational or irrational in their actions. Most of the chapters, however, are more difficult to classify. They combine personal reflections with conceptual observations, anecdotes with discussion of research and research trends. The sequence of these chapters is sometimes arbitrary.

What is not arbitrary is the authority of each of the contributors. In his introductory remarks at the Yosemite conference, the first editor described these unique scholars as "the makers of social psychology, those who helped to shape the field; a 'dream team' of social psychologists whose names we repeat over and over again in our social psychology courses . . . those who, in their work, not only enhanced the status of social psychology as a science, but also provided inspiration to so many other researchers and trained so many other students, who now disseminate their ideas, their findings, and their teaching."

Eudora Welty, in the autobiography *One Writer's Beginnings,* observed: "Through travel I first became aware of the outside world; it was through travel that I found my own introspective way into becoming a part of it." In the nine chapters that follow, we are offered reflections from some of the keenest of observers who have traveled the history of experimental social psychology. One of the great figures of travel writing, Nathaniel Hawthorne's Wakefield, went on the road so he could see what was "true" about the home he left. Here are what nine of the most important makers of social psychology see when, like Wakefield, they look back at what is true there.

Aroldo Rodrigues
Robert V. Levine

Notes

1. More specifically, the date of Triplett's most often referenced publication on the topic is 1897–1898: Norman Triplett, "The Dynamogenic Factors in Pacemaking and Competition," *American Journal of Psychology, 9,* 507–533.

2. Tony Hiss, *The Experience of Place* (New York: Vintage Books, 1990), p. xi.

3. A videotape of the Yosemite conference is available from the authors.

Acknowledgments

We wish to thank a number of individuals for making both the Yosemite conference and this book possible. First, we thank President John Welty, former provost Alex Gonzalez, and Dean K. P. Wong of California State University, Fresno, for their generous support of the conference. We also wish to thank Lynnette Zelezny, Chris Wilhite, Tom Breen, Sergio Aguilar-Gaxiola, Connie Jones, Bev Karau, Sheri Osborn, and Wanda Patton for their crucial and extraordinary work both leading up to and during the conference. Thanks are also due to our many other colleagues who supported this conference from the beginning and to the students—including John Thomas, Barbara Martinez, Robyn Williams, Albert Rodriguez, Poh Chua, and Kim Khoo—who helped us at the meeting and later, in preparations for this book. We thank John Boyd for his magic and dedication in producing a film of the conference. We thank Lisa Wigutoff for her extremely capable stewardship through the final months of this project and Alice Colwell for her superb copyediting. And we are, of course, very grateful to editor Cathy Murphy of Westview Press for having first recognized the importance of bringing to light the reflections of a "dream team" of social psychologists upon a field that owes so much to them.

A. R.
R. V. L.

1   A Personal Perspective on the Development of Social Psychology in the Twentieth Century

Morton Deutsch

Reflecting on his career as a social psychologist, Morton Deutsch guides us through a remarkable number of significant events that have shaped the field. He begins with his experiences under the leadership of Kurt Lewin and the impact of the intellectual atmosphere that prevailed at the Research Center for Group Dynamics, which shaped not only his dissertation but his entire value orientation as a social psychologist. He tells of his later work within the more applied atmosphere of the National Training Laboratory led by Ron Lippitt, describing his own particular research and many of the indelible contributions he has made to the field. Deutsch observes that his career as a social psychologist has centered on two continuing themes: cooperation, competition, and conflict on the one hand and distributive justice on the other. He concludes his reflections with the hope that future social psychologists will achieve a successful integration of three of the intellectual heroes of his youth: Freud, Marx, and Lewin.

My life almost spans the existence of modern social psychology. My commentary on social psychology will be from the personal perspective of a reflection on my career as a social psychologist and the factors, social and personal, that influenced its development. However, I shall precede my autobiographical reflection with a brief commentary on the development of social psychology prior to my exposure to it.

Although modern social psychology was born in the first decades of the twentieth century, its ancestry in social philosophy can be traced back to ancient times. (For an excellent review of the precursors of modern social psychology, see Allport, 1954a). It is a child of psychology and sociology, having been conceived in the ambivalent mood of optimism and despair that has characterized the scientific age. The rapidly expanding knowledge, the increasing confidence in scientific methods, the ever quickening technological change with its resulting opportunities and social problems, the development of new social organizations and of social planning, the social turmoil, the repeated disruption of communities and social traditions—all these helped to create both the need for social psychology and the awareness of the possibility that scientific methods might be applied to the understanding of social behavior.

Charles Darwin's theory of evolution dominated the intellectual atmosphere of the time, and it became a model for early theorists in social psychology, who also set as their goal the achievement of a broad, encompassing theory of social behavior. The programmatic statements of theorists such as Charles Cooley (1902), Gabriel Tarde (1903), William McDougall (1908), and Edward Ross (1908) were grandly ambitious in scope but meager in detail. Many of the initial explanations of social behavior were made in terms of such processes as sympathy, imitation, and suggestion, which, in turn, were thought to be instinctually determined. The "herd instinct," the "instinct of submission," the "parental instinct," and a host of other instincts were invoked as innate, evolutionarily derived causes of behavior.

The instinctual doctrines, however, did not last long. By the middle of the 1920s, they were in retreat. The prestige of the empirical methods in the physical sciences, the point of view of social determinism advanced by Karl Marx and various sociological theorists, and the findings of cultural anthropologists all contributed to their downfall. The two emphases in the rebellion against the instinctivist position, the rejection of the notion of instinctually caused behavior and the methodological stress on empirical procedures, still color contemporary social psychology. Empiricism is an inheritance from psychology; environmentalism is a legacy of sociology.

Opposition to the doctrine of instincts and, along with it, the minimization of genetic as compared to environmental influences upon social behavior led to many studies that illustrated the effects of social factors on individual psychological processes. (Bartlett's [1932] "Social Factors in Recall," Sherif's [1936] "Group Influences Upon the Formation of Norms and Attitudes," and Piaget's [1948] "Social Factors in Moral Judgment" are classic studies of this genre.) In consonance with the rapid social changes so characteristic of the modern period, investigations by social psychologists challenged long-held views about the fixity of human nature and about the innate superiority or inferiority of any social class, national group, or race. Social psychologists were not initially unsympathetic to J. B. Watson's (1930) extravagant assertion that "there is no such thing as inheritance of capacity, talent, temperament, mental constitution, and characteristics." More recently, there has been recognition that any full explanation of the development of human behavior must take into account the genetically determined biological equipment with which individuals confront their environment; even more lately, the emergence of "evolutionary social psychology" reflects this emphasis. Yet almost all social psychologists still reject the view of innate superiority-inferiority and the notion that social behavior is "fixed" by instinct.

The rejection of abstract theorizing about social behavior in favor of empirical investigation provided the stimulus for the development of a variety of methods for studying social behavior: questionnaires of various sorts to measure opinions and attitudes; systematic interviews to obtain information about the motivations underlying behavior; controlled observational procedures to describe and classify behavior in social situations; methods of content analysis to analyze speeches, documents, and newspapers; sociometric techniques to study the social bonds and patterns of social interaction within a community; projective instruments for the study of personality patterns; and so forth. These methods have been extensively applied in public opinion polling, consumer research, studies of morale, investigations of prejudice and discrimination, personnel selection, and the like.

This revolt against armchair theorizing led many social psychologists not only to leave their armchairs but also to stop theorizing. Or perhaps it is more accurate to say that social psychologists who began to engage in empirical research in the 1920s and early 1930s did little to connect their research with theoretical ideas. During this same period, the psychoanalysts and also the early theorists abandoned their armchairs mainly for the lecture podium.

Toward the end of the 1930s, under the enthusiastic but gentle leadership of Kurt Lewin, modern experimental social psychology began to flourish. Lewin and his students demonstrated that it is possible to create and study groups in the experimental laboratory that have important features in common with real-life groups. In doing so, they stimulated an interest in social psychological experimentation and attracted many experimentalists to work in this area.

Autobiography: Presocial Psychology

I was born, prematurely, in 1920 into a Jewish middle-class family in New York City, the last of four sons. I was always eager to catch up with my older brothers, feeling like an underdog, so I skipped through elementary and high school and entered the City College of New York (CCNY) in 1935 at the age of fifteen: two and a half years younger than most students.

I started off as a pre-med major with the idea of becoming a psychiatrist, having been intrigued by the writings of Sigmund Freud, some of which I read before college. I was drawn to psychoanalysis undoubtedly because it appeared to be so relevant to the personal issues with which I was struggling, and also because it was so radical and rebellious (it seemed to be so in the early and mid-1930s). During my adolescence, I was also politically radical and somewhat rebellious toward authority, helping to organize a student strike against the terrible food in the high school lunchroom and, later, a strike against the summer resort owners who were exploiting the college student waiters, of whom I was one.

The 1930s were a turbulent period, internationally as well as domestically. The economic depression; labor unrest; the rise of Nazism and other forms of totalitarianism; the Spanish civil war; the ideas of Marx, Freud, and Albert Einstein; as well as the impending second world war were shaping the intellectual atmosphere that affected psychology. Several members of the psychology faculty at CCNY were active in creating the Psychologist League, the precursor to the Society for the Psychological Study of Social Issues. Thus when I became disenchanted with the idea of being a pre-med student after dissecting a pig in a biology lab, I was happy to switch to a psychology major: It was a simpatico faculty. Psychology was a part of the Department of Philosophy at CCNY when I started my major in it. Morris Raphael Cohen, the distinguished philosopher of science, was the leading intellectual figure at CCNY, and his influence permeated the atmosphere.

At CCNY Max Hertzman introduced me to the ideas of Kurt Lewin and other Gestalt theorists. And under Walter Scott Neff's direction, I conducted my first laboratory experiment, a variation on Sherif's study of social norms, employing the autokinetic effect. As I now recall, in it I introduced a stooge who constantly judged the stationary speck of light in a dark room as having moved a substantial distance in one direction. (Most subjects see the light as moving small distances in varying directions.) The stooge has a considerable impact on the judgments made by the naive, majority of subjects. The findings of this pilot study anticipated later research by Serge Moscovici on minority influence.

My first exposure to Lewin's writings was in two undergraduate courses, taken simultaneously: social psychology and personality and motivation. In the social psychology course, one of our textbooks was J. F. Brown's *Psychology and the Social Order* (1936). This was an ambitious, challenging, and curious text that tried to apply to the major social issues of the 1930s Lewinian and Marxian ideas, with a sprinkling of the Riemanian geometry employed by Einstein in his theory of relativity. To a naive seventeen-year-old undergraduate student like me, it was a very impressive and inspiring book showing how social science could shed light on the urgent problems of our time.

In the personality and motivation course, I read Lewin's *Dynamic Theory of Personality* (1935) and *Principles of Topological Psychology* (1936). I also read his *Conceptual Representation and Measurement of Psychological Forces* (1938) as an undergraduate, but I cannot recall when. I and others experienced great intellectual excitement on reading these books more than fifty years ago. *A Dynamic Theory of Personality* consisted of a collection of independent articles, previously published in the early 1930s, whereas the other books made a brilliant but flawed attempt to articulate the foundations of a scientific psychology with the aid of topology. They were mind openers. These books are permeated by a view of the nature of psychological science different from what was then traditional. The new view was characterized by Lewin as the "Galilean mode of thought," which was contrasted with the classical "Aristotelian mode." In my writings on field theory (Deutsch, 1968), I have characterized in some detail Lewin's approach to psychological theorizing, his metatheory.

Although I was impressed by Lewin's writings, my career aspirations in psychology were still focused on becoming a psychoanalytic psychologist as I decided to do graduate work in psychology. My undergraduate experiences, in as well as outside the classroom, led me to believe that an integration of psychoanalysis, Marxism, and scientific method, as exemplified by Lewin's work, could be achieved. In the 1930s such influential figures as Wilhelm Reich, Erich Fromm, Max Horkheimer, Theodor Adorno, and Else Frenkel-Brunswik, as well as many others, were trying to develop an integration of psychoanalysis and Marxism. Also at this time, some psychoanalytic theorists such as David Rappaport were intrigued by the idea that research conducted by Lewin and his students on tension systems could be viewed as a form of experimental psychoanalysis.

I am not sure why I was advised to go to the University of Pennsylvania to take my master's degree. Possibly it was because it had a well-established psychological clinic and two faculty members, Frances Irwin and Malcolm Preston, who were sympathetic to Lewin's ideas. I had some interesting clinical experiences there working with children, largely without supervision, but the course work seemed dull and antiquated in comparison with my undergraduate courses at CCNY. I earned the reputation of being a radical by challenging what I considered to be racist statements about Negro intelligence in a course on psychological measurement given by Morris Viteles.

After obtaining my M.A. degree in 1940, I started a rotating clinical internship at three New York state institutions: one was for the feebleminded (Letchworth Village), another for delinquent boys (Warwick), and a third for psychotic children as well as adults (Rockland State Hospital). During my internship I became skilled in diagnostic testing and clinical interventions with a considerable variety of inmates, more widely read in psychoanalysis, and more aware of how some capable inmates were unjustly retained in the institution because of the valuable services they performed for it or its staff.

I also had the good fortune to meet Clark Hull (the famous learning theorist) while he was visiting a former doctoral student of his, a staff psychologist at Letchworth Village. He was a remarkably generous and tolerant person. We had several long discussions, one related to his recently published book developing a hypothetico-deductive system for rote learning. I had read the book and was somewhat critical of it from two perspectives: the perspective of Gestalt psychology and of Morris Cohen and Ernst Nagel's book on scientific method, both of which I had been thoroughly indoctrinated in while I was an undergraduate at CCNY. Hull seemed genuinely interested in what I had to say even though I was an overly brash twenty-year-old pipsqueak. We had another interesting discussion in which he gave me advice on how to seduce a woman. He told me that, on a date, I should carry a handkerchief permeated with perspiration. He explained that sweat and sexual feelings were associated together because of their joint occurrence during sexual intercourse and that sweat would arouse sexual feelings. In retrospect, I realize that he must have been joking since his suggestion never worked for me.

When Pearl Harbor occurred in December 1941, I was still in my psychology internship. Shortly thereafter, I joined the air force. My first assignment was to a psychological research unit at Maxwell Field in Alabama, which did psychological testing of aviation cadets to classify them for training as pilots, navigators, or bombardiers. I soon became bored with testing and wanted to participate directly in action against the Nazis. I became a cadet and was trained as a navigator. To get to our combat base in England, our crew flew to and stopped at bases in such exotic spots as Trinidad; Fortaleza and Belém in Brazil; Dakar and Marrakech in Africa; and Scotland. What an eye-opening cross-cultural experience; I had never been outside the Northeastern part of the United States before joining the air force.

I flew in thirty bombing missions against the Germans. During combat I saw many of our planes as well as German planes shot down, and I also saw the massive damage inflicted by our bombs and those of the Royal Air Force on occupied Europe and Germany. Moreover, being stationed in England, I saw the great destruction wreaked by the German air raids and felt the common apprehensions while sitting in air-raid shelters during German bombings. Although I had no doubt of the justness of the war against the Nazis, I was appalled by its destructiveness.

After my combat tour of duty was completed, I returned to the United States and was assigned as a clinical psychologist to an Air Force Convalescent Hospital and served as such until shortly after V-E Day. I was demobilized early as the result of being one of the few nonpatients at the hospital who had been in combat and had amassed a substantial number of demobilization points.

After my demobilization, I contacted some psychology faculty members I knew at CCNY to ask for advice with regard to resuming graduate work in psychology. I discussed with them my somewhat confused interests in getting clinical training, in studying with Lewin because of his work on democratic and autocratic leadership, and in doing psychological research. As a result of these conversations, I decided to apply for admission to the doctoral programs at the University of Chicago (where Carl Rogers and L. L. Thurstone were the leading lights), at Yale University (where Donald Marquis was chairman and where Clark Hull was the major attraction), and at MIT (where Kurt Lewin had established a new graduate program and the Research Center for Group Dynamics). As one of the first of the returning soldiers, I had no trouble in getting interviews or admission at all three schools. I was most impressed by Kurt Lewin and his vision of his newly established research center and so decided to take my Ph.D. at MIT.

My Autobiography as a Social Psychologist

I date the start of my career as a social psychologist to my first meeting with Lewin, in which I was enthralled by him and committed myself to studying at his center. He had arranged for me to meet him for breakfast at a midtown hotel in New York in August 1945. Even though it was very hot, I dressed formally—with jacket and tie—to meet with this distinguished professor. Our meeting time was 8:30 A.M., but he did not appear until about 9:00 A.M. He came bustling in, cheerfully looking around for me, his face bright pink from a recent sunburn. He was not wearing a jacket or a tie, and his manner was quite informal. I recognized him from a picture that I had seen and introduced myself, and we set off for the hotel's dining room. But they would not admit us because he had no jacket or tie (how things have changed). We then went to a nearby coffee shop. I do not remember much about the conversation other than that I described my education, experience, and interests, and he described his plans for the new center. I was being treated as an equal; I felt somewhat courted; I was experiencing a trancelike sensation of intellectual illumination with new insights constantly bubbling forth from this brilliant, enthusiastic, effervescent, youthful, middle-aged man. He spoke a colloquial American, often with malapropisms, and he was both endearing and charming. I left the interview with no doubt that I wanted to study with Lewin. I also left in a dazed sense of enlightenment, but I could not specifically identify what I was enlightened about when I later tried to pin it down for myself.

I had a similar experience a month later when I went to MIT to study and work with Lewin. He discussed with me some work he was then doing with the Commission on Community Interrelations of the American Jewish Congress (a commission he helped to establish) to reduce anti-Semitism and other forms of prejudice. His discussion of the issues was intensely illuminating when I was with him, but I could not define it afterwards when I was alone. At the end of our meeting, he asked me to prepare a review of the essence of the literature on prejudice, and he indicated that it should be brief and that he needed it in three days. I felt good. I was being treated as a serious professional and was given a responsible and challenging task. Lewin's treatment of me was, I believe, typical of his relations with his colleagues and students. He would discuss a topic with great enthusiasm and insight, he would ignite one's interest, and he would encourage one to get involved in a task that was intellectually challenging, giving complete freedom for one to work on it as one saw fit.

Shortly after arriving at MIT, I noticed a very attractive young woman, named Lydia Shapiro, who would occasionally pop into the center. She was working under Lewin's direction as an interviewer for a study on self-hatred among Jews. We started to get to know one another over cherry Cokes and jelly donuts. Being supported on the GI bill, I was a cheapskate, and she did like jelly donuts. I don't recall the specifics, but somehow I was assigned to supervise her work. After learning that she spent much of her supposed work time sunning herself on the banks of the Charles River, I fired her. About a year and a half later, on June 1, 1947, we got married. Stan Schachter and Al Pepitone, with whom I was sharing an apartment, were my best men at the wedding. In moments of marital tension, I have accused Lydia of marrying me to get even, but she asserts it was pure masochism on her part. In our fifty years of marriage, I have had splendid opportunities to study conflict as a participant observer.

Immediately after our honeymoon in Quebec, we went to Bethel in Maine for the first National Training Laboratory (NTL). I served on its research staff with other students from the RCGD at MIT and from the Harvard Department of Social Relations. Lydia and another woman were the rumrunners for the workshop; Bethel was a dry town, and they had to drive 20 miles to buy the liquor to keep the workshop staff and participants well lubricated.

The first NTL was a natural follow-up of the Connecticut Workshop on Intergroup Relations held during the summer of 1946. As I now recall it, the training staff consisted of Ron Lippitt, Ken Benne, and Lee Bradford, and the research staff consisted of Murray Horowitz, Mel Seeman, and myself. One evening, following a lengthy workshop day, Lewin, the workshop participants, the trainers, and the researchers were all sitting around a conference table when one of the participants turned to the researchers and asked us what we were doing. We said that we were keeping track of the patterns of interaction among the group. He then asked us to describe what we had noted; Lewin suggested that would be an interesting thing to do. We summarized our impressions, and this led to a lively, productive discussion among the participants that all of us felt was a valuable, insightful, learning experience. This was the embryo of the T-group and sensitivity training that was given birth at the first NTL in 1947.

I would now say that the researchers at the first NTL did not fully appreciate the importance of the new procedures and new movement being developed. The evangelical tone of some of the trainers appalled many of us, with the result that there was considerable unhappiness among the researchers that summer of 1947. Today many of us recognize that NTL as the birthplace of much of applied social psychology, especially in the area of organizational psychology.

The Research Center for Group Dynamics

Lewin assembled a remarkable group of faculty and students to compose the Research Center for Group Dynamics at MIT. For the faculty, he initially recruited Dorwin Cartwright, Leon Festinger, Ronald Lippitt, and Marian Radke (now Radke-Yarrow). Jack French and Alvin Zander were to join later. The small group of twelve students included Kurt Back, Alex Bavelas, David Emery, Gordon Hearn, Murray Horowitz, David Jenkins, Albert Pepitone, Stanley Schachter, Richard Snyder, John Thibaut, Ben Willerman, and myself. These initial faculty and students were extraordinarily productive, and they played a pivotal role in developing modern social psychology in its applied as well as its basic aspects. As I write these last two sentences, it strikes me that all of the students and the key faculty members were male. This was quite a change for Lewin; in Berlin most of his students were female (e.g., Bluma Zeigarnik, Tamara Dembo, Eugenia Hanfmann, Maria Ovsiankina, Anitra Karsten). It is interesting to speculate how modern social psychology's development might have differed if the student group included a substantial number of women.

Lewin died suddenly on February 11, 1947, of a heart attack. The RCGD had been functioning for considerably less than two years when he died. Yet in this brief period of time he had established an institution that would strongly influence the development of modern social psychology. Let me offer some thoughts about why the Research Center for Group Dynamics was so remarkably productive.

Reasons for the Center's Effectiveness

First, Lewin was an unusually effective scientific "tribal leader" (to borrow a phrase from Donald Campbell). As I have indicated in describing my personal contacts with him, he was enthusiastic, inspiring, and persuasive. He led those working with him to feel they were involved in an important, promising enterprise that could have valuable consequences for both social science and society. He treated his faculty and students as colleagues: giving them autonomy and responsibility and a sense of being actively involved, individually and collectively, in creating the new field of group dynamics. He also encouraged open and vigorous conflict about ideas and methods among his faculty and students in the never ceasing attempt to get to a deeper understanding of the issues involved.

This was most evident in the loosely organized research seminars, named the *Quasselstrippe* (or winding string), that he led for the faculty and students. In the *Quasselstrippe* a faculty member or student would typically present some research or some theoretical issue that he or she was involved in, and a lively controversy would erupt. Sometimes the controversy was related to the presentation, but frequently the discussion wandered off into other issues. Not infrequently the most heated exchanges took place between Leon Festinger and Ronald Lippitt, who had rather different views of the nature of science and research. During these vigorous disputes, Lewin would be smiling benignly as he watched his intellectual offspring squabble. Almost invariably at the end of these wandering, disputatious research seminars he would emerge from his role as an observer, and in an active way he would offer a deeper, integrating perspective that would provide a basis for synthesizing the conflicting viewpoints.

It was not only Lewin's leadership style but also his ideas that contributed to the productivity of the RCGD. Very much influenced by Ernst Cassirer, the German philosopher of science, he thought "the taboo against believing in the existence of a social entity is probably most effectively broken by handling this entity experimentally" (Lewin, 1951, p. 193). The concept of "group," as well as other concepts relating to social psychological phenomena, had little scientific status among psychologists in the 1930s and 1940s when Lewin was first turning his attention to social psychology. He believed the "reality" of these concepts would be established only by "doing something with them." So at the center there was strong pressure to do something with the concepts related to groups and not merely to talk about these ideas. And, of course, the faculty and students did many experiments to demonstrate that one could, in a sense, capture for science such phenomena as "styles of group leadership," "social influence," "cooperation and competition," "group cohesiveness," "pressure for uniformity," "trust and suspicion," "social comparison," and so on. The pressure to do something with the concepts was directed not only toward experimentation but also toward application, namely, to show that these concepts could be employed to change existing social reality—to improve group functioning, to reduce prejudice, or to train more effective leaders.

Lewin's metatheory, his conceptual language, as well as his specific theoretical ideas were also important influences on the members of the center while they were at MIT. More than thirty years later, in the spring of 1978, there was a reunion at Columbia University of almost all of the surviving RCGD members. The participants included Kurt Bach, Dorwin Cartwright, Leon Festinger, Jack French, Gordon Hearn, Harold Kelley, Ronald Lippitt (via tape), Albert Pepitone, Stanley Schachter, and myself. At that reunion the participants were asked to indicate Lewin's effect on their work. From the discussion, it was evident that all of us had been very much influenced by Lewin's way of thinking about science and by his general orientation to psychology. Elsewhere I have described the key elements of Lewin's metatheory—in other words, his field-theoretical approach to psychology. This is what had most impact on the participants. Few were still involved with Lewin's conceptual language or terminology, with topological and vectorial psychology. Some had been stimulated to do work that related to Lewin's specific theoretical ideas, particularly those relevant to tension systems, level of aspiration theory, social interdependence, group leadership, group decisionmaking, changing individual attitudes, and quasi-stationary equilibria. And several were stimulated by Lewin to be concerned with articulating the connection between social psychology theory and change in social practice.

Nevertheless, the common thread that linked our group of past RCGD members together was a Lewinian way of thinking. It emphasized the importance of theory; the value of experimentation for clarifying and testing ideas; the interrelatedness between the person and the environment; the interdependence of cognitive structures and motivation; the importance of understanding the individual in his or her social (group, cultural) context; the usefulness of theory for social practice; and the value of trying to change reality for the development of theory. These emphases are not unique to the Lewinian way of thinking; they characterize good social science and good social practice. But Lewin was the one who introduced them to social psychology.

The RCGD fostered a sense of pioneering elitism among its members. We felt we were working on the frontiers of social psychological knowledge, creating new research methods, and capturing new phenomena for science. This fostered a narcissistic arrogance in many of us that permitted us to venture on untrodden paths and to feel rather superior to the work being done by our friends and neighbors in Harvard's Social Relations Department as well as elsewhere.

In addition, of course, the center had a critical mass of active researchers among its faculty and students, so that the publications of this group dominated the early work in experimental and applied social psychology. Alfred Marrow (1969), in his biography of Kurt Lewin (*The Practical Theorist*), listed over 100 publications and dissertations connected with the RCGD during the period of 1945–1950. In a sense, apart from whatever merits we had, we were so influential because we were lucky enough to be active early in the development of modern social psychology, when there were comparatively few others who were doing research and publishing in this field.

Lewin recruited a very able and congenial group of mature students who, for the most part, had done previous graduate work in psychology and had served in the armed forces in World War II. They were prepared to take responsibility and to work with the faculty as colleagues. The relatively young faculty were unusually accessible and open to collaborative working relations with the students. As students, we were quickly involved in the design and execution of experiments and research on the training workshops; some of us were also rapidly thrust into the role of conducting training workshops on group processes and group leadership. The students comprised a small, cohesive group that provided much mutual support even as we had intense intellectual discussions about the new ideas and techniques that were being developed.

Lewin also recruited a remarkably gifted younger faculty. I assume that he purposefully created a faculty that had some tension as well as some unifying elements within it, a faculty within which there would be productive tension in theory, research, and application. As suggested earlier, Festinger and Lippitt had fundamental disagreements, and while he lived, Lewin served as an integrating force, intellectually as well as administratively. After his death, Cartwright maintained administrative integration, but there was little intellectual common ground between the disparate perspectives of Festinger and Lippitt. For many students, Festinger became a symbol of the tough-minded, theory-oriented, pure experimental scientist, whereas Lippitt became a symbol of the fuzzy-minded, do-gooder, practitioner of applied social psychology. These were unfortunate caricatures of both Festinger and Lippitt. Such distortions were, I believe, one of the contributing causes to the estrangement between basic and applied social psychology in the United States during the 1950s and early 1960s. I doubt that these caricatures would have developed if Lewin had lived longer. As my earlier quotation from him indicated, he saw an intimate, two-directional link between the development of theory and practice.

My career in social psychology has been greatly affected by Kurt Lewin and my experiences at the Research Center for Group Dynamics.[1] First, I probably would not have been a social psychologist were it not for the inspiring interview with him in the summer of 1945. Second, the intellectual atmosphere created by Lewin at the

RCGD strongly shaped my dissertation and my value orientation as a social psychologist. Lewin was not only an original, tough-minded theorist and researcher with a profound interest in the philosophy and methodology of science, but he was also a tenderhearted psychologist who was deeply involved with developing psychological knowledge that would be relevant to important human concerns. Lewin was both tough-minded and tenderhearted; he provided a scientific role model that I have tried to emulate. Like Lewin, I have wanted my theory and research to be relevant to important social issues, but I also wanted my work to be scientifically rigorous and tough-minded. As a student, I was drawn to both the tough-mindedness of Festinger's work and to the direct social relevance of Lippitt's approach and did not feel the need to identify with one and derogate the other.

My Dissertation Study

My dissertation started off with an interest in issues of war and peace (atomic bombs had been dropped on Hiroshima and Nagasaki shortly before I resumed my graduate studies) and with an image of the possible ways that the nations composing the newly formed United Nations Security Council would interact. The atmosphere at the center, still persisting after Lewin's premature death, led me to turn this social concern about the risk of nuclear war into a theoretically oriented, experimental investigation of the effects of cooperative and competitive processes. The specific problem that I was first interested in took on a more generalized form. It had been transformed into an attempt to understand the fundamental features of cooperative and competitive relations and the consequences of these different types of interdependencies in a way that would be generally applicable to the relations among individuals, groups, or nations. The problem had become a theoretical one, with the broad scientific goal of attempting to interrelate and give insight into a variety of phenomena through several fundamental concepts and basic propositions. The intellectual atmosphere at the center pushed its students to theory building. Lewin's favorite slogan was, "There is nothing so practical as a good theory."

As I reflect back on the intellectual roots of my dissertation, I see it was influenced not only by Lewin's theoretical interest in social interdependence but also by the Marxist concern with two different systems of distributive justice: a cooperative egalitarian and a competitive, meritocratic one. In addition, the writings of George Herbert Mead affected my way of thinking about cooperation and its importance to civilized life.

This study,[2] in addition to being the takeoff point for much of my subsequent work, has helped to stimulate the development of a movement toward cooperative learning in the schools under the leadership of David and Roger Johnson. Although cooperative learning has many ancestors and can be traced back for at least 2,000 years, my dissertation helped to initiate the development of a systematic theoretical and research base for cooperative learning. Hundreds of research studies have since been done on the relative impact of cooperative, competitive, and individualistic learning (see Johnson & Johnson, 1989). These various studies are quite consistent with one another and with my initial theoretical work and research on the effects of cooperation-competition (Deutsch, 1949a, 1949b) in indicating favorable effects upon students. Through cooperative learning, students develop a considerably greater commitment, helpfulness, and caring for one another regardless of differences in ability level, ethnic background, gender, social class, and physical ability. They develop more skill in taking the perspective of others, emotionally as well as cognitively. They develop greater self-esteem and a greater sense of being valued by their classmates. They develop more positive attitudes toward learning, school, and their teachers. They usually learn more in the subjects they are studying by cooperative learning, and they also acquire more of the skills and attitudes that are conducive to effective collaboration with others.

The Research Center for Human Relations

After obtaining my Ph.D. from MIT in the summer of 1948, I joined the Research Center for Human Relations (then at the New School) headed by Stuart Cook. The war against Nazism had stimulated a considerable interest among psychologists in understanding prejudice and how to overcome it, and financial support for research in this area was available from Jewish organizations such as the American Jewish Congress as well as from federal agencies. Among the many groups receiving funding for work in this area were members of the Berkeley Public Opinion Study and the former Frankfurt Institute of Social Research, who produced *The Authoritarian Personality* (Adorno, Frenkel-Brunswik, Levinson, & Sanford, 1950); Lewin's MIT Center, which developed not only the first workshop for reducing prejudice and improving intergroup relations but also action research "to help social agencies that were developing programs aimed at reducing prejudice and discrimination"; and the Harvard group working with G. W. Allport (1954b) on creating an integrated overview of the nature of prejudice and ways of reducing it.

The Research Center for Human Relations was in 1948 also mainly funded by agencies interested in reducing prejudice. As soon as I joined, I became involved in a study of interracial housing that I conducted with Mary Evan Collins. We started with an "experience survey" of knowledgeable public housing officials to identify the important factors affecting interracial relations in housing projects. On the basis of this survey, we decided that the residential pattern—whether the races were segregated or integrated within the housing project—was a critical determinant. We then set out to identify housing projects that were otherwise similar but differed in terms of whether black and white residents lived in separate buildings or were integrated within each building. We were able to identify biracial segregated public housing developments in Newark, New Jersey, and racially integrated ones in New York City that were roughly similar. We then did an extensive interview and a small observational study in the projects, and by the use of various controls we created a quasi–ex post facto experiment. Despite the obvious methodological limitations of such a study, it was clear that the two types of projects differed profoundly in terms of the kinds of contacts between the two races and the attitudes that they developed toward each other.

This study (Deutsch & Collins, 1951) had important social consequences. As the executive director of the Newark Public Housing Authority stated in a postscript to our book, *Interracial Housing*, "The partial segregation which has characterized public housing in Newark will no longer obtain. In large measure, this change in fundamental policy reflects the impact of the study reported in this book. The study has served as a catalyst to the re-examination of our basic interracial policies in housing and as a stimulus to this change." It also led me to become active on a Society for the Psychological Study of Social Issues (SPSSI) committee concerned with intergroup relations. Over the next several years, this committee gave talks before policy-oriented groups as well as helped lawyers who were challenging racial segregation in various suits brought before federal courts. The committee also contributed material to the legal brief that was cited in the 1954 Supreme Court decision *Brown v. the Board of Education*, which outlawed racial segregation in schools and other publicly supported facilities.

In 1949 the Research Center for Human Relations moved to New York University (NYU), and I became a member of its graduate faculty in psychology. Here I worked collaboratively with Marie Jahoda and Stuart Cook on an SPSSI-sponsored textbook, *Research Methods in Social Relations* (Jahoda, Deutsch, & Cook, 1951), one of the earliest—if not the earliest—of its kind. To help me overcome my Kafkaesque, Germanic style of writing, Mitzi pinned on my wall a slogan that stated, "You don't have to write complex sentences to be profound." It was a good reminder as well as a subtle way of deflating my pompous persona of theorist-basic researcher with which I had emerged from my graduate studies.

At NYU I also worked collaboratively with Harold Gerard on a laboratory study of normative and informational influence on individual judgment (Deutsch & Gerard, 1955) and a study of decisionmaking among high-level air force officers. In addition, with support from the Office of Naval Research, I was able to start a program of research on factors affecting the initiation of cooperation. Hal had introduced me to Howard Raiffa, who in turn introduced me to the Prisoner's Dilemma (PD), which I soon turned into a useful research format for investigating trust and suspicion (Deutsch, 1958, 1962a, 1973). I was probably the first psychologist to use the PD game in research. Unfortunately, the PD game (like the Asch situation and the Skinner box) became an easy format for conducting experimental studies, and as a result a torrent of studies followed—most of which had no theoretical significance.

I added to my busy schedule by undertaking training as a psychoanalyst at the Postgraduate Center for Mental Health, which had an eclectic orientation rather than being committed to one or another school of psychoanalysis. It involved not only my own analysis (three times per week) but also six to nine hours of classes, twenty hours of doing psychoanalytic psychotherapy, and two to three hours of supervision per week. It was hectic, but I was young. It was an extremely valuable supplement to my work as an experimental social psychologist, which gives perspectives only on very narrow cross-sections of people's lives. Psychoanalysis provided a longitudinal, developmental view in addition to glimpses into the internal psychodynamics underlying a person's behavior in conflict situations. My psychoanalytic work stimulated my research interest in such topics as trust and suspicion and conflict. It has been a two-way street. My social psychological work on conflict, negotiation, and mediation has affected my therapeutic approach to the conflicts experienced by patients as well as my approach to marital therapy. I continued a small private practice until about ten years ago, when I wanted to have more freedom to travel. The practice was personally rewarding. I helped a number of people, it enabled me to stay in touch with my own inner life, and it provided a welcome supplement to my academic salary.

During my tenure at New York University, most of my salary was paid out of soft money, from research grants or other monies from outside sources. As McCarthyism developed increasing strength in the early 1950s, social science and social scientists became targets of attack, being labeled as "radical," "fellow travelers," "communist sympathizers," and the like. If your personal library contained books by Karl Marx, if you had participated in interracial groups challenging segregation, if a friend was or had been a member of the Communist Party, and so on, you were suspect and might be purged from your position. During the height of the McCarthy period, many funding agencies no longer were willing to support research dealing with prejudice or interracial relations, and there was much talk of reducing federal support for social science research. Thus I was happy to accept when Carl Hovland, in 1956, invited me to help establish a new basic research group in psychology at the Bell Telephone Laboratories. Bell Labs had an excellent reputation for its support of basic research, and this is what I wanted to do, without the constant problem of raising money.

Much to my surprise, even during the worst part of McCarthyism I never had any problems, nor did my funding from the Office of Naval Research or the air force stop. Although never a communist, I had many of the characteristics of the "usual suspect." Possibly, I was not harassed because I had received a security clearance from the air force before doing research on decisionmaking in the early 1950s.

The Bell Laboratories

Bell Labs was, by academic standards, a luxurious place to work. I received a good salary and had no trouble getting research assistants, equipment, secretarial help, and travel money as well as much freedom to do what I wanted. I was able to hire Bob Krauss and Norah Rosenau, then graduate students at NYU, to work as my research assistants. I was also able to add Hal Gerard and Sy Rosenberg to our research staff. It was a productive group. At Bell Labs, Bob Krauss and I developed and conducted research with the Acme-Bolt Trucking game; we also started on our book, *Theories in Social Psychology* (Deutsch & Krauss, 1965). I did various other studies including "The Interpretation of Praise and Criticism" (Deutsch, 1961), "Dissonance or Defensiveness" (Deutsch, Krauss, & Rosenau, 1962), and "The Effects of Group Size and Task Structure Upon Group Process and Performance" (Deutsch & Rosenau, 1963). This last was a fine study that was never written up for publication because of Norah Rosenau's premature death and my change of interests as I moved to Teachers College in 1963.

In addition, while at the Bell Labs, I was its unofficial peacenik, criticizing the strategic thinking among establishment intellectuals and coediting the book *Preventing World War III* (Wright, Evan, & Deutsch, 1962). During this period I was quite active in SPSSI, articulating some of the social psychological assumptions underlying our national policy and even becoming its president.

Although Bell Labs was in many respects a fine place to work, it had its problems. Compared to a university, it was a stiff organization: It had a clear hierarchical structure; it had fairly set hours of work and vacation (from which I was a tolerated deviant); the lab had no small, offbeat, informal eating places that served wine or beer; there were few students and little ethnic or racial diversity.

In addition, there were specific problems related to our psychological research unit. Although it was located in the Bell Labs in Murray Hill, New Jersey, the Personnel Research Group at AT&T had been instrumental in getting the unit established and thought that we should be primarily working closely with them on problems with which they needed help. None of us who had come to Bell Labs at Carl Hovland's urging had this view, nor apparently did Carl. The administrative head of our unit was a former member of the AT&T Personnel Group. An uncomfortable power struggle developed about what we should be doing, which Bell Labs ultimately won. But because of the dispute and also because we were the oddballs of the Bell Labs (which was composed mainly of physical scientists and mathematicians), we were the constant object of high-level attention. We had visits from the president of AT&T, the president of Western Electric, the presidents of various Bell Telephone Companies, and so on, and at each visit our group would have to put on a show, lasting one or two days, in which we would demonstrate our research. During one of these visits, when a committee came in order to make a recommendation about the future of our group, we received word that Bob and I had just been awarded the American Association for the Advancement of Science (AAAS) sociopsychology prize for the research we had done at the Bell Labs with the Acme-Bolt Trucking game (Deutsch & Krauss, 1962). This apparently laid to rest the doubts about our group.

In addition to the people I recruited for my research group on interpersonal processes, Alex Bavelas, another key staff member selected by Hovland, recruited Herbert Jenkins, a Skinnerian who did his research on learning using pigeons.

Herb must have had several people a day ask him, jokingly, "Going to replace the telephone with pigeons, eh?" After a year or so, Bavelas quit the labs, feeling that it was not a receptive environment for what he wanted to do. Jenkins then recruited Roger Shepard, who started his brilliant work on multidimensional scaling there.

While at the labs, I was consulted by its administration on problems such as how to improve the creativity of their researchers, how to apply social science knowledge to improve the functioning of the various telephone companies, and how to improve race relations. As I recall, I gave many potentially useful suggestions, none of which were implemented. I also suggested that they hire Henry Riecken to establish a social science development group to develop existing social science knowledge for use in the Bell system. Although Bell interviewed Riecken, they did not implement this idea either.

Hovland died in 1961, and about a year later I started to think about leaving the labs. I was getting tired of commuting from New York City to Murray Hill; I missed working with graduate students as well as the looser, less hierarchical atmosphere of a university; and I was bored by the special attention that our group was receiving. My memory of the specifics are unclear, but around this time I was approached by Teachers College to consider an appointment to replace Goodwin Watson, who was retiring, and to head its doctoral program in social psychology. Teachers College was attractive to me because Lydia and I were determined to continue living in New York, I would have freedom to create a new social psychology program, and I was interested in education. I received other feelers from nearby institutions (the Department of Management at Yale University and the Department of Psychiatry at the Albert Einstein College of Medicine) that would have provided higher salaries and more affluent settings, but they did not have the lure of shaping a social psychology program.

Teachers College

When I joined Teachers College in September 1963, I had a strong view of what I wanted the new social psychology program to be like. I wanted it to attract students and turn out graduates who would be tough-minded and tenderhearted, who would be as knowledgeable and expert in theory and research as the best of the "pure," experimental social psychologists and also socially concerned with developing and applying social psychological knowledge to the urgent and important social problems of our time. In other words, I wanted to develop a program that would overcome the split that had developed between the laboratory and applied social psychology during the 1950s and the early 1960s. As I have indicated earlier, the differences between the sharp-minded and sharp-tongued Festinger and the evangelical, unsystematic Lippitt were precursors of this split, which widened into a chasm in the decade after Lewin's death (see Deutsch, 1975 for a more extensive discussion of this rift).

Although the split was understandable in terms of the insecurities of both sides in a young discipline, it was harmful and stupid from my perspective. It polluted the atmosphere of social psychology. When I left Bell Labs (a tough-minded institution) to join Teachers College (a tenderhearted one), I thought that my experimental colleagues would consider this to be a loss of status for me and that my new colleagues would be concerned that I would be overly critical and scientistic (rather than scientific) as well as out of touch with practical realities. However, by the time I came to Teachers College, I felt sufficiently secure in my own identity as a social psychologist not to be concerned by colleagues who would deprecate either tenderheartedness or tough-mindedness.

I was fortunate when I came to Teachers College in several respects. First, although Teachers College, like most schools of education, has relatively little money for research by its faculty or stipends for its graduate students, I was able to bring in outside funding to get the social psychology program off to a good start: The National Science Foundation (NSF) gave funds to build a well-equipped social psychology laboratory, the Office of Naval Research (ONR) supported my research, and the National Institute of Mental Health (NIMH) provided a training grant that would support most of our graduate students. Second, we were able to attract many excellent students who fit our criteria of being tough-minded and tenderhearted, including Harvey Hornstein, David Johnson, Jeffrey Rubin, Roy Lewicki, Barbara Bunker, Madeleine Heilman, Kenneth Kressel, Charles Judd Jr., Janice Steil, Michelle Fine, Ivan Lansberg, Louis Medvene, Susan Boardman, Sandra Horowitz, Susan Opotow, Eben Weitzman, Martha Gephart, and Adrienne Asch. Third, our program was initially small enough for us to be a very cohesive group that mainly worked cooperatively on interrelated research projects under my direction. We could have frequent informal lunches together during which we discussed politics, diets, Jackie Ferguson (our fascinating secretary who mothered us all), and research and theory. Many good ideas emerged from these lunches. Finally, the change from Bell Labs to Teachers College accelerated a shift in focus and labeling of my research. At the Bell Labs, I and others came to view the Acme-Bolt Trucking game as a bargaining game, so I began to think of studies that employed it as bargaining or negotiation and more generally as conflict studies. This was a shift away from labeling them as studies of the conditions affecting the initiation of cooperation.

With a change in labeling, I began to reframe the question underlying much of my research from, "What are the conditions that give rise to cooperation rather than competition?" to "What are the conditions that give rise to constructive rather than destructive processes of resolving conflict?" At a conceptual level, the two questions are very similar. Nevertheless, the latter phrasing is much sexier; it resonates directly to many aspects of life and to the other social sciences as well as psychology. And it is also directly connected to many of the social issues with which I was concerned: war and peace, intergroup relations, class conflict, and family conflict.

It was a productive reframing that led to much research in our social psychology laboratory by my students and myself. My book *The Resolution of Conflict: Constructive and Destructive Processes*, published in 1973, summarizes much of this research and had a considerable impact in the social sciences. It helped to provide a new way of thinking about conflict and broadened the focus of the field to include constructive conflicts as well as destructive ones.

Our research into the question central to *The Resolution of Conflict* started off with the assumption that if the parties involved in a conflict situation had a cooperative rather than competitive orientation toward one another, they would be more likely to engage in a constructive process of conflict resolution. In my earlier research on the effects of cooperation and competition upon group process, I had demonstrated that a cooperative process was more productive than a competitive process in dealing with a problem that a group faces. I reasoned that the same would be true in a mixed-motive situation of conflict. A conflict could be viewed as a mutual problem facing the conflicting parties. Our initial research on trust and suspicion employing the Prisoner's Dilemma game strongly supported my reasoning, as did subsequent research employing other experimental formats. I believe that this is a very important result that has considerable theoretical and practical significance.

At a theoretical level, it enabled me to link my prior characterization of cooperation and competitive social processes to the nature of the processes of conflict resolution that would typically give rise to constructive or destructive outcomes. That is, I had found a way to characterize the central features of constructive and destructive *processes* of conflict resolution; doing so represented a major advance beyond the characterization of *outcomes* as constructive or destructive. This not only was important in itself, but it also opened up a new possibility: that we would be able to develop insight into the conditions that initiated or stimulated the development of cooperative-constructive versus competitive-destructive processes of conflict. Much of the research my students and I have done has been addressed to developing this insight.

Much of our early research on the conditions affecting the course of conflict was done on an ad hoc basis. We selected independent variables to manipulate based on our intuitive sense of what would give rise to a cooperative or competitive process. We did experiments with quite a number of variables: motivational orientation, communication facilities, perceived similarity of opinions and beliefs, size of conflict, availability of threats and weapons, power differences, third-party interventions, strategies and tactics of game playing by experimental stooges, the payoff structure of the game, personality characteristics, and so on. The results of these studies fell into a pattern that I slowly began to grasp.

All of these studies seemed explainable by the assumption, which I have labeled "Deutsch's crude law of social relations," that *the characteristic processes and effects elicited by a given type of social relationship (cooperative or competitive) also tend to elicit that type of social relationship.* Thus cooperation induces and is induced by a perceived similarity in beliefs and attitudes, a readiness to be helpful, openness in communication, trusting and friendly attitudes, sensitivity to common interests and deemphasis of opposed interests, an orientation toward enhancing mutual power rather than power differences, and so on. Similarly, competition induces and is induced by the use of tactics of coercion, threat, or deception; attempts to enhance the power differences between oneself and the other; poor communication; minimization of the awareness of similarities in values and increased sensitivity to opposed interests; suspicious and hostile attitudes; the importance, rigidity, and size of the issues in conflict; and so on.

In other words, if one has systematic knowledge of the effects of cooperation and competitive processes, one will have systematic knowledge of the conditions that typically give rise to such processes and, by extension, to the conditions that affect whether a conflict will take a constructive or destructive course. My early theory of cooperation and competition is a theory of the *effects* of cooperative and competitive processes. Hence, from the crude law of social relations stated earlier, it follows that this theory provides insight into the conditions that give rise to cooperative and competitive processes.

The crude law is *crude*. It expresses surface similarities between effects and causes; the basic relationships are genotypical rather than phenotypical. The crude law is crude, but it can be improved. Its improvement requires a linkage with other areas in social psychology, particularly social cognition and social perception. Such a linkage would enable us to view phenotypes in their social environments in such a way as to lead us to perceive correctly the underlying genotypes. We would then be able to know under what conditions "perceived similarity" or "threat" will be experienced as having an underlying genotype different from the one that is usually associated with its phenotype.

Although the gaming conflicts in the laboratory during this period (1963–1973) were relatively benign, the conflicts in the outside world were not. During this period the cold war escalated; the Berlin crisis occurred; the brothers John and Robert Kennedy and Martin Luther King Jr. were assassinated; the United States was increasingly involved in the Vietnam War; there were teach-ins, campus upheavals, race riots, Woodstock, love-ins, communes, the emergence of the new left, and so on. I was not immune to the effects of these events, personally or professionally.

Professionally, as a result of *Preventing World War III* (of which I was coeditor), my activities in SPSSI, my various speeches, and our conflict studies, I became identified as one of the psychologists (along with Ralph White, Charles Osgood, Irving Janis, Jerome Frank, and Herbert Kelman) concerned with war and peace issues. I was invited to participate in meetings on the Berlin crisis, arms control, deterrence, Soviet-U.S. relations, and so on. Some involved high-level diplomats, others involved people in the defense establishment, others were at the UN, and still others were with citizen groups or social scientists. During the 1960s I was also trying to get more of my fellow psychologists involved in these issues. I took the opportunity of several addresses to speak to these issues: My 1960 SPSSI presidential address was "Psychological Alternatives to War" (Deutsch, 1960); my 1966 New York State Psychological Association talk was "Vietnam and the Start of World War III: Some Psychological Parallels" (Deutsch, 1966); my 1968 Eastern Psychological Association presentation was "Socially Relevant Science" (Deutsch, 1969b); and my Kurt Lewin Memorial Award address was "Conflicts: Productive and Destructive"[3](Deutsch, 1969a).

About the time I was finishing the manuscript for my conflict book, in May 1972, I received from Melvin J. Lerner, then at the University of Waterloo, an invitation to participate in a conference entitled "Contributions to a Just Society." Mel had been an NYU social psychology student who had worked with Isadore Chein but had taken some courses with me. Shortly after the conference, he asked me to contribute to the *Journal of Social Issues* volume on the justice motive that he was editing. The two papers I wrote as a result of his urgings were "Awakening the Sense of Injustice" (Deutsch, 1974) and "Equity, Equality, and Need: What Determines Which Value Will Be Used as the Basis of Distributive Justice?" (Deutsch, 1975). In preparing these papers, I reviewed the existing work on the social psychology of justice and became quite dissatisfied with the dominant approach to this area: equity theory. My dissatisfaction led me to write an extensive critique of equity theory in 1977 (Deutsch, 1978, 1979) and, with the support of the National Science Foundation, to embark on a program of research on the social psychology of distributive justice. This program was, without my full recognition, something I had been engaged in for many years. Like Molière's bourgeois gentleman, I had been "speaking justice" all the time without being aware of it. My dissertation study could be thought of as a study of two different systems of distributive justice, cooperative-egalitarian and competitive-meritocratic. Our research on bargaining and conflict had direct relevance to a central question in the social psychology of justice, namely, What are the conditions that facilitate the establishment of a stable system of justice among interactants that they will consider to be fair?

Our research program had three main components: (1) experimental studies of the effects of different systems of distributive justice, (2) research into the determinants of the choice of distributive systems, and (3) investigations into the sense of injustice. The theory and research that emanated from this program has been presented mainly in my 1985 book, *Distributive Justice*. I believe the it is an important extension of the work I had done on conflict.[4]. The book received extremely favorable reviews, but I was disappointed that it did not create as much of a stir as I had hoped, despite some of its interesting ideas and provocative research findings. Possibly this was due to my having included in the book many theoretical papers that had been published earlier.

The year 1982 was particularly outstanding for me. I made two important addresses. In one, my presidential address to the International Society of Political Psychology, I developed the concept of "malignant conflict" and described the processes involved in such conflicts and used this discussion as a basis for analyzing the cold war between the United States and the Soviet Union (Deutsch 1983, 1985). The reaction of the audience was very gratifying. In various follow-ups (e.g., interviews, talks, conferences, pamphlets) it received considerable attention.

The second address was my inaugural lecture as the E. L. Thorndike Professor of Psychology and Education at Teachers College. I admired Thorndike both as a psychologist and as a person (after reading an extensive biography of him), but I felt his views about race reflected the ignorance and bigotry prevalent in his time. In my opening remarks, I expressed my admiration for Thorndike but dissociated myself from his statements about racial and ethnic groups. My address was essentially a review of my work in social psychology. However, in a concluding section, I indicated my intention to help to further develop the educational implications and applications of my work on cooperation and conflict resolution. To this end, I proposed establishing a center at Teachers College that would foster cooperative learning and constructive conflict resolution in the schools. At that time I vainly hoped that I might be able to induce a former student of mine to direct, administer, and raise funds for such a center; I never liked administrative work or raising funds, even though I had been reasonably successful in doing so during my career. In 1986, with the aid of a small grant from President Michael Timpane ($9,600), I started the center that I later ambitiously named the International Center for Cooperation and Conflict Resolution (ICCCR).

In 1982 I also published a paper, "Interdependence and Psychological Orientation," that integrated several strands in my work. Mike Wish and I (while Mike was on the faculty at Teachers College) did some initial work on characterizing the fundamental dimensions of interpersonal relations. This work grew out of some research that my students and I were doing on marital conflict; we felt it would be useful to go beyond personality descriptions of the individual spouses so that we would be able to characterize the couple as a couple in terms of their relations to one another. Using various data-collection procedures and multidimensional scaling methods, we (Wish, Kaplan, & Deutsch, 1976) came up with five dimensions: cooperation-competition, power distribution, task-oriented versus social-emotional, formal versus informal, and intensity of the relationship.

Previously, I had done much to characterize the social psychological properties of the first dimension, cooperation-competition. Now I sought to do this for the others. Undoubtedly influenced by the popularity of the cognitive approach, I labeled my first attempt "modes of thought." But this title did not seem to be sufficiently inclusive. It appeared to me evident that cognitive processes differ in types of social relations, and I wanted to sketch the nature of some of these differences. However, I also thought that the psychological differences among the types of social relations were not confined to the cognitive processes: Various motivational and moral dispositions were involved as well. It had been customary to consider these latter predispositions as more enduring characteristics of the individual and to label them "personality traits" or "character orientations." Since my emphasis is on the situationally induced nature and, hence, temporariness of such predispositions, these labels did not seem fitting either. Thus I settled on the term "psychological orientation" to capture the basic theme of this paper, namely, that people orient themselves differently to different types of social relations and that these orientations reflect and are reflected in various cognitive processes, motivational tendencies, and moral dispositions.

At the time I was not doing research in cognitive social psychology, but I was sympathetic to it for two reasons. First, as someone greatly influenced by the Gestalt psychologists as well as by Lewin and Fritz Heider, I felt perceptual and cognitive processes were very important. Second, I felt it was a healthy reaction to the antimentalist views of B. F. Skinner and his followers, which were quite popular in psychology in the 1960s and 1970s. My sympathies for the cognitive approach possibly unconsciously led me to suppress the significant differences between it and my emphasis on psychological orientations. Psychological orientations involve the cognitive but also motivational and moral orientations. In the 1980s, cognitive social psychologists neglected both the motivational and moral aspects of people's orientations to social relations.

More recently, there has been increasing recognition of the importance of motivation, even belated recognition of the relevance of Lewin's approach, which integrates cognition and motivation. However, psychologists have not yet acknowledged that there is a moral, normative feature to every type of social relation and that any reasonably full characterization of the psychological orientation associated with a social interaction (or its perception) will include the person's moral orientation as well as his or her cognitive and motivational orientations. My work in the area of justice, of course, has helped to sensitize me to the importance of moral norms in social situations. I speculate that the neglect of the moral component of psychological orientations is linked to the fact that the study of justice has not been central in the social psychological research literature. The flurry of interest in equity theory died down in the late 1970s with the decrease of interest in dissonance theory. The dissonance component of equity theory was its most interesting psychological feature.

After publishing *Distributive Justice* in 1985, I sought funding from NSF for a program of basic research related to some of the ideas in my paper "Interdependence and Psychological Orientation." Unfortunately, my proposal was not funded. By this time our NIMH-supported, predoctoral training program was no longer in existence; NIMH's interest had turned toward postdoctoral training. Teachers College provided no funds for research or for graduate research assistants and little secretarial support or money for travel or equipment. It was also a period in which academic appointments became scarce. The consequence was that our doctoral students increasingly became part-time students who often had full-time jobs. In addition, they became more interested in nonacademic positions and more frequently decided to specialize in the organizational rather than in the social psychology component of our doctoral program in social and organizational psychology.

In this context I discontinued my basic research, which had been primarily conducted in the laboratory. From 1985 on, I continued to write and publish papers mainly for small conferences related to conflict or justice, several as award addresses for honors I was receiving and a number by invitation of editors of books or special journal issues. Among the thirty articles I have published since 1985, several titles stand out: "On Negotiating the Non-Negotiable"; "Psychological Consequences of Different Forms of Social Organization"; "The Psychological Roots of Moral Exclusion"; "Sixty Years of Conflict"; "Equality and Economic Efficiency: Is There a Trade-Off?" "Kurt Lewin: The Tough-Minded and Tender-Hearted Scientist"; "Educating for a Peaceful World"; "The Effects of Training in Cooperative Learning and Conflict Resolution in an Alternative High School"; "Constructive Conflict Resolution: Theory, Research, and Practice"; (with Peter Coleman) "The Mediation of Interethnic Conflict"; "William James: The First Peace Psychologist"; and "Constructive Conflict Management for the World Today" (see citations in the References).

The International Center for Cooperation and Conflict Resolution

In 1986 I started the center that I promised in my Thorndike inaugural address. Our first activity was a workshop to which I invited the superintendents of school districts in and around New York City as well as representatives of several foundations who might become interested in financing the activities of our center. In addition to introductory remarks made by the president of Teachers College and myself, the workshop consisted of a series of miniseminars chosen to reflect the kinds of activities in which our center would engage: cooperative learning, the constructive use of controversy in teaching, conflict resolution training in schools, the training of student mediators, and research evaluation of programs. Each seminar was conducted by a leading expert (e.g., David and Roger Johnson led the seminars on cooperative learning and the constructive use of controversy).

As the result of this workshop, one of the superintendents invited us to develop a program of cooperative learning in his wealthy, suburban school district and to evaluate the program. We sought without success to broaden the program to include conflict resolution training. However, the superintendent was helpful in arranging for us to meet with the superintendent of a nearby, comparable school district that would serve as a control. We approached several foundations for funds but were rejected until I noticed in a publication that Hank Riecken was on the board of the W. T. Grant Foundation. I contacted Hank and told him of our plans and hopes, and he arranged for me to meet with the president and himself. Both were enthusiastic about our plans, which called for support for five years at a level of $200,000 per year, and they asked me to write a detailed proposal for submission to the board. The board approved the project for three years and indicated that after the first year we should obtain half our funds from other sources. At the time I did not realize that this was a customary but nasty policy of many foundations—forcing one to remain continuously in a fund-raising mode.

We began the project with a preliminary workshop in which David Johnson got a group of senior, influential teachers involved in cooperative learning. They became enthusiastic supporters. Our next step, which proved to be fatal, was to introduce the questionnaires, observational measures, and other recorded data we wished to obtain. We needed permissions from the school board as well as from the school personnel and parents of the students. When the school board learned that we were not only interested in academic achievement but also in measuring social skills, social relations, and psychological adjustment, they were horrified and canceled permission to do the study in their district. As the superintendent regretfully explained, the political attitudes of the board members were to the right of Attila the Hun, and they thought of mental health as a dangerous, explosive topic.

At this point I was sorry that I had left the social psychology laboratory to do research in field settings. However, Ellen Raider, who had joined our center as training director after we were funded, came up with the center-saving suggestion that we move our project to an inner-city, alternative high school where she knew the principal and associate principal. Luckily, the foundation was happy to approve the move; they preferred that our research be done with inner-city youth.

I shall not describe the many headaches and heartaches we had in carrying out our research other than to indicate that we were training overworked and fatigued but dedicated teachers, most of whose students lived in poor and difficult circumstances and often did not have the reading or writing skills necessary for successful work as high school students. Also, to put it bluntly, the physical conditions of the school and neighborhood were horrible. Many aspects of the project were not executed as well as we had planned: the training of the teachers; the measurement of the effects on students; the duration of the study; the records kept by the school on student attendance, dropouts, disruptions, and so on. By the standards of a laboratory experiment, it was very unsatisfactory research. Yet I must say that I came out of this study with a great deal of appreciation of those researchers who are foolhardy enough to leave the laboratory. They must have the kind of administrative and social skills, flexibility, ingenuity, statistical wizardry, and frustration tolerance rarely required in laboratory studies.

Despite our problems, much to our surprise, we were able to demonstrate that our training had important and significant effects on the students. In brief, the data showed that as students improved in managing their conflicts (whether or not because of the training in conflict resolution and cooperative learning), they experienced increased social support and less victimization from others. This improvement in their relations with others led to greater self-esteem as well as a fewer feelings of anxiety and depression and more frequent positive feelings of well-being. The higher self-esteem, in turn, produced a greater sense of personal control over their own fates. The increases in their sense of personal control and in their positive feelings of well-being led to higher academic performances. There is also indirect evidence that the work readiness and actual work performance of students were also improved. Our data further indicated that students, teachers, and administrators had generally positive views about the training and its results.

This study was the first longitudinal study of the effects of cooperative learning and conflict resolution training conducted in a very difficult school environment. It was also the first to go beyond the measurement of consumer satisfaction. Its positive results were consistent with our theoretical model and with results obtained in smaller, brief studies in experimental classrooms. In part because the study was conducted in the New York City school system, the city's board of education made a contract with ICCCR in 1992–1994. The contract specified that ICCCR would train two key faculty or staff people from every high school in New York City so that one would become sufficiently expert to be able to train students, teachers, and parents in constructive conflict resolution and the other would become sufficiently expert in mediation to be able to establish and administer an effective mediation center at the school, with students functioning as mediators.

Ellen Raider and her staff conducted the training, which took place for fifty hours over ten sessions, for a total of 300 people in cohorts over a year and a half. The training methods were based on a model and manuals developed by Ellen Raider and Susan Coleman. The principals of the various high schools also received training in conflict resolution and mediation in three-day workshops, abbreviated versions of the larger sessions.

Although ICCCR was not provided with funds to conduct a research evaluation of its training, the research division of the board of education and the Dispute Resolution Center of John Jay College were able to conduct some relevant research. The research indicated that within two years of training almost all of the more than 150 high schools who participated had established mediation centers in their schools (fewer than 5 percent had not). In addition, most of the schools had introduced into their curriculum education in constructive conflict resolution , and thousands of students had exposure to such education. All participants in the research believed that the program had a positive impact on personal relationships and school climate overall. Cited were improvements in the way students dealt with anger and resolved conflicts, heightened respect for differences, better communication skills, and increased understanding of students' needs on the part of the school staff. Some people noted that the school atmosphere was calmer and more collaborative. Peer mediators, disputants, and students who had participated in lessons in cooperative negotiation all commented on positive changes in their own interactions with others, both within and outside of school. Most telling, perhaps, was that disputants had enthusiastically recommended peer mediation to their friends, and curriculum students believed that all students should be required to take lessons in conflict resolution.

ICCCR continues to do conflict resolution training in various school systems and in other contexts, such as the United Nations. More recently, as a prelude to offering graduate studies in conflict resolution at Teachers College, Ellen Raider conducted workshops on conflict resolution with various members of the faculty. The graduate studies now exist as one of the concentrations in the degree programs in social and organizational psychology as well as a certificate program for nondegree students. I have continued to teach a theory course entitled "Fundamentals of Cooperation, Conflict Resolution, and Mediation." Ellen and her staff have been conducting our various practica courses in this area.

I have also been the organizer for a faculty seminar on conflict resolution from which a book is now in preparation, "The Handbook of Constructive Conflict Resolution: Theory and Practice," to be published by Jossey-Bass in 2000. I have written four chapters for it, and I am serving as its editor along with Peter Coleman, who is the new Director of ICCCR. As I have reduced my academic responsibilities (less teaching, no more faculty meetings, only one or two highly selected doctoral students whom I supervise), Lydia and I have been doing considerably more traveling and dining in superb restaurants.

Conclusion

As I look back upon my career, several things stand out for me:

Luck.   I was lucky to go to CCNY, which had two young faculty members, Max Hertzman and Walter Scott Neff, who stimulated my interest in Lewin and in social psychological research. I was extremely lucky to be a student at the RCGD at MIT, where I was able to become part of a small, innovative group of faculty and students who had a major impact on the development of modern social psychology. Moreover, my career got off to a quick start largely as a result of the prodding of Stuart Cook, who had me involved in writing two books shortly after I obtained my Ph.D. Also, I was very fortunate to be able to receive financial support for my research throughout most of my career. In addition, I have had the opportunity to work with many excellent, productive students who have stimulated me and contributed much to my research. Not least, I was lucky enough to marry a woman whose esthetic sensibility and practical skills helped to create a congenial and supportive home environment that enabled me to focus my attention on scholarly activities rather than on such household activities as fixing things (which I never could do anyway).

Continuing Themes.   My work on social psychology has been dominated by two continuing themes with which I have been preoccupied throughout my career. One is my intellectual interest in cooperation and competition, which has been expressed in my theorizing and research on the effects of cooperation and competition, our studies of conflict processes, and our work on distributive justice. I have continued to believe that these foci are central to understanding social life and also that a "social" social psychology rather than an "individual" social psychology would have these as its fundamental concerns. The second continuing interrelated theme has been developing my work so that it has social relevance to key social problems. Sometimes images, derived from such social problems as war and peace, prejudice, marital conflict, and injustice, would be the starting point for the development of a theoretical analysis or an experimental study. At other times I would use theory and research (other social scientists' as well as mine) in an attempt to shed light on important social issues. The two themes of my career have contributed to important applications, particularly in the field of education, where I am considered to be one of the parents of cooperative learning and conflict resolution training.

Episodic Research.   Occasionally, I strayed from the two themes just described, to do single studies that expressed my reservations about some of the fashionable theorizing and research. I took potshots at Solomon Asch's neglect of group factors in his conformity studies, at Festinger's omission of defensiveness in his dissonance theorizing, at equity theory's assumption of greater productivity when people are rewarded in proportion to their performance, at social perception studies that ignored the social and institutional context in which social acts are imbedded, and at Henri Tajfel's initial assumption that the mere awareness of a difference among a collection of individuals will promote group formation. My straying was usually short-lived because my primary interests were in the two themes described above and I was not sufficiently energetic to take on additional themes.

Familial Context.   As I look back on my career, I am impressed by how much its themes have been influenced by my experiences within my family as well as what was occurring in the broader society. Within my family, I was the youngest of four sons, and I felt a strong need to catch up with my next older brother (two and a half years older), believing that if I did not I would be excluded. In fact, one of my earliest memories focuses on injustice. I was about three and a half years old. We were all staying at a resort in the Catskills, and a counselor organized a game of softball for the older kids (the six- to eight-year-olds). I was excluded from it because I was too young and was asked to stay on the side. I was very mad, and when a foul ball was hit near me, I recall picking it up, running with it, and throwing it as far as I could in a direction away from the players. I trace my passionate feeling about injustice to such early experiences as this one. In my attempts to keep up with the older kids, as a child and youth I was quite competitive. However, it was a strain, and when I lost I felt injured and when I won, surpassing my older brother and his friends, I could feel their sense of hurt and shame. My questioning of the value of competition undoubtedly arose from these episodes. This questioning was reinforced by the favorable attitude toward socialism that was held by my parents and many of their friends. My father became rabidly antiunion during my rebellious adolescence, and, perversely, this strengthened my favorable view of unions, cooperatives, and socialism.

The Social Context.   I grew up in a time when, as a Jew, I experienced many instances of prejudice, blatant as well as subtle, and could observe the gross acts of injustice being suffered by blacks. In my youth and adolescence, there was the economic depression, union organizing, the Spanish civil war, and the emergence of fascism, Nazism, and Stalinism. I was politically engaged—contributing lunch money to the Spanish loyalists, organizing strikes in high school and in a summer resort, participating in a sit-in against the fascist ambassador, and so forth. It is no wonder that I was attracted to Lewin, whom I saw as taking psychology in a direction that would enable it to contribute to the development of a democratic, cooperative society that was free of prejudice.

The activist theme in my career as a social psychologist undoubtedly reflects the social context of my youth. The social context also helps to explain why I did not become a political activist or union organizer. In my family, among my fellow (mostly Jewish) students, and in my high school and college, there was a strong emphasis on ideas and intellectual achievement. Our heroes were those who contributed to the world through their ideas—Darwin, Marx, Freud, and Einstein. They had exemplified Lewin's dictum, recalled earlier, that "there is nothing so practical as a good theory." This has been the second theme of my career.

One final note: Every society has its own implicit assumptions of which its members are usually not aware. We live in a highly individualistic society. Its ethos is that of the lone, self-reliant, enterprising individual who has escaped from the restraints of an oppressive community so as to be free to pursue his or her destiny in an environment that offers ever expanding opportunity to those who are fittest. I think this image has influenced much of American social psychology, which has been too focused on what goes on in the isolated head of the subject, with a corresponding neglect of the social reality in which the subject is participating.

The socialist ethos incorporates the view that the human being is a social animal whose nature is determined by the way people are related to one another in their productive activities in any given community. Its vision is of social beings free to cooperate with one another toward common objectives because they jointly control the means of production and share the rewards of their collective labor. This vision is a useful supplement to the dominant emphasis in American social psychology. However, it is neglectful of the characteristics of individual persons—characteristics that are determined mainly in the course of interaction between the biological person and his or her social environment.

I conclude with the hope that future social psychologists will be more concerned than we have been with characterizing the socially relevant properties of individuals and the psychologically relevant attributes of social structures. To oversimplify it, I hope that they will provide a successful integration of the orientations of three of the intellectual heroes of my youth: Freud, Marx, and Lewin.

Notes

1. Lewin was widely admired by other psychologists. In the summer of 1947, after his death, there was a meeting of the Topological Circle at Smith College. At this meeting there were such eminent psychologists as Fritz Heider (the host), Edward Chace Tolman, and David Rappaport, as well as many of the faculty and students of the RCGD. At that meeting Heider presented the ideas that are at the core of his subsequently published book. Heider was a shy and somewhat inarticulate public speaker, but the profundity of his ideas gripped us all. The meeting also provided us the opportunity to have lively informal discussions with Tolman and Rappaport (who offered me a job at Austen Riggs).

2. One sour note in connection with my dissertation: For it, I had developed an observation schedule and manual describing the "functions of participation" for characterizing the behavior of group members. It included a description and detailing of various task, group, and individual functions. I also used this material in analyzing observational data in connection with the research done on the first NTL. Much to my surprise, shortly before my dissertation defense in the summer of 1948, an article by Kenneth Benne and Paul Sheats entitled "The Functional Role of Group Members" appeared in the *Journal of Social Issues*. This article was mainly a reprint of my manual with some elaboration; my authorship received no acknowledgment. When I brought this to the attention of Benne and Sheats, they acknowledged that their article was based on my manual, but since it did not have my name on it, they thought it was some impersonal product of NTL. They apologized for their error, but when the article was widely reprinted in books, there was no attempt to undo their error. When I published my dissertation, I included a footnote indicating that some of my dissertation material had been published in "The Functional Role of Group Members."

3. In 1968 I also gave this address at a meeting of social psychologists from the West (the United States and Western Europe) and from Eastern Europe. We met in Prague shortly after the Soviet Union had sent its troops into Czechoslovakia to squash an incipient rebellion against Soviet domination. Despite our misgivings, we came at the strong urging of our Czech colleagues who wanted to maintain their contacts with the West. My paper included a section on what strategies and tactics were available to "low-power" groups when confronting "high-power" groups. The Czechs loved it and widely circulated a tape recording they made of it.

Leon Festinger, in contrast, asked me, "Is this science?" I replied, "Leon, you and I have a different conception of the nature of science." My conception, I believe, was more inclusive than his. Leon and his followers were always puzzled by me: They thought I did fine theoretical and experimental work, but they did not understand my willingness to apply the best available social science knowledge to important social issues even when that knowledge was not firmly rooted in experimental research.

The meeting in Prague was sponsored by the Transnational Social Psychology Committee of the Social Science Research Council (SSRC). Leon was its chair, and under his leadership it did much to stimulate the development of social psychology in Western Europe.

However, Leon was very much annoyed and harshly criticized Henri Tajfel for his manuscript "Experiments in a Vacuum" and Serge Moscovici for his "Society and Theory in Social Psychology," both of which were critical of American social psychology. This occurred during a committee meeting in West Germany in 1971.

The committee also exerted some efforts to develop social psychology in Latin America. We held a seminar in Chile for Latin American social psychologists during the tumultuous period just prior to Salvador Allende's coming to power. After Leon resigned as the committee chairman, I was asked to take on this role. We had another East-West meeting in Hungary, in a small resort village about 20 miles from Budapest. We also held a conference in Majorca that led to the book *Applying Social Psychology* (Deutsch and Hornstein, 1975). About this time, SSRC decided to end its financial support for the committee (it had had a rather extended life by SSRC's usual standards for committees). The committee, however, was not quite ready to quit. Martin Irle hosted a small meeting in Mannheim, Germany. I hosted an even smaller one in my beach house in East Hampton, New York, and Jujuji Misumi hosted an even smaller one in Japan.

This traveling committee, which met mainly outside the United States (so as to stimulate the development of social psychology elsewhere), included—at different times—such people as Leon Festinger, John Lanzetta, Stanley Schachter, Harold Kelley, Henry Riecken, and myself from the United States as well as Serge Moscovici, Henri Tajfel, Jaap Kookebacker, Martin Irle, Ragner Rommetweit, Jujuji Misumi, and Jaromir Janousek from other parts of the world. Throughout much of its existence, Jerome Singer was the committee's witty and tolerant administrator for SSRC.

During much of the same time, there was another traveling committee funded by the Office of Naval Research, through Luigi Petrullo, which met to discuss research on conflict. About half of its members were from the United States and the other half from Western Europe. Its U.S. members included Harold Kelley, Gerald Shure, John Thibaut, John Lanzetta, Dean Pruitt, and myself. Among the Europeans were Serge Moscovici, Henri Tajfel, Claude Faucheux, Claude Flament, and Josef Nuttin Jr. We met about twice a year, alternating locales between Europe and the United States. We had many good discussions, excellent wine and food, and formed some lasting friendships. We also did a cross-national experiment on bargaining that has rarely been cited. It was a wonderful period to be a social psychologist.

4. Among the many students who contributed directly to this book were Rebecca Curtis, Michelle Fine, Sandra Horowitz, Ivan Lansberg, Brian Maruffi, Louis Medvene, Dolores Mei, Marilyn Seiler, Janice Steil, Bruce Tuchman, Janet Weinglass, William Wenck Jr., and Cilio Ziviani. Other students in my work group on justice who have contributed indirectly to this volume include Lorinda Arella, Adrienne Asch, Susan Boardman, Ellen Brickman, Ellen Fagenson, Martha Gephart, Cheryl Koopman, Jay Kantor, Eric Marcus, Susan Opotow, Jorge da Silva Ribeiro, Rony Rinat, Shula Shichman, and Rachel Solomon.

References

Adorno, T. W., Frenkel-Brunswik, E., Levinson, D. J., & Sanford, R. N. (1950). *The authoritarian personality*. New York: Harper.

Allport, G. W. (1954a). The historical background of modern social psychology. In G. Lindzey (Ed.), *Handbook of social psychology* (Vol. 1). Cambridge, MA: Addison-Wesley.

_____. (1954b). *The nature of prejudice.* Reading, MA: Addison-Wesley.

Bartlett, F. C. (1932). *Remembering: A study in social and experimental psychology.* Cambridge: Cambridge University Press.

Brown, J. F. (1936). *Psychology and the social order: An introduction to the dynamic study of social fields.* New York: McGraw-Hill.

Cohen, M., & Nagel, E. (1934). *An introduction to logic and scientific method.* New York: Harcourt.

Coleman, P., & Deutsch, M. (1995). The mediation of interethnic conflict. In W. D. Hawley and A. W. Jackson (Eds.), *Toward a common destiny: Race relations in America, 1995.* Jossey-Bass.

Cooley, C. H. (1956). *Human nature and the social order.* Glencoe, IL: Free Press.

Deutsch, M. (1949a). An experimental study of effects of cooperation and competition upon group processes. *Human Relations, 2,* 199–231.

_____. (1949b). A theory of cooperation and competition. *Human Relations, 2,* 129–151.

_____. (1954). Field theory in social psychology. In G. Lindzey (Ed.), *Handbook of social psychology* (pp. 181–222). Cambridge, MA: Addison-Wesley.

_____. (1958). Trust and suspicion. *Journal of Conflict Resolution, 2,* 265–279.

_____. (1960). Psychological alternatives to war. *Journal of Social Issues, 18,* 97–119.

_____. (1961). The interpretation of praise and criticism as a function of their social context. *Journal of Abnormal and Social Psychology, 62,* 391–400.

_____. (1962a). Cooperation and trust: Some theoretical notes. In M. Jones (Ed.), *Nebraska Symposium on Motivation* (pp. 275–318). Lincoln: University of Nebraska Press.

_____. (1962b). Dissonance or defensiveness? *Journal of Personality, 30,* 16–28.

_____. (1966). Vietnam and the start of World War III: Some psychological parallels. Presidential address before the New York State Psychological Association, May 6, New York.

_____. (1969a). Conflicts: Productive and destructive. *Journal of Social Issues, 25,* 7–41.

_____. (1969b). Socially relevant science: Reflections on some studies of interpersonal conflict. *American Psychologist, 24,* 1076–1092.

_____. (1973). *The resolution of conflict: Constructive and destructive processes.* New Haven, CT: Yale University Press.

_____. (1974). Awakening the sense of injustice. In M. Lerner & M. Ross (Eds.), *The quest for justice.* New York: Holt.

_____. (1976). Equity, equality, and need: What determines which value will be used as the basis for distributive justice? *Journal of Social Issues, 31,* 137–150.

_____. (1978). The social psychology of justice. In *Proceedings of the international symposium on social psychology* (pp. 23–46). Kyoto, Japan: Japanese Group Dynamics Association.

_____. (1982). Interdependence and psychological orientation. In V. Derlega & J. L. Grzelek (Eds.), *Cooperation and helping behavior: Theories and research* (pp. 15–42). New York: Academic Press.

_____. (1983a). Conflict resolution: Theory and practice. *Political Psychology, 4,* 431–453.

_____. (1983b). Current perspectives on justice. *European Journal of Social Psychology, 13,* 305–319.

_____. (1983c). Preventing World War III: A psychological perspective. *Political Psychology, 3,* 3–31.

_____. (1985). *Distributive justice: A social psychological perspective*. New Haven, CT: Yale University Press.

_____. (1988). On negotiating the non-negotiable. In B. Kellerman & J. Rubin (Eds.), *Leadership and negotiation in the Middle East* (pp. 248–263). New York: Praeger.

_____. (1989). Equality and economic efficiency: Is there a trade-off? In N. Eisenberg, J. Reykowski, & E. Staub (Eds.), *Social and moral values*. Hillsdale, NJ: Erlbaum.

_____. (1990a). Psychological consequences of different forms of social organization. In H. Himmelweit & G. Gaskell (Eds.), *Societal psychology* (pp. 157–176). London: Sage.

_____. (1990b). Sixty years of conflict. *International Journal of Conflict Management, 1,* 237–263.

_____. (1991). Egalitarianism in the laboratory and in the workplace. In R. Vermunt & H. Steensma (Eds.), *Social justice in human relations* (Vol. 1, pp. 195–210). New York: Plenum Press.

_____. (1992a). *The effects of training in cooperative learning and conflict resolution in an alternative high school*. New York: International Center for Cooperation and Conflict Resolution, Teachers College, Columbia University.

_____. (1992b). Kurt Lewin: The tough-minded and tender-hearted scientist. *Journal of Social Issues, 48,* 31–43.

_____. (1993a). Educating for a peaceful world. *American Psychologist, 48,* 510–517.

_____. (1993b). The effects of training in cooperative learning and conflict resolution in an alternative high school. *Cooperative Learning, 13,* 2–5.

_____. (1994a). Constructive conflict management for the world today. *International Journal of Conflict Management, 5,* 111–129.

_____. (1994b). Constructive conflict resolution: Theory, research, and practice. *Journal of Social Issues, 50,* 13–32.

_____. (1995). William James: The first peace psychologist. *Peace and Conflict: Journal of Peace Psychology, 1,* 17–26.

Deutsch, M., & Collins, M. E. (1951). *Interracial housing: A psychological evaluation of a social experiment*. Minneapolis: University of Minnesota Press.

Deutsch, M., & Gerard, H. B. (1955). A study of normative and informational influences upon individual judgment. *Journal of Abnormal and Social Psychology, 51,* 629–636.

Deutsch, M., & Hornstein, H. (Eds.). (1975). *Applying social psychology: Implications for research, practice and training*. Hillsdale, NJ: Erlbaum.

Deutsch, M., & Krauss, R. (1960). The effect of threat upon interpersonal bargaining. *Journal of Abnormal and Social Psychology, 61,* 181–189.

_____. (1962). Studies of interpersonal bargaining. *Journal of Conflict Resolution, 6,* 52–76.

_____. (1965). *Theories in social psychology*. New York: Basic Books.

Johnson, D. W., & Johnson, R. T. (1989). *Cooperation and competition: Theory and research*. Edina, MN: Interaction.

Lewin, K. (1935). *A dynamic theory of personality*. New York: McGraw-Hill.

_____. (1936). *Principles of topological psychology*. New York: McGraw-Hill.

_____. (1938). *The conceptual representation and measurement of psychological forces*. Durham, NC: Duke University Press.

_____. (1951). *Field theory in social science*. New York: Harper.

Marrow, A. (1969). *The practical theorist: The life and work of Kurt Lewin*. New York: Basic Books.

McDougall, W. (1908). *An introduction to social psychology*. London: Methuen.

Piaget, J. (1948). *The moral judgement of the child*. Glencoe, IL: Free Press.

Ross, E. A. (1908). *Social psychology*. New York: Macmillan.

Selltiz, C., Jahoda, M., Deutsch, M., & Cook, S. W. (1959). *Research methods in social relations* (2nd ed.). New York: Holt and Dryden.

Sherif, M. (1936). *The psychology of social norms*. New York: Harper.

Tarde, G. (1903). *The laws of imitation*. New York: Henry Holt.

Watson, J. B. (1930). *Behaviorism* (rev. ed.). New York: W. W. Norton.

Wish, M., Deutsch, M., & Kaplan, S. (1976). Perceived dimensions of interpersonal relations. *Journal of Personality and Social Psychology, 33,* 409–420.

Wright, Q., Evan, W. M., & Deutsch, M. (Eds.). (1962). *Preventing World War III: Some proposals*. New York: Simon and Schuster.

2   *Fifty Years in Social Psychology: Some Reflections on the Individual-Group Problem*

Harold H. Kelley

Harold Kelley's contributions to the field of social psychology are both broad and profound. In this chapter he uses the metaphor of reflections to argue that the field stands between two counterimposed mirrors—the mirror of the individual and that of the group. How we look into these mirrors illustrates four ways of phrasing the subject matter of social psychology: the individual or the group, the individual versus the group, the individual from the group, and the individual against the group. Kelley describes how social psychology and his own research have navigated through these four reflections. He begins with his experiences at Yale, where, along with several other notable social psychologists, he helped bring a group focus to the study of mass communication processes. He emphasizes his close and long-lasting association with John Thibaut and their numerous works on interdependence. Kelley regards his work on attribution—most notably the development of the famous Kelley cube—as an example of the tradition of research on the individual versus the group. He tells how his 1978 book with Thibaut, on interdependence patterns and how they may define and shape individual differences, is in the tradition of the approach emphasizing the individual from the group. Kelley shows how some of his studies at Yale, as well as his ANOVA model, are examples of how individuals may resist group influences.

My reflections are not scholarly, researched conclusions. They're the ways I remember things and feel about them now. This egocentric approach seemed to be the surest way to avoid redundancy with the other authors of these reflections.

"Reflections" is an apt metaphor for some of the major themes of social psychology. Located as it is between the social and the psychological, we can think of social psychology as standing between two counterposed mirrors, the one the mirror of the individual and the second the mirror of the group. We can look into the one, or we can look into the other. But when we look into either one, we see reflections from the other, including its reflections of the mirror we're viewing directly.

Using that metaphor (and with apologies to Charles Horton Cooley), I've located my comments under four counterposings of the individual and the group:

1. The individual *or* the group? (What is the proper focus of our field? Which mirror do we look directly into?)
2. The individual *versus* the group? (The "person" versus the "interpersonal situation" as causes of behavior? When we see behavior, in which mirror does its image originate?)
3. The individual *from* the group? (How are individual differences related to or derived from the group? When we look into the individual mirror, what are we seeing from the other side?)
4. The individual *against* the group? When are individuals independent of the group? When are images in the individual mirror independent of those in the other?

Those four themes have been important in social psychology over the twentieth century and are, to varying degrees, reflected in my own fifty years of work. In discussing them, I include a few stories along the way. These are my recollections about why certain things went as they did during those years.

First a few comments about my background. Unlike the other authors in this book, I came from a rural area. My father was a farmer in the small town of Delano, California, located some 90 miles south of Fresno. Like most college-bound youngsters there, from Delano High School I went on to Bakersfield Junior College and then to "Cal," that is, Berkeley. I can no longer reconstruct exactly why I became a psychology major, but I did well in my studies. On graduating with a master's degree in 1943, I had the good fortune to go directly into the Aviation Psychology Program of the U.S. Army Air Force. There I worked under the direction of Stuart Cook ("Captain Cook" in those days), developing selection tests and analyzing how various aircrew members did their jobs (e.g., landing a plane, interpreting airborne radar signals).

Heider (1983) concludes his autobiography with a reference to a "friendly spirit" that arranged the sequence of events in which fortune was so kind to him. I resonate strongly to Heider's comment because it applies to my life as well. Surely the relationship with Stuart Cook was the work of such a spirit. I came to trust his judgment fully, and it was on his strong urging that, at the end of the war, I enrolled in the group psychology program at MIT. That decision landed me in what became one of the most influential groups of social psychologists and gave me a head start on a productive career in the field.

Now, let me return to my four "reflection" themes.

The Individual or the Group

This concerns the basic question of what is the proper subject matter of "social psychology." At MIT we were taught that a group is more than the sum of its parts. Our version of social psychology was focused on "dynamic wholes," closely interconnected—that is, interdependent—sets of individuals. By virtue of their past or their ongoing interaction, they have complex and dense ties: linkages via communication networks, influence via sociometric and status positions, and so on. That focus contrasted with that of earlier social psychologists who argued that only individuals are real and a group is no more than the sum of individuals' actions.

In research the individual focus was illustrated by Triplett's and similar work that examined such things as the effect of observers on a person's activities. In this tradition experiments usually used strangers as subjects, and the interaction was highly constrained and, generally, brief.

The group focus is well illustrated by the leadership studies at Iowa; by Festinger, Schachter, and Kurt Back's study of a housing project at MIT; by Deutsch's study of contrasting classroom incentive systems; and by Thibaut's laboratory study using gangs from Boston neighborhoods. (My own work on first impressions wasn't in that vein, though, like Mort Deutsch and several others, I received a Ph.D. from MIT in *group* psychology.) The studies were marked by the use of ongoing groups and by the effort put into documenting the processes within those groups. That stands in contrast to the individually oriented work with strangers, short time spans, and concern with end products rather than process.

From 1950 to 1955, my role at Yale, in Carl Hovland's program, was to bring a "group" focus to bear on mass communication processes. That was in contrast to Hovland's orientation (with its learning-theoretic focus on the individual's comprehension, learning, and retention of information) and Irving Janis's similar individualistic focus on personality and psychodynamics. The group and individual orientations were never brought into confrontation. They existed side by side, which reflected Carl's open personality and the value he attached to eclecticism.

In the late 1940s and the 1950s, the major focus was the "group" one, set in place mainly by the group dynamics people. But then, I think it is clear, the group focus began to blur and was gradually pretty much replaced by the individual focus. This shift occasioned Ivan Steiner's famous question in 1974: "Whatever happened to the group in social psychology?" In this shift, much of the study of groups has been left to neighboring disciplines (sociology, communication, education, management, etc.).

That shift leads me to think that the "group" focus in social psychology does not afford a stable intellectual orientation for psychologists. To mix metaphors a bit, it is not a firm place for us to stand. Ned Jones wrote that "in a curious way, social psychology has always been ambivalent about the study of groups per se"

(Jones, 1985, p. 77). I offer two possible reasons for this instability of our attention to groups:

1. An institutional reason concerns the relative prestige of various locations in the scientific hierarchy. In the reductionistic aspects of our shift toward the individual, perhaps there is a seeking of hard-science legitimacy and prestige—a disengagement from the softer (perhaps, the more sociological) parts of social psychology and an identification with the physical and biological sciences.

2. The other reason may be found in the problem that Bob Cohen identified as "bubbe psychology," the natural desire to try to surprise and impress one's bubbe (Yiddish for "grandmother") and one's colleagues. I would argue (as I have in Kelley, 1992) that avoiding the commonplace or "obvious" takes us in one or both directions away from the intermediate level of observable behavior in groups—either to more micro (reductionistic) levels or to more macro (collective, cultural) levels. Leon Festinger's scientific career might be examined in these terms, with his moves away from groups, first downward to microlevels of individual motivation, then later to motion of the eyeball, and finally upward to the macrolevels of paleontology and history.

In the Thibaut and Kelley collaboration that began in 1953, John and I *did* achieve a stable focus on phenomena at the group level. We did so by hitting upon a comprehensive and systematic theory, the elements of which others might regard as mundane but the combinatorial structure of which brings order to numerous interpersonal and intergroup phenomena.

So another friendly spirit story concerns the Thibaut and Kelley collaboration and how it came about. In 1952 Gardner Lindzey wrote me at Yale, asking me to write a chapter on groups for the new *Handbook* he was editing and suggesting that I ask Irv Janis to be a coauthor. I posed the question to Irv, and he declined. I then asked Thibaut (who had been a fellow graduate student at MIT), and he accepted. John and I found that we greatly enjoyed working together, our minds and temperaments meshed well, and we produced a chapter of which we were rather proud. On the merits of that chapter (at least in part), we were invited to the Ford Center (the Center for Advanced Studies in the Behavioral Sciences, or CASBS, in Stanford) as a team. We intended to write a textbook on groups, perhaps along the line of Homans's *Human Group*. But we got sidetracked into economic models (I remember drawing numerous indifference curves on the blackboard), and then got caught up with payoff matrices. Luce and Raiffa had just written their survey of game theory, and we studied a draft copy then available at the center. Our book turned out to be a theoretical work that in its use of outcome matrices (in a more relaxed way than the payoff matrices are used in game theory) provided a strongly analytic and organizing approach to group interdependence—an approach we eventually came to call "interdependence theory."

Our collaboration was importantly determined by some good luck and helpful accidents—Janis's other competing tasks; the formation of the Ford Center at that time, which gave us the year to work together; the Luce and Raiffa manuscript; and so on. The Thibaut and Kelley collaboration surely had the benefit of arrangements by one of Heider's friendly spirits.

That collaboration continued until John's death in 1986. Further developments in our theory are described below. Over the years, we continued our joint theoretical work, but our respective lines of empirical work diverged rather markedly. I became increasingly obsessed with the dyad, which I felt I could eventually master intellectually. Reflecting his longtime interests in moral and political philosophy, John's work increasingly consisted of experimental studies of social organizations, norms, and processes. Prominent among those was his brilliant work, with Laurens Walker (a colleague from the University of North Carolina Law School), on procedural justice. I have no doubt that Thibaut was the single most important intellectual influence on my career and work in social psychology.

The Individual Versus the Group (as Causes of Behavior)

This second counterposing of individual and group refers to the "person versus situation" attribution problem. The "situation" almost always involves one or more other persons, so the "person-situation" contrast is a special case of the individual-group contrast. Is an observed behavior due to the "person," or is it due to the "group," that is, due to pressures from other persons? This, of course, is one of the central questions raised by the attribution perspective in social psychology.

My role in the development of attribution theory was that of bringing together under one tent a number of lines of prior and ongoing work. So a brief story about why and how the Kelley cube came about: At Minnesota we "social relations" people (Stan Schachter, Ben Willerman, Ken Ring, John Arrowood, Jerry Singer, Ladd Wheeler, and others) had read and discussed Heider's book, and I had reviewed it for *Contemporary Psychology*. I had long been a fan of Thibaut and Henry Riecken's paper on perception of conformity to requests for help from more and less powerful people, and then at the University of California at Los Angeles (UCLA), Ken Ring and Arie Kruglanski had done doctoral theses taking off from some of Thibaut's work. From Minnesota days, I was familiar with Schachter's arousal-affect work, which lent itself to attributional interpretations. I had studied "From Acts to Dispositions," by Jones and Davis (1965). And I interacted at UCLA with Melvin Seeman, a sociology colleague steeped in Rotter's locus of control ideas. So my head and notes were full of causal perception– and attribution-related stuff. Then came the invitation to write a paper for the Nebraska Symposium on Motivation, and I did the obvious thing, which was to draw together those various strands of thought.

Now, pardon a homely metaphor: The theoretical fruit was hanging high in the tree, ripe and ready for picking, and I happened to be in the orchard at the top of the ladder (good imagery for Fresno, and it comes naturally to a farm boy from Delano). My point is that possessing the particular combination of information and opportunity I had, almost any respectable social psychologist could have written that attribution paper. (This point is also suggested by Ken Ring's and Daryl Bem's subsequent comments, which implied that a similar synthesis was close to the surface of their thinking.) Again, Heider's friendly spirit smiled on me. I should add that the Kelley cube was included only at the last minute, as a visual aid for the lecture. If I had relied entirely on words, as I had originally intended, people wouldn't have had the Kelley cube to play hacky-sack with all these years.

To back up a little, until it was discouraged by Cronbach's critique of the methodology, much of the earliest work on person-perception after World War II was concerned with the *accuracy* of judgments of other people. Then, following leads in Asch's early work, there came the extensive study of judgments of nouns and adjectives, as illustrated by Norman Anderson's work and Charles Osgood's monumental studies of the meaning of concepts.

The attribution approach was different from the earlier work in that it avoided issues of accuracy and from the later work in that it dealt with interpretations of behavior rather than adjectives. The new questions concerned the causal explanation for the behavior—whether due to the individual and, therefore, informative about that person or due to the group or situational context. Equally important about the attribution perspective was that it was clear that such attributions make a difference. This was shown in the work on misattributions (inspired by Schachter's work on labeling of arousal) and, soon, in Bernie Weiner's studies of affect, moral judgments, and behavior in relation to person-situation attributions.

The major impact of the ANOVA (analysis of variance) model was not in its direct use but in the broader questions it stimulated. Raised first by Leslie MacArthur's research, these questions concerned biases in the use of the covariance information and in the tendency to make "person versus situation" attributions. Those issues came to the forefront in the attribution book I coedited (Jones et al., 1972)—the "orange" book.

Schachter was, in some ways, the friendly spirit responsible for that book. When I happened to be in New York, he suggested that I invite Dick Nisbett and Stuart Valins to come out to UCLA to discuss attribution problems. It was natural and easy, the executive secretary of the appropriate NSF review panel at that time being Kelly Shaver, to get funds for a workshop on attribution. I also invited Ned Jones and two other UCLA participants—Bernie Weiner and Dave Kanouse. We met at UCLA in August 1969 and continued a bit later at Yale. Again, my (i.e., our) good luck held, and the attribution book was quite influential. You may remember that it was printed on beige paper, for which we must credit Hurricane Agnes, which in the summer of 1972 produced floods in Pennsylvania that reduced the printer's supply of paper to that lovely creamy stock.

Most directly traceable to that workshop and most notable in its influence was the Jones and Nisbett chapter on the actor-observer discrepancy, the hypothesis being that actors tend to attribute their behavior to the situation but observers tend to attribute it to the actors. The latter became the focus of much of Ned's subsequent work on insufficient discounting (or "correspondence bias," as he called it) and the basis of work that led to Lee Ross's famous concept of the "fundamental attribution error." (So we see that questions of accuracy crept back into social perception work after all.)

The Individual from the Group

This third counterposing of "individual" and "group" concerns how individual differences are related to—derived from—the group. Here I want to describe my own shift in attitudes toward individual difference and personality research and how the Thibaut and Kelley analysis of interdependence patterns became a platform for analyzing how individual differences are defined and shaped by interdependence.

As I remember it, in the early days we experimentalists were rather supercilious in our attitudes toward colleagues who used personality measures and studied individual differences. We were "real" scientists, using the experimental method, drawing firm conclusions about cause and effect, and not fooling around with mushy correlational data. (A not uncommon and hypocritical exception was made when we used "take measures"—a highly relevant and contemporaneous individual difference assessment—to sort our experimental subjects and "clarify" our experimental results.)

I shared that attitude. Yet individual differences played a crucial role in one of my best studies—with Tony Stahelski—on cooperators versus competitors, their interaction in the Prisoner's Dilemma game, and the behavioral assimilation of the cooperators to the competitors. In their interplay, cooperators quickly begin to act like competitors, but this assimilation goes unnoticed by the competitors and serves only to substantiate their misanthropic beliefs that almost all people are, deep down, competitive like themselves.

That was a nice model. And it was a first step in bringing together my interests in interdependence and attribution—interests I had previously tended to keep separate. Not long after, I tired of laboratory experiments with gamelike tasks and turned to using questionnaires to study real dyads—young couples in love and in ongoing relationships. My first interest was in whether we could extract from their reports the two-by-two outcome matrices latent in the problems they encountered in their lives. The answer is, "Well sort of—but two-by-two matrices aren't quite adequate for the job," that is, the job of describing natural interpersonal situations. Far better descriptions are provided by transition lists, presented in my 1984 paper.

In the course of that work, it became clear that people's satisfactions/dissatisfactions with each other are greatly influenced by the general interpersonal dispositions they attribute to each other. So "attribution" shifted from a peripheral to a central position in my work on interdependence. It began to make sense to think of people as being outcome-interdependent not only in their actions but also in their attitudes and dispositions.

That view of interdependence was reflected in Thibaut's and my 1978 book. With an advance from Wiley, we moved our families to Morelia, Mexico, for a month, and then quickly lost interest in the original plan, which was to write a revision of our 1959 book. Instead, we worked on two new ideas: (1) a thorough analysis of the domain of two-by-two outcome patterns—to identify all the major problems, opportunities, dilemmas, and so on that such situations present to interdependent people; and (2) a causal model of behavior in such situations. That model distinguishes between the underlying ("given") situation and the transformed ("effective") situation. The latter reflects the new situation created by the attitudes they bring to bear on the concrete problem—such attitudes as cooperativeness, fairness, and dominance. This is a systematic, logical way of identifying and distinguishing the individual differences that are relevant to interdependent life. We were heavily influenced in that elaboration of the theory by Chuck McClintock and his colleagues' work on social orientations—work that continues to be very useful in its explanation and prediction of social interaction.

I might note that in writing the 1978 book, John Thibaut and I became increasingly aware of how greatly our theory depended on various key ideas from Kurt Lewin's writings. Those ideas include, for example, interdependence, contemporaneity, taxonomy of situations, cognitive restructuring of the field, goal conflict, motivational properties of conflict, and (in transition lists) locomotion through a "space" defined by paths and goals. The relation of our theory to Lewin's had been questioned by various commentators over the years, and some writers had even regarded us as disloyal renegades from the Lewin camp. Our experience in belatedly appreciating our theoretical indebtedness to Lewin piques my interest in the recent resurgence of attention to Lewinian "field theory," as evidenced by the very active Society for the Advancement of Field Theory (with much leadership from two other MIT fellow students, Kurt Back and Albert Pepitone); Ross and Nisbett's use of Lewinian ideas in their 1991 book, *The Person and the Situation*; and the 1996 Society of Personality and Social Psychology (SPSP) symposium on Lewin held in San Francisco.

In our 1978 book and my 1979 *Personal Relationships* volume, our "group" focus merged with an "individual" focus. In a sense, we became able to look into both mirrors at once, though for our purposes the group mirror was the primary one, the images in the individual mirror being closely coordinated with those on the group side. In brief, the Thibaut and Kelley theory expanded to include a psychology of individual differences. So I now see a basis for creating tight theoretical linkages between social and personality psychology. The idea, expressed in the 1982 Cartwright symposium paper and developed somewhat further in two recent papers (Kelley, 1997a, 1997b), is to derive logically the relevant personal dispositions from the problems and opportunities presented by situations. Accordingly, the dispositions a person is likely to have are a function of the sample of interdependence situations that person has experienced and of the pattern of tendencies the person has been able to "negotiate" with the various partners in those situations.

My research on young couples naturally led to contact with other social psychologists working on relationships. Another brief story concerns the increasing involvement of social psychologists in the close or personal relationship field, that is, in work on love, jealousy, commitment, arguments, divorce, and so on. The pioneers in this involvement were Elaine Walster and Ellen Berscheid. Despite encountering considerable prejudice against the scientific study of "personal" phenomena, in the 1970s they published impressive research on feelings of fairness, interpersonal attraction, and love. At a conference at Vanderbilt, John Harvey suggested to Berscheid and me that a group should be assembled to write a broad-gauge book for the field of close relationships. Again, NSF supported a workshop at UCLA; we assembled a cadre of nine fine social, clinical, and developmental psychologists; and after some Sturm und Drang published *Close Relationships* (Kelley, 1983). In the meantime there were the beginnings of interdisciplinary organizational activities in that field. A signal event was a 1982 conference on relationships at Wisconsin, arranged by Steve Duck and Elaine Walster. That was the first in a series of meetings that evolved into an ongoing international organization, the International Society for the Study of Personal Relationships (ISSPR), which brought experimental social psychologists into contact with researchers from sociology, family studies, and communication. Partly through the ideas in *Close Relationships* and through the authors' participation in that organization, the influence of social psychologists—their theories and their methods—have become diffused through what has come to be known as the "personal relationship" field. Again, the friendly spirit smiled on us.

The Individual Against the Group

The broad question here concerns when a group member can stand up against the group, maintaining independence of behavior or belief while still retaining membership.

The Festinger program on cohesiveness and pressures toward uniformity (with Schachter and Kurt Back) emphasized the effectiveness of groups in bringing their members into line. A similar emphasis on the power of the group setting was present in many of the key studies in the 1950s and 1960s—those by Solomon Asch, Stanley Milgram, Theodore Newcomb, Muzafer Sherif, Philip Zimbardo, and others.

Several of my studies at Yale raised questions about when an individual might resist those pressures, for example, by being highly valued in the group or by having strong direct evidence from his or her own senses. A similar counteremphasis existed (implicitly) in the risky shift studies and (explicitly) in Moscovici's work on minority group influence—the influence of an initially divergent minority.

The same issue was raised later in my ANOVA model, which explicitly counterposed group versus individual information sources, in the form, respectively,
of the consensus versus consistency criteria. One of my favorite studies, with
John Harvey, provided a neat experimental demonstration of the effect of informational consistency on confidence in one's judgment—something we demonstrated experimentally where before it had been indicated only by correlational
evidence.

The possible behavioral independence of a person was, of course, one of the
major questions for interdependence theory. The (logical and perhaps mundane)
generalization was that behavioral independence is possible when you are less dependent on others than they are on you. This generalization proves to have implications for a variety of basic events in close relationships, such as who has the
most say in its affairs, who is most free to deviate from its norms, who is least likely
to worry about being left by the partner, and who, indeed, is most likely to leave.

Interdependence, Lewin's criterion for a real "group," comes in several forms.
The Thibaut and Kelley 1959 book focused on outcome interdependence, but as
our second, 1968 *Handbook* chapter emphasized, social psychology also yielded a
great deal of evidence about information interdependence, for example, in the
Bavelas-inspired communication network studies, the sharing of information in
Elliot Aronson's jigsaw classes, and recent studies of jury decisions.

It has now become clear to me that the analysis of the interdependence between an individual member and the group requires even further differentiation.
They are interdependent in their concrete outcomes, but they are also interdependent in how they use their outcome control (as in being cooperative or competitive, altruistic or selfish). They are interdependent in their control over movement into, through, and out of situations, but they are also interdependent in
how they use those controls (as in being a leader or follower, active or passive).
Similarly, they are interdependent in the information they control (i.e., to which
they have access) but also in how they use that information (in their attentive-
ness, carefulness of analysis, etc.). Particularly important is their interdependence
in the communication of information (as in being open, honest, and trusting or
secretive, deceitful, and suspicious).

These comments are not meant to overwhelm the reader with the obvious but
merely to highlight the multidimensional nature of the relation between the individual member and the group. At each of these nexuses of interdependence, the
member has power over the group and they over him or her. (So it is not surprising that my distinctions among components of interdependence begin to resem-
ble Bert Raven's very useful distinctions among various bases of power.)

For the question at hand, of when a member can stand up against a group,
these distinctions suggest that the social influence effects from the earlier work
(by Festinger, Asch, Milgram, and others) are not subject to simple interpretations. Over the years we have been much impressed by those results and have
placed various dramatic interpretations on them. However, I believe that we do

not yet know what mix of factors separate the conformers from the nonconformers under the various conditions. The utilitarian, coordinative, solidarity, ethical, reality, and self-regard factors in most acts of conformity versus resistance are, in my judgment, quite complex. Given this list of factors, it is not surprising that, for example, the subjects in Asch's line-judging experiment were deeply disturbed by discrepancies between their own and their fellows' judgments. That disturbance surely reflected, in part, their puzzlement about reality considerations. But they must also have been perplexed about possible concrete rewards and costs, group incoordination, demonstrating "good membership," the ethics of their fellows, and the consequences of their verbalizations for their self-regard. This multidimensional perspective leads me to warn against blithely oversimplified and, too often, cynically misanthropic interpretations of conformity.

Concluding Comment

By now the reader will probably have been overdosed on the friendly spirits and my stories. However, in these comments I have not exaggerated my feelings about how and why my career proceeded as it did. It is clear to me that the course of my work and the roster of people I've worked with have been influenced very much by various chance events and timely opportunities. Perhaps the stories suggest that the *process* of my work—the interactions, meetings, working groups—are more salient in my memories than are the *results* of that work. That is not entirely correct. I have decided not to use this occasion to lay out the cumulative results of the theoretical work that John Thibaut and I began and that I continue to this day. In that regard, I'm hoping that the benevolent causal structure of my world will continue to be what it has been in the past and that there will be a few more smiles from the friendly spirits. But that is to challenge fate, and I do better to wish for the spirits to smile on the future of social psychology.

References

Heider, F. (1983). *The life of a psychologist: An autobiography.* Lawrence: University Press of Kansas.

Jones, E. E. (1985). Major developments in social psychology during the past five decades. In G. Lindzey & E. Aronson (Eds.), *Handbook of social psychology* (3rd ed., pp. 47–107). New York: Random House.

Jones, E. E., & Davis, K. E. (1965). From acts to dispositions: The attribution process in person perception. In L. Berkowitz (Ed.), *Advances in experimental social psychology* (Vol. 2, pp. 220–266). New York: Academic Press.

Jones, E. E., Kanouse, D. E., Kelley, H. H., Nisbett, R. E., Valins, S., & Weiner, B. (Eds.). (1972). *Attribution: Perceiving the causes of behavior.* Morristown, NJ: General Learning Press.

Kelley, H. H. (1979). *Personal relationships: Their structures and processes.* Hillsdale, NJ: Erlbaum.

_____. (1992). Common-sense psychology and scientific psychology. *Annual Review of Psychology, 43,* 1–23.

_____. (1997a). Expanding the analysis of social orientations by reference to the sequential-temporal structure of situations. *European Journal of Social Psychology, 27,* 373–404.

_____. (1997b). The "stimulus field" for interpersonal phenomena: The source of language and thought about interpersonal events. *Personality and Social Psychology Review, 1,* 140–169.

Kelley, H. H., Berscheid, E., Christensen, A., Harvey, J. H., Huston, T. L., Levinger, G., McClintock, E., Peplau, L. A., & Peterson, D. R. (1983). *Close relationships.* San Francisco: W. H. Freeman.

Kelley, H. H., & Thibaut, J. W. (1978). *Interpersonal relations: A theory of interdependence.* New York: Wiley.

3 A Social Psychologist Examines His Past and Looks to the Future

Harold B. Gerard

Harold Gerard begins by pondering the succession of events that determined the direction of his career, recalling the prominent role that happenstance often played at critical junctures along the way. He reviews his work at Bell Labs and in academia, ranging from explorations of the dynamics underlying the Asch paradigm to his collaborations with Ned Jones (which led to their well-known text on the foundations of social psychology text), to his work on dissonance theory, to his large-scale investigation of the effects of school desegregation in the Riverside, California, school district. He reviews his "last major effort working in mainstream social psychology"—his study with Orive at UCLA, published in 1987, on the dynamics of opinion formation based on dissonance and social comparison theories. After these studies, Gerard became increasingly involved in psychoanalysis. He tells how and why this came about and mentions his recent attempts to apply the methods of experimental social psychology in exploring psychoanalytic dynamics in early mental development. He argues for the crucial importance of psychodynamics in understanding social interaction, concluding with the hope that social psychology will return to the "natural connection between personality and social behavior."

The cognitive revolution in psychology, which was instigated in part by social psychologists beginning in the late 1950s, has all but eliminated concern with the psychodynamics that underlie how we perceive and behave toward others. Nearly fifty years ago, when Bert Raven, another contributor to this volume, and I were in the graduate program in social psychology at the University of Michigan, our reading list for the social psychology preliminary exam included much in the way of psychodynamics. We read Sigmund Freud, Anna Freud, Karen Horney, Erich Fromm, Clara Thompson, Harry Stack Sullivan, Heinz Hartmann, Ernst Kris, and others. Both Theodore Newcomb and Daniel Katz, the senior faculty in the program, held the conviction that the personality dynamics studied by psychoanalysis were important determinants of social behavior. As further acknowledgment of that, one of the core courses in the program was in personality theory, taught by Gerald Blum, that was wholly psychoanalytic. Nowadays psychodynamics is a complete blank in the curriculum of graduate training in social psychology. There had been a long tradition linking social psychology with both personality theory and psychopathology. The premier publication outlet for research in social psychology was for many years the *Journal of Abnormal and Social Psychology,* an explicit acknowledgment of the connection between psychopathology and social behavior.

What I hope to do in this chapter is to describe some of my work in mainstream social psychology and more recent work by myself and my students that is designed to reopen consideration of the crucial importance of psychodynamics in social interaction.

The Early Years

As a backdrop to what I have to say, I want to briefly trace my haphazard academic history, emphasizing crucial turning points, to give you an idea how I got into all of this. I entered Brooklyn College in the fall of 1939 at age sixteen, declaring myself a physics major. Immediately after Pearl Harbor, I dropped out of college in order to become an aviation cadet. I had the flying bug. Family resistance prevented me from enlisting, so instead I went to work in a defense plant, the Johns-Hartford Tool Company in Hartford, Connecticut, which manufactured punches and dies for stamping out shells for bullets of various calibers. I was a setup man for the lathes and milling machines. I did enlist in the signal corps in March 1942. I took a crash course (crash courses of all kinds were whipped up in those early days of the war) in electrical engineering at New York University, after which I was sent to the Lexington Signal Depot in Lexington, Kentucky, for another crash course in radar. I remember being totally fascinated with what was designated the SCR547(SCR for "signal corps radio"), a large ground-radar station. After my tour of duty in Lexington, I was determined to pursue a career in electrical engineering after the war.

I was finally able to apply to become an aviation cadet, but by the time I was accepted I was in Newport News, Virginia, awaiting overseas shipment, which, to my dismay, put me in a high-priority category, out of reach of the army air corps. I tried every which way to transfer from the signal corps to the air corps, but it was a lost cause. I even pleaded for help to the army chaplain in the Newport News embarkation camp. I was told to reapply once I got overseas, which I tried to do, but further complications intervened. It was just not meant to be. When I was eventually shipped overseas in January 1944 to take part in the invasion of Europe, I was, through no design of my own but because of my engineering background, assigned to teach electronics and radio repair at the American School Center in Shrivenham, England. I finally got into the war itself after the Battle of the Bulge, but that's another story.

After I was discharged in December 1945, I immediately returned to Brooklyn College. Hiroshima and Nagasaki cured me of wanting to be a physicist or an engineer. I decided instead to become a social scientist to help me make some sense of the war experience, which I found so devastating. I was haunted by the Holocaust and still am. I became completely caught up in some of the courses I was taking at Brooklyn College. In a philosophy course I read *An Introduction to Logic and Scientific Method* by Morris Cohen and Ernest Nagel (1934). I still own and treasure that original copy, which is now quite tattered. Nothing I read before or since had the impact on me of that book. It literally changed my way of seeing the world. I began to devour everything Morris Cohen had written, including his wonderfully sweet autobiography, *A Dreamer's Journey* (1949), which began with his childhood in Russia. Even though I never met Cohen, I consider him, along with Leon Festinger, one of my mentors. Cohen, incidentally, was one of Festinger's teachers at New York's City College, where Cohen taught for many years. When I eventually went to work with Leon, he suggested that I read Cohen and Nagel. I assured him that I had already internalized it.

I was a veritable sponge in my postwar stint at Brooklyn College, soaking up everything. I took a course in economic analysis and was encouraged by the instructor, Eli Shapiro, to follow him for graduate work to the University of Chicago, where he had just taken a job. Chicago was *the* place to study economic analysis and still is, I suspect. Shapiro invited me to his apartment for a steak dinner and to meet his wife. My wife-to-be, Dorothy (I had just gotten engaged) would not consider living in Chicago. It was windy and full of gangsters and meat-packing houses.

I was nearly sidetracked into art history by a course I took with Leo Balet, an inspired teacher who also took a shine to me. Sidney Siegel, the instructor in the introductory sociology course I was also taking, encouraged me to become a sociologist. So instead of economics at Chicago, I opted to go to Columbia University in sociology, which turned out to be a mistake. That was the easy way out, since we would remain in New York.

Graduate School

In my first semester at Columbia, I had courses with Robert MacIver, Robert Lynd, Theodore Abel, Paul Lazarsfeld, and Robert Merton. Quite a lineup! Merton's lectures were the most impressive. He was erudite, well organized, and dynamic—one of the best lecturers I had ever heard. I wanted desperately to work with him. So I approached him after one of his lectures and, miraculously, he put me to work. He turned me loose with a deck of IBM cards that held data from a housing study of his that was supported by the Lavenberg Foundation. He also gave me a key to the facilities of the Bureau of Social Research, which was located in the scary Hell's Kitchen part of Manhattan. I was as green as it gets as a first-year graduate student, and I was to somehow make sense of those data. I would go to the bureau nearly every evening, when the place was dark and totally deserted, and run my cards through the countersorter over and over again, looking for relationships in the data. It was strictly a fishing expedition.

I was given a fixed appointment time every week with Merton, during which I would report my latest findings. He was as cold and severe face to face as he was warm and engaging behind the lectern. Gradually I came to dread those weekly meetings and was looking for a way to quit. I was rescued by an unfortunate turn of events; Merton had a heart attack—not the first, I learned—which put him out of commission for some time. I just never went back to him, and I never did find out what happened to the work I had already done.

When I was finally able to get an appointment with Robert Lynd, the coauthor, with his wife, of the famous Middletown study, to discuss a proposal I had for a master's thesis, he threw me for a loop. At the time Dorothy and I were living in a predominantly black housing project in Queens, and I wanted some guidance for conducting a participant observation study of racial contact. With his experience, Lynd seemed like the perfect mentor. When I described my proposal to him, his response, which I remember verbatim, was, "Son, that's like pissin' through a knothole." He suggested that instead I do a study of how Keynesian economic principles would meet obstacles if applied to the United States. (He was evidently enamored of the English Fabians.) What a topic for a greenhorn like me! So that was that. Lazarsfeld's course was taught most of the time by his assistant, Patricia Kendall, whom I believe he eventually married. Columbia's Sociology Department had all those stars, but I found it a disconcerting, anomic, and uncongenial place.

In my second semester at Columbia, I took a course with Margaret Mead. On the basis of a term paper I wrote for the course, she offered to sponsor me if I would switch to the Anthropology Department. She even offered me a Viking Fund fellowship to support my future fieldwork. Again, Dorothy prevailed on me to refuse Mead's offer because she did not want to spend a year or two somewhere like central New Guinea contracting malaria. Incidentally, Mead suffered periodic bouts of malaria, which she had contracted in New Guinea, so there was something to Dorothy's concern.

Mead and Ruth Benedict were jointly involved in a program of Research on Contemporary Cultures (RCC). A number of their graduate students had conducted their dissertation research on various ethnic groups such as contemporary Japanese, Polish, Italian, German, Syrian, East European, and Middle Eastern Jews. Mead had discussed some of that research in class. So when it came time for me to select a topic for a term paper, I decided to study differential ethnic reactions to a single crisis situation, to see if the conclusions reached in the RCC research rang true as regards how people from different ethnic backgrounds reacted to the same crisis. Mead agreed to give me access to the RCC materials.

I made a historical search for a crisis to which people from a number of ethnic groups that were represented in the RCC materials were exposed. Initially, I considered physical calamities such as earthquakes, hurricanes, or tidal waves, but I was unable to come up with one that filled the bill. Someone, I don't remember who, suggested labor strikes as a possibility—a great suggestion. I finally found the Lawrence, Massachusetts, textile strike of 1912. To my delight, workers representing seventeen ethnic groups were involved, and the Lawrence Library had an extensive archive of materials on the strike, mostly in the form of newspaper accounts of the day. The Lawrence strike was one of the most bitter, most protracted strikes in American labor history. It was organized by the International Workers of the World, or the Wobblies, the forerunner of the American Communist Party.

To make a long story short, I traipsed up to Lawrence with Dorothy and spent many hours perusing the archival materials. I also interviewed Elizabeth Gurley Flynn, who had been one of the strike's organizers, at the American Communist Party headquarters in New York City. I was unable to interview the other two organizers, Joe Ettor and Arturo Giovanitti. Ettor had moved to California to make wine, and Giovanitti, a brilliant poet who named his firstborn son Lenin (they call him Len), refused to see me. I tried to get Len, who was an organizer for the ILGWU, the garment workers' union, to help me, to no avail. His father had refused to speak to him for years. In any event, I was able to discuss the strike with Flynn, a beautiful and remarkable woman, in the inner sanctum of Communist Party headquarters. Her memory of the strike and the principals involved was still vivid after thirty-five years.

The paper I wrote for Mead represented my very first halting research effort. I attempted to tie in events occurring during the strike, that is, the behavior of the strikers, to the RCC materials. The workers did behave true to form. For example, the Italians were the first to strike. The Germans spent most of their time arguing politics in their beer hall. The Polish women made a cordon by locking arms and pushed scabs off the sidewalks. The Jews shipped their firstborn sons off to New York City. Unexpectedly, the only suicide was a Pole. Recently, while clearing my files, I came across my copy of the paper, which is quite long. If I must say so myself, it's not half bad. Mead evidently liked it because, on the strength of it, she invited me to spend a day with her at the Museum of Natural History, where she had her offices. She was one of the museum's curators. I arrived there bright and early and left after dark, exhausted. My memory of that day is still crystal clear. Mead held me in thrall for the entire day as I accompanied her on the whirlwind of her various activities. I got a real sense of what a day in the life of a serious academic is like. Unlike me, she didn't waste a minute.

When I called Mead the following day to refuse her offer to sponsor me, she asked me, "Well, then, what *do* you want to do?" She seemed to be interested in furthering my career. I had recently read the Lewin and Lippitt (1938) article on experimentally created autocratic, democratic, and laissez-faire group atmospheres in groups of young boys, which had so impressed me. Also, while at Brooklyn College, I had attended a lecture given by Lewin to the Psychology

Club. More than fifty years later, I still remember that lecture on what he called quasi-stationary equilibria. I answered Mead's question about what I wanted to do by saying that I would like to study with Lewin. She informed me that, unfortunately, he had just died, but that Ronald Lippitt, a coauthor of the paper I had read, was at the University of Michigan and that she knew Lippitt quite well since they had worked on a project together during the war. She picked up the phone and called Lippitt, and that's how the ball got rolling. Eventually, I formally applied to the social psychology program at the University of Michigan and was accepted. I'm sure a good word from Margaret Mead helped.

I had applied to two graduate programs, Michigan's and Cornell's School of Industrial and Labor Relations. I had also recently read William Foote Whyte's stunning *Street Corner Society* (1955), a detailed study of a street-corner gang. I remember an intriguing and important finding of a positive relationship between the members' bowling scores and their relative status in the gang. The initial status of the members did not depend on how well they bowled. Status expectations had somehow induced pressures that influenced performance. Since Whyte was in Cornell's labor relations school, I applied to study with him. Cornell also accepted me but could not guarantee financial support. Since Michigan guaranteed me a paid assistantship in the Research Center for Group Dynamics, I chose Michigan. I would also have $75 a month on the GI Bill. I'm not sure what I would have done had Cornell come through with money at the last minute. To this day I'm still intrigued by Whyte's finding, which may reflect a general tendency for performance in a group to be influenced by status expectations.

My first job as a graduate student was working with Ronald Lippitt on a study of a group of young Germans who had been brought to this country to be "democratized." However, as a born experimentalist, I was soon drawn to the work Leon Festinger and his research group were doing. Bert Raven and Hal Kelley were in that group. Luckily, I was able to switch to working with Leon. Thus began a forty-year career thinking about and designing experiments to study social influence processes and attitude change.

When I joined Festinger's research group, they were hard at work testing derivations from his theory of "informal social communication" (Festinger, 1950), which grew out of the study Festinger and two of his students had conducted in a student housing community (Festinger, Schachter, & Back, 1950). The general idea behind the theory was that in any group, over time, differences of opinion will tend to equilibrate. Furthermore, certain group characteristics will affect how quickly and to what extent opinion equilibration will occur. The mediating conceptual variable, *pressures toward uniformity*, will be moderated by the *cohesiveness* of the group and the degree of *homogeneity* of the group members, that is, how similar in background they are to one another. Other factors external to the group that bring pressure to bear on it, such as the importance of being steadfast in the face of confrontation, will also tend to intensify and hasten movement toward uniformity of opinion.

Festinger had an idée fixe from the time of his doctoral dissertation: his concern with how people cope with discrepancy. In his dissertation he studied, in a laboratory context, how the knowledge that the performance of a superior, inferior, or same-status group was different from his or her own performance on a task affected a person's level of aspiration. In a subsequent experiment (Festinger, 1947), he studied the effect on a person's voting behavior of knowing that others in various comparison groups had voted differently. The work he was doing when I joined him was in the same vein but in an experimental context with considerable refinement that enabled us to track the process of opinion equilibration over time.

Where did this equilibration model come from? Festinger's mentor, Lewin, had developed a model of the person that took into account both the person's momentary needs and the activities available to him or her through which those needs could be satisfied. Lewin conceived of the inner person as having what he called a need system, which consists of need regions that may be in various degrees of tension in relation to one another. If a particular need is in tension relative to the rest of the system, the person will tend to engage in some activity that will reduce the tension in that need region, that is, satisfy that need, so that need tension across the entire need system would tend to equilibrate. Lewin also argued that the boundaries between adjacent regions are what he called semipermeable, borrowing a term from cell biology. To the degree that need region boundaries are permeable, tension in the system will tend to spread rapidly across boundaries. In Festinger's opinion equilibration model, the group's degree of cohesiveness played a conceptual role analogous to Lewin's notion of semipermeability between adjacent need regions. Equilibration models in psychology were not new. In his *Project for a Scientific Psychology*, written in 1895, part of which I discuss later, Freud argued that the function of the entire nervous system is, through activity, to reduce excitation, that is, to equilibrate excitation across the system.

As what must have seemed a natural segue, Festinger much later followed his concern with discrepancy to an even more fundamental phenomenal level—perception—in which, for example, he used prismatic distortion to study the effects of discrepant information from two different sensory modalities, tactile and visual perception (Coren & Festinger, 1967; Miller & Festinger, 1967). In carrying out that work, he devised some ingenious "brass instrument" apparatus, which impressed me when I visited him at the New School for Social Research, his last academic position.

In his last book, which is on archeology, Festinger (1983) transposed his concern with discrepancy to human history, examining how prehistoric and ancient humans solved the problem posed by the growing discrepancy between a burgeoning population and a limited food supply. Agriculture was the solution. In his inimitable fashion, he turned the pessimistic Malthusian dilemma on its ear by arguing from historical data that through humans' intrepid ingenuity, our species will survive.

In the research we carried out at the University of Michigan in the early 1950s, we devised methods for manipulating characteristics of the group, such as the degree of cohesiveness and member homogeneity, and studied the way in which and how quickly opinion equilibration occurred. I must say those were heady days. We were at the frontier of attitude and opinion research and the effects of the group on its members. We were inventing new research paradigms to test hypotheses derived from a general theory of social influence processes, something no one before had ever done.

The only other previous attempt to test derivations from a general theory of social influence was the work of the towering intellect Emile Durkheim. The French sociologist's classic study of suicide published in 1897 (Durkheim, 1897/1951) was the first piece of research of a social phenomenon based on systematic data collection. Durkheim argued that "social facts," which he also called "collective representations," arise sui generis as a consequence of group life, and the greater the number of collective representations a group has, such as beliefs and rituals, the less the anomie experienced by its group members and therefore the less likely will a group member be to commit suicide. Based on this theory, Durkheim predicted and found that Catholics were least likely and Protestants most likely to commit suicide. Jews fell in the middle.

Festinger's term "group standards" is really synonymous with the term "collective representations" coined by Durkheim. Since Festinger and Durkheim were after the same thing, the effects on the individual of the beliefs and behavior of group members, it is not surprising that there is an underlying similarity in their conceptions. The unique aspect of what we were doing, however, was that we created experimental situations within which to study the process. Durkheim took the process as a given, whereas we studied the process by creating social contexts and manipulating moderating variables. The laboratory research on opinion comparison was begun at the Massachusetts Institute of Technology and carried forward at Michigan, where I did my apprenticeship, participating in three studies (Festinger, Gerard, Hymovitch, Kelley, & Raven, 1952; Gerard, 1953, 1954). Since my dissertation required two people to run it, Leon allowed me to hire someone to help me. That someone was Bob Zajonc, who was paid something like 65 cents an hour. At the time, Bob was a student in the Sociology Department. Yes, that's true. The rest is history.

When Festinger left Michigan for the University of Minnesota in 1951, he offered to take me with him, but I was happy in Ann Arbor. However, I did want to finish my dissertation with him. My doctoral committee agreed to let me use a preliminary study as my dissertation. I therefore finished with Leon as my chair in the record time of a year and a half. I may still hold the record.

In Minnesota Festinger (1954) extended the theory of social comparison processes to encompass how we come to assess our abilities. He and his students at Minnesota devised ability comparison experiments that were analogous to the earlier opinion comparison ones. Those experiments revealed clear tendencies for the person to use the performance of others as referents for judging his or her ability. In this research Festinger made a full circle back to his dissertation research on level of aspiration. He had once again demonstrated the social determinants of self-ability estimates. One of Festinger's former students, Stanley Schachter (1959), extended the theory even further to the comparison of emotions.

Return to New York

I reluctantly left Ann Arbor in the fall of 1952 (Michigan was such a nurturing environment) to take my first postgraduate school job working with Morton Deutsch at New York University. Mort had a contract with the air force to study group formation and group functioning, and my salary was paid out of that contract. Along with Jim Farr and Phil Lichtenberg, we conducted a number of laboratory studies on group formation. In addition, Mort and I studied staff work at Mitchell Air Force Base on Long Island; at Maxwell Air Force Base, Alabama; and in the Pentagon. We spent a great deal of time on that study and wrote a lengthy report for the air force. The report was classified "top secret," so I couldn't read it after I had helped write it; my security clearance was only up to "confidential." I never found out why I hadn't received "top secret" clearance, but I suspect it was because a close family member belonged to the Communist Party. I had also signed petitions that were suspect and, when I was much younger, had marched in a May Day parade. When Eisenhower took office in 1953, he appointed Charles Wilson as secretary of defense. Wilson, in deciding to tighten up the defense budget, zeroed in on psychological research and, bingo, Mort lost his contract and I, of course, lost my job. When I was hired, Stuart Cook, the director of the Research Center for Human Relations where Mort was a staff member, assured me of at least five years of employment. Cook rushed to make good on his promise by offering me another position in the research center working with Isadore Chein on a long-term drug study, but I declined the offer. I was determined to remain an experimental social psychologist.

I remember vividly the American Psychological Association meeting that September. So many people were in my boat because of Charlie Wilson and were scurrying around looking for jobs. I had a wife and two young children to feed, so I literally took the first job that came along, an assistant professorship in the Psychology Department at the University of Buffalo for the munificent salary of $5,500 a year—a mistake, not because the job was bad but because Dorothy found the winter unbearable. I must say I wasn't prepared for all that snow either.

But to backtrack to NYU, while I was there I got to puzzling over Solomon Asch's (1952) classic conformity experiments. Asch had framed the problem in strictly informational terms. What is the person going to do when confronted by unanimous disagreement about something from a group of peers? He found that fully a third of the subjects yielded at least part of the time to the discrepant group judgments, even though they were clearly wrong. Festinger also couched his "informal social communication" theory in informational terms. I had the strong suspicion that in Asch's experiments and in ours, strong normative pressures were also operating. In both experimental paradigms, subjects were in face-to-face contact with the other subjects (or paid participants in Asch's studies and in some of ours). Both types of face-to-face encounters must have been rife with concern by each of the group members as to how he or she would be regarded by the others. As I saw, it there were probably two motives operating: the desire to make a correct judgment and the desire to be accepted by the others.

In our studies one of the key variables was group cohesiveness. The experimental manipulation of cohesiveness we used in most of those studies was to try to convince subjects in the "high cohesive" condition that on the basis of premeasures we took they would like each other and should get on well together. The instructions to the "low cohesive" groups were very lukewarm. (Of course, assignment to conditions was made on a random basis.) Clearly, those instructions would tend to induce differential status concerns, with the subjects in the "high cohesive" groups being more concerned about how they would be regarded by other group members. Yet Festinger insisted he was studying the effects of the opinions of others about the matter at hand, for example, how to treat "Johnny Rocco," a delinquent boy who had committed a crime. He virtually ignored the effect of normative pressures.

I decided to tease apart the effect of normative versus informational influence, and I asked Mort to collaborate with me. Given that I had acquired some electrical know-how in the army, I built the conformity apparatus that Mort and I used in the first experiment and I used in a number of subsequent ones. It was designed to eliminate normative pressures. Most psychologists are familiar with the setup. Richard Crutchfield and others later built other, similar versions of it. It was actually ultrasimple. Four subjects were run at a time, each seated in a cubicle facing the front of the room where the stimulus material was displayed. We used Asch's stimuli, which consisted of a single line at the left and three comparison lines of different lengths presented on the right, one of which was equal in length to the single line on the left. Each subject indicated his or her choice of correct comparison line by depressing one of three switches. The choices of "the others" were displayed on a three-by-four matrix of red bull's-eye lights on a panel in front of the subject. The subterfuge was that all four subjects were told that they were "subject number 3," and all of them responded simultaneously. I ran the experiment, and Mort was hidden behind a screen feeding in a prearranged sequence of judgments (the same sequence Asch used) for subjects "1," "2," and "4," such that subject "3" found that he or she disagreed with a unanimous majority on twenty-four of the thirty-six trials. Mort also recorded their choices.

In order to compare the cubicle treatment with Asch's original setup, we ran an approximately equal number of subjects, four at a time, in the face-to-face situation, three of whom were paid participants. As we predicted, the combined effect of informational and normative influence in the face-to-face situation produced much more yielding as compared with the cubicle situation, which we referred to as the "anonymous" treatment. "Anonymous" was really a misnomer, since the subjects saw each other when they arrived for the experiment and, more important, assumed that they would see each other again before leaving the laboratory. That expectation must have induced normative pressures. A subject who deviated from the majority might have been concerned about what the others would think of him or her and how they would react to him or her after the experiment was over. So my hunch is that the cubicle situation served to reduce normative pressures considerably but certainly did not eliminate them completely. In order to reduce them even further, a situation would have to be created in which subjects did not see each other either upon arriving or leaving. Such a situation, however, might arouse suspicion that the experiment was rigged.

The one really positive event of my yearlong sojourn in Buffalo was meeting Edward Jones. Ned grew up in Buffalo. His father, Edward Sr., was a longtime member of the Psychology Department. By the time I joined the department, Ed had retired. One day he called, insisting that Dorothy and I come to lunch to meet his son and his son's wife, Ginnie. I didn't realize it at the time, but that was a fateful meeting. A year or so later, I received a letter from Ned telling me that he was bogged down trying to write a social psychology textbook and asked if I would collaborate on it with him. I flatly refused, saying that writing textbooks is not part of my self-image or some such disclaimer. He wouldn't take no for an answer and proceeded to send me drafts of chapters on perception that he had already written. As I read the material, I became more and more intrigued; my resistance melted away. I was very impressed with the level of Ned's scholarship and his grasp of the field of what was then called social perception. That was in the pre–attribution theory days. More about the book later.

Dorothy and I were rescued from the next Niagara frontier winter by an offer of a Fulbright Fellowship to the Netherlands. Bert Raven had been there during the year we were in Buffalo, and he paved the way for us. We had an absolutely wonderful year in Holland and met some lovely people. Jacob Rabbie was assigned to me as my assistant, and we managed to do some research together. I was so impressed with him that I helped him work out graduate training at Yale. When he finished his Ph.D., he was offered the professorship of social psychology at the University of Utrecht. He recently retired from that position.

While in Holland, we were not relishing a return to Buffalo; one traumatizing winter was enough. I had an offer from my alma mater, Brooklyn College, with a much higher salary than Buffalo's, but the teaching load was onerous: five courses a semester. Olive Lester, the chair of the Buffalo department, had twisted the dean's arm to give me a raise. He did, $150 for the year—$12 and change a month!

One reason for returning to Buffalo was that I was to begin medical school that fall. I had started some research on emotion using physiological measurement within the context of the Asch conformity paradigm and also following up

Schachter's work on the social comparison of emotion. Rightly or wrongly, I concluded that if I wanted to really immerse myself in that work, medical training would give me a leg up. The dean of the medical school had worked out a decelerated program for me that would enable me to take the medical courses and continue my teaching and research. Even so, we both dreaded at least six more snowy and windy winters in Buffalo.

The Bell Labs

As luck would have it, Mort Deutsch came to our rescue. With the guidance and stewardship of Carl Hovland, AT&T had decided to form a Social Science Communication Department to be housed at the Bell Telephone Laboratories in Murray Hill, New Jersey. Carl got the labs to hire Mort, and Mort hired me. When I asked the powers that were at the labs why in the world they wanted to support research in social psychology, I received a simple answer: "Since there are 750,000 people working in the Bell System, whatever you may discover about people and how they relate to one another is potentially useful to us." An acceptable answer. Our department was unique in corporate America. There were 3,500 members of technical staff in the labs, only 150 of whom were in the Research Department, to which we eight belonged. We were part of an elite group. Those not in the Research Department were involved in applications to the communication industry.

I spent a very happy and productive six years at the labs, mostly exploring more fully the psychology underlying the Asch conformity paradigm. I made a foray into the use of physiological measurement, work I had begun in Buffalo, in order to study the emotional impact of the situation on the subject. I kept coming back to an experience with one subject in the face-to-face treatment in the experiment I ran with Mort at NYU. When he entered the laboratory room, the subject was extremely friendly toward the three paid participants, who, he believed, were also naive subjects like himself. When he found himself in disagreement with them on most trials, he became quite upset. At some point he asked to leave the room. When he returned, he looked sick and visibly shaken. I became worried and suggested that we discontinue the session. He absolutely refused to stop and continued through all thirty-six trials, not yielding to the others on a single trial. After the experiment was over and I explained the subterfuge to him, his entire body relaxed and he sighed with relief. Color returned to his face. I asked him why he had left the room. "To vomit," he said. He did not yield, but at what a price! He wanted so much to be accepted and liked by the others and was afraid he would not be because he had stood his ground against them. There you have normative pressure operating with a vengeance. It was very important for this subject to be both correct and liked. At the Bell Labs, I began to study the emotional consequences of deviation and yielding, inspired by my memory of that subject.

The work situation at the Bell Labs was as perfect as it gets. The people were great and so was my salary. If I needed anything, all I had to do was requisition it.

One of the engineers designed an impressive new version of the conformity apparatus that ran and collected data automatically. During my sixth year there, however, a change in the administration at AT&T occurred, and the new vice president in charge was not as supportive of our department as was the previous VP. Pressure began to build, mostly in subtle ways, for us to do something that would be directly useful to the Bell system. Mort actually did do some consulting for one of the so-called operating companies. While at the labs, I received job offers from time to time that I turned down since things at the labs were going along so swimmingly.

The Move West

When the "do something for Ma Bell" pressure began to build, I happened to be approached by the Riverside campus of the University of California. After a very pleasant visit there, I decided to take the job. So in the fall of 1962 my family and I made the trek to California, and I was back in academia. As part of the negotiation with Riverside, they agreed to my taking a leave of absence for a year after the first year. Ned Jones and I had been working fairly steadily on the textbook and had reached a point where we needed to spend time together to finish it. We managed to wangle an invitation for both of us to the Center for Advanced Studies in the Behavioral Sciences at Stanford for the academic year 1963–1964. So after a year in Riverside, we headed north to Stanford.

Working with Ned every day was a joy. We saw eye to eye on most everything, which was surprising since we had come out of different traditions. Ned was trained more or less as a clinician at Harvard, and I had come out of the Lewinian tradition. I consider that year one of the high points of my career. We did manage to nearly finish the book, and both of us were pleased with the fruits of our labor. We were each responsible for writing first drafts of eight chapters. Each time one of us finished a chapter, he would give it to the other to work it over. Both of us were ruthless in revising each other's work. After the revision, the chapter was given a going-over by the original author of the chapter, and back and forth it went. In that way each chapter went through four or five revisions, until it was acceptable to both of us. Ned challenged me and I him at every step of the way. My gray matter got a real workout. I haven't been as intellectually stimulated since.

One of the chapters in the book for which I had primary responsibility was entitled, "Action, Choice, and Dissonance," which necessitated my digging into the mushrooming literature on dissonance theory. What most intrigued me was the controversy between Festinger and his followers on the one side and critics like Irving Janis and Milton Rosenberg on the other, who argued that the counterintuitive finding of the inverse relationship between attitude change and reward, as reported by Festinger and Carlsmith (1959) and Brehm and Cohen (1962), was due to various artifacts.

I remember one occasion when I drove Festinger from Stanford (he had moved to Stanford by then) to the San Francisco airport. We had some time to kill before his departure and decided to have a drink while we waited for his plane. I questioned him about the Janis and Rosenberg studies, which he dismissed with some simple but telling criticism. "Aren't you going to take them on?" I asked. He answered by saying something to the effect that he had more fertile fields to plow or other fish to fry. That was about the time he was getting heavily involved in the perception research, so we went on to discuss how to implement an ocular system for producing prismatic distortion. So that was that. Given Festinger's considerable impact on social psychology—arguably more than anyone else's—it is rather amazing that he spent so little time—about twenty years—working among us, from the early 1940s to the early 1960s.

When I arrived back in Riverside, I had the good fortune to work with three talented graduate students, Edward Conolley, Linda Fleischer, and Roland Wilhelmy, and several exceptionally good undergraduates, among them Jon Atzet and Grover Mathewson. The three graduate students did their dissertations on problems related to dissonance theory, as did Mathewson. Conolley and Wilhelmy tested derivations from a general theory we were developing that encompassed both dissonance and incentive effects, and Fleischer, using a pupillary dilation measure, studied what Jones and I called the "basic antinomy"—the radical change, as described by Festinger, of the psychology underlying the pre- versus postdecisional situation. We eventually published an account of the theory and the supporting experimental studies (Gerard, Conolley, & Wilhelmy, 1974).

The Riverside school district was at that time in the post–*Brown v. Board of Education* turmoil. The school board eventually voted unanimously to desegregate the schools, a decision that put me in a quandary. There I was, on the spot, literally. In my naiveté, I was convinced that desegregation would give a boost to minority students' academic performance. I was in a position to document the change and study the mediating processes that would presumably produce it. But did I want to leave the pristine confines of the laboratory for the messiness and unpredictability of the real world? I knew that a study in the schools would take a great deal of time and money—I didn't realize then how much of each would be involved—but I decided to do it. (When Leon heard about my involvement in the study, he said, "Hal, I thought you were an intelligent man.") A number of us on the campus, including Norman Miller, formed a consortium with personnel in the school district and began to mount the study in 1965, the year before desegregation was to be implemented, in order to take premeasures. The California State Department of Education came through with money, as did the National Institute of Child Health and Human Development.

We selected a sample of 1,800 children from all the elementary grades that included the three major ethnic groups: Mexican American, black, and what we dubbed Anglo. We tracked the children yearly from 1965 through 1971, taking measures not only on the children but also on their teachers and parents as well. In most of the schools, there wasn't any space that we could use for testing the children, so we rented air-conditioned trailers that were set up in the school yards. Our staff grew to 150. I was called on the carpet twice by the dean, once because our computer programmer was caught shoplifting a pair of shoes and again because a member of our testing staff was accused of molesting one of the children. Somehow I was to blame for not having screened prospective employees carefully enough. I was so wiped out by that first year's effort that I ended up in the hospital.

A number of publications came out of the work, including a volume edited by Norman Miller and myself (Gerard & Miller, 1975). Most of the measures we used were bootstrapped. (We received very little help from the existing developmental literature.) There are enough data from our study to plum for the next 100 years—literally. We had time only to skim the surface, looking at the most obvious relationships. Generally speaking, the results were pretty depressing. Comparing cross-sectional achievement data for the pre-desegregation year with the longitudinal post-desegregation data made it clear that, overall, the performance gap between the Anglos and the two minority groups did not change; there was no apparent salutary effect of desegregation on school performance. As the children moved through the grades, the achievement gap widened as it had for the pre-desegregation data.

We did find an interesting relationship between the degree of the teacher's prejudice and the academic performance of the minority children in her class and their acceptance by their Anglo classmates. We used an unobtrusive measure of the teacher's prejudice from the way in which she evaluated the academic ability of the children in her class. Each teacher rated all the children in her class on twenty-seven semantic differential type scales, a number of which tapped her evaluation of the child's intelligence and academic performance. By comparing those evaluations with objective measures of performance from the state-mandated achievement tests, we were able to generate a prejudice ratio for each teacher based upon how much she underestimated the performance of minority versus Anglo children in her class. Nearly all teachers underestimated minority performance, some more than others. The measure seemed to work like a charm. We found impressive correlations between a teacher's prejudice score and how well a minority child did in her class, as measured by the change in the child's performance before and after being in her class, and also with how well accepted the child was by his or her Anglo peers, as reflected by sociometric measures. The teacher apparently modeled for the children. It is therefore not surprising that the achievement gap widens as children move through the grades. This is not the place to go into the full panoply of the data, but those nuggets do stand out.

On to UCLA

My last major effort working in mainstream social psychology is reported in Gerard and Orive (1987). We developed an overall theory of the dynamics of opinion formation that encompasses both social comparison and dissonance processes. The basic notions behind the model are that an opinion represents a preparatory set for action and that a given action has some required level of opinion preparedness (OP). Requiredness level (RL), which is the cornerstone of the theory is, in turn, a function of both the immediacy and the importance of the anticipated action. The theory relies heavily on earlier conceptions of the nature of conflict as formulated by Lewin (1931, 1935, 1938), Hull (1938), and Miller (1944, 1959) and on Allport's (1924) theory of the reciprocal effects of what he called social projection.

In Jones and Gerard (1967), cognitive dissonance is cast within a framework of action with a pragmatic, functional basis. We view dissonance, which Festinger (1964) argued is strictly a postdecisional state of mind, as instead induced by cognitions having incompatible behavioral implications. After a decision, the negative features of the chosen alternative and the positive features of the rejected one(s) induce action tendencies in the person (P)—approach toward the rejected alternative(s) and avoidance of the chosen one—that are incompatible with maintaining an unequivocal behavioral orientation (UBO) toward transaction with the chosen alternative, interfering with effective transaction with it. Viewed in this light, dissonance reduction is an attempt to reduce or eliminate these incompatible tendencies in the service of maintaining UBO. The imperative induced by an impending transaction with X requires that P develop a well-formed opinion toward X, enabling P to transact unconflictedly with X.

As far back as 1931, Lewin proposed what he called a "force field" analysis of conflict that he subsequently elaborated further (Lewin, 1935, 1938). In this analysis he proposed that as P moves closer to transaction with X, its positive features gradually loom larger, and if there are anticipated negative consequences attendant on transaction, those features loom larger still. In effect, if anticipated transaction portends both positive and negative consequences, two psychological gradients develop, a positive one, which starts early and increases with a shallow slope as P nears transaction, and a negative one, which starts later and increases more sharply with decreasing distance.

Lewin gives the example of a little boy at the beach whose rubber swan is floating near the water's edge. (In Germany they must have rubber swans rather than rubber ducks.) As the boy moves closer to the swan, its attractiveness increases; I assume that is due to the anticipated growing joy of finally having it. The boy, as it happens, is afraid of the water, and as he approaches the swan, his fear of the water mounts rapidly, more rapidly than his joy at getting closer to the swan. Because of the configuration of force fields of the swan and the water, the boy will stop at the point where the force fields are equal and opposite; in gradient terms, where the positive and negative gradients cross. If the boy moves forward of the equilibrium point, his fear of the water will increase relative to his desire for the swan, so he will retreat. If he retreats beyond the equilibrium point, his desire for the swan will be greater than his fear of the water, which will move him forward again. All of this will result in his vacillating near the water's edge.

In order for the child to resolve his conflict, a restructuring of the gradient configuration is necessary. He has to overcome his fear of the water, that is, lower the negative gradient or raise the positive one so that it is everywhere above the negative gradient. This cognitive restructuring will enable the child to enter the water and fetch the rubber swan.

As demonstrated by White and Gerard (1981), dissonance arousal is not inherently a postdecisional mental state, although it is often that, but it is induced by an awareness that accommodation is necessary in order for UBO to be maintained in the face of transaction. In the White and Gerard experiment, the subject chose between two closely valued alternatives, anticipating immediate or delayed transaction, either ten minutes or thirty minutes later, with the chosen one. The typical postdecisional spreading apart in value of the alternatives, the chosen one increasing relative to the rejected one, occurred only when anticipated transaction was to be immediate but not when it was delayed, even though subjects in all three conditions had made a decision. It was analogous to the problem of the little boy and his rubber swan. In order to enable him to fetch the swan, which he wanted immediately, he had to do the cognitive work necessary to enter the water. Subjects in the "immediate" condition in the experiment were under the gun, so to speak.

Lewin argued that there are two basic kinds of conflict, one in which the positive and negative force fields emanate from separate sources, as in the boy and swan example: the positive force field from the swan and the negative one from the water. The other basic conflict situation is one in which one activity embodies both positive and negative features, as would be the case when a boy wants to climb a tree but is afraid of falling out of it or someone wants to eat a gooey hot fudge sundae but is concerned about its calories. The so-called forced compliance paradigm invented by Festinger and Carlsmith (1959) is prototypical of the first kind of conflict; the subject is offered a positive inducement to lie to the next subject, a negative counterattitudinal act. In order for the subject to engage in the lie, some form of accommodation is necessary; the less the inducement to lie, the greater will be the accommodation in order to maintain UBO. Rabbie, Brehm, and Cohen (1959) found that when the subject merely agreed to engage in counterattitudinal behavior, without actually engaging in the behavior itself, it was enough to induce accommodation. Since transaction was to be immediate, an opinion-forming imperative was induced.

In an experiment utilizing a double approach-avoidance conflict (each alternative embodied both a positive and a negative feature), Gerard and White (1983) found that postchoice dissonance reduction consists of reducing ambivalent feelings toward the chosen alternative but not toward the rejected one, which is in line with the results of the previously described study. Consistent with our theoretical framework, the subject's efforts were focused primarily on the negative feature of the chosen alternative, attempting to increase its value. Both the positive and negative features of the rejected alternative and the positive feature of the chosen one did not change appreciably in value. Festinger would have predicted that in addition to the decrease in the negativity of the chosen alternative, the positive feature of the rejected alternative would be denigrated, which did not occur.

In our model of opinion dynamics, cognitive work is necessitated when there is a discrepancy between P's RL for the transaction facing him or her and his or her OP for that transaction. When OP is at or above RL, P is sufficiently prepared for transaction, therefore no increase in net support is necessary. When OP is below RL, however, P will be motivated to reduce the discrepancy. Two basic strategies for doing that are possible: lowering RL or raising OP (or both). Lowering RL may be possible either by postponing transaction with X, if that is possible, or reducing X's importance (or both), the two factors that determine RL. A result of lowering RL is a tendency to reduce opinion extremity. This follows from two related consequences: RL lowering reduces the level of opinion preparedness needed to reach the RL, and since there is a monotonically increasing relationship between OP and net support, the lower the OP, the less extreme will be the opinion. Early important work by Suchman (1950) on the relationship between opinion intensity and opinion extremity clearly shows that the two variables are related in a U-shaped function, such that more extreme opinions, either pro or con, are held with greater intensity. By this line of reasoning, it therefore follows that a less extreme opinion will result from lowering RL, a consequence that can easily be tested. It would also follow that lowering RL will tend to make P more vulnerable to social influence, another consequence that can easily be tested. Indirect evidence for it is offered by Petty, Cacioppo, and Goldman (1981), who found that the greater the importance of an issue for P, the stronger the arguments required to change P's attitude. In addition, subjects for whom an issue had low importance were vulnerable to weak arguments presented by a highly credible source but not to the same arguments presented by a source of low credibility. This suggests that an "expert" can have such an effect, in spite of weak arguments, because RL is low. Initial opinion was not firm, making the subject more vulnerable to persuasion.

In addition to RL lowering, opinion uncertainty may induce information generation in the service of lowering the OP-RL discrepancy, which , in turn, will result in a tendency for P to polarize his or her opinion. This is the basis for Petty and Cacioppo's (1981) contention that thought is required for durable opinion change, which is supported by Cialdini and colleagues (1976), who found that enduring opinion polarization emerged only for an important transaction that could not be delayed. In effect, net support had increased because of the action imperative, which polarized the subject's opinion.

Support for an opinion may be provided by direct, issue-relevant information or by indirect social support. P may increase direct support by adding supportive cognitions, by subtracting nonsupportive ones, or by changing the weights of cognitions related to the issue. Indirect support may consist of the opinion of an expert, group consensus, or fabricated consensus.

Although his description of the process was incomplete, F. H. Allport (1924) was, to my knowledge, the first to describe fabricated consensus through a process he called social projection. He developed the theory as a way of understanding crowd behavior, which was one of the central concerns of early social psychologists. Allport identified three steps: projection, reciprocal consensus, and increased opinion extremity. The tendency for P to project his or her opinion onto others is at the heart of informational social comparison. In the early social comparison studies, the manipulation of both cohesiveness and homogeneity was tantamount to providing the subject with differential opportunity to project his or her opinion on the other group members. Social projection occurs irrespective of whether or not P is below his or her RL. It may provide an avenue of increasing opinion preparedness by adding fabricated consensus information as supporting cognitions. And if P's OP is below RL, it will tend to polarize P's opinion.

Allport's analysis helps us understand the social dynamics underlying crowd behavior, but he left out two critical features. First, in order for P to project his or her opinion onto others, they must be judged by P to be cooriented with him or her, that is, to share the same vantage point (or values) with regard to X, the issue at hand. Second, in order for P's opinion to polarize, his or her OP must be below his or her RL. The first condition can be seen as the necessary and the second the sufficient condition for polarization to occur.

Wolfgang Wagner, an Austrian postdoc who worked with me, ran two experiments that are reported in Gerard and Orive (1987), in order to study the effect of coorientation, opinion importance, and measurement delay on opinion polarization. In the first study, subjects were run in same-sex groups of four in which, with false feedback, the subject was led to believe that the others shared his or her value perspective or did not. This would presumably influence the degree to which the subject could utilize social projection to fabricate a consensus in order to increase OP. In order to vary RL, which would affect the degree to which the subject would be motivated to engage in information generation, Wagner utilized a manipulation I had used in my dissertation (Gerard, 1953). Subjects were told that they were each going to debate someone not in their present group on the opinion issue, the "Johnny Rocco" case, immediately after the present session, next week, or possibly not at all. Following that, the subject indicated his or her opinion on a seven-point scale as to whether Johnny should receive harsh or lenient treatment for his crime. The subjects never actually discussed the case, nor did they have the debate. The results were in line with the theory. It was only under high similarity and anticipated immediate confrontation that opinions polarized significantly. RL was high and social projection was possible, confirming the necessary and sufficient conditions Allport had failed to note.

The work of Tesser (1978) and his colleagues on opinion polarization utilized a situation in which several subjects were run simultaneously and told that they would be quizzed later about their opinions. These circumstances had created a situation with both high similarity (similar students) and a high RL (the quiz), which is ripe for social projection. Tesser ran subjects under an immediate opinion measurement treatment and another in which there was a ninety-second measurement delay. Tesser predicted greater polarization in the ninety-second treatment since, he argued, subjects would have time to pare away inconsistent information, which would render opinions that were less ambivalent and hence more polarized, which is what he found.

We argued that the greater polarization in the ninety-second treatment was instead likely due to the fact that the subjects in that treatment had been given a greater opportunity to project their opinions onto the other subjects who were present than those in the immediate measurement treatment and would therefore experience a reciprocal consensus effect that would tend to polarize their opinions. In order to counterpose our interpretation of the results with Tesser's, Wagner varied group similarity and measurement delay. Subjects were led to believe either that the others were similar or dissimilar, under immediate or delayed measurement. He also ran subjects alone with immediate or delayed measurement. It was only in the condition of high similarity and delayed measurement that subjects polarized their opinions as compared to the other five conditions, which clearly supports our interpretation of Tesser's results. Tesser, on the basis of his paring-away explanation, would have predicted opinion polarization in all three delay conditions, including the alone condition. Clearly, then, it is highly likely that social projection was the mediator of opinion polarization in Tesser's studies, rather than a paring-away process. His subjects were attempting by the means available to them to reach their RLs, which were high because they expected a quiz: social projection by virtue of the presence of similar others.

Psychoanalysis Enters the Picture

In 1969 I married for the second time to a psychoanalytically minded clinical psychologist who was determined to get me interested in psychodynamics. We met at the Interamerican Congress of Psychology in Montevideo on April Fool's Day 1969.*

I resisted Desy as long as I could but eventually capitulated to acknowledging the importance of personality dynamics in social interaction, especially of emo-

---

*The editors have shortened this section because of space constraints and editorial judgment. The original draft of this chapter contained considerably more detail of psychoanalytic theory as it bears on Gerard's later work. The interested reader can obtain the full version from the author.

tions, that we social psychologists had all but ignored. By the 1970s, social psychology had become dominated by the cognitive revolution that had swept most of psychology. My own work, which I've already discussed, fit the prevailing cognitive cast. I began to have a strong, sneaking suspicion that an important ingredient of social life was missing from our work. Social psychology had ignored the gut, where we really live. A sad commentary is that the study of personality, which tends to focus on affect, has nearly faded out of existence in American academic psychology. At UCLA we no longer have a personality area.

As part of her campaign to convert me, Desy got me hooked into the psychoanalytic doings in Los Angeles. I took a course with her, taught by a local analyst, on the work of Melanie Klein and Wilfred Bion, which was an eye-opener. I began to familiarize myself with that literature. Also, Desy was in supervision with the leading Kleinian analyst in town and tape-recorded her supervision sessions with him. She cajoled me into listening to the tapes. Her campaign was compelling. More and more, I developed a sinking feeling that we social psychologists were missing the boat. There is much more to social interaction than is represented in the research in mainstream social psychology.

It took a lot of doing for me to overcome my stereotype of clinicians as softheaded in order for me to become one. I decided that if I were going to develop some kind of purchase on the emotional underpinnings of social interaction, I ought to go whole hog into the enterprise. So in 1982, at age fifty-nine, I entered psychoanalytic training, one of the oldest candidates ever, if not the oldest. I finished my training ten years later, finding I *had* developed a sense of how the mind functions from being both on the couch and behind it.

On the one hand, I had become dissatisfied with the bland cast that had overtaken social psychology. But now I was confronted by the lack of both rigor and systematic research in the psychoanalytic literature. The question as I saw it was how was I going to marry my newfound knowledge of the mind with my background as an experimentalist in order to bring some harder science into the new field I had entered.

I had just gotten wind of a doctoral dissertation conducted by Cynthia Patton (1992) at the University of Buffalo under the direction of an old friend, Joe Masling. The study, a laboratory experiment, showed that bulimic-tending women eat more than nonbulimics when exposed to the subliminal stimulus "Mommy is leaving me" but not to the same stimulus presented supraliminally. No such effect occurred for a neutral stimulus. As I saw it, the subliminal stimulus was able to enter the early primitive unconscious level of mind and had stimulated separation anxiety, whereas when that same stimulus was presented above awareness, its effect was blunted by the subject's focusing on its details or mustering conscious defenses against it.

I was excited by Patton's results because I believed that she was studying one of the two basic situations confronted by the infant as described by Freud (1895/1966) in his seminal *Project for a Scientific Psychology*. Since Patton had studied the effect of one of the two basic situations described by Freud, the baby's experience with the absent breast, I decided to get my feet wet using subliminal activation by attempting to replicate her study. We were able to confirm her results (Gerard, Kupper, & Nguyen, 1993), which gave me confidence in the efficacy of subliminal activation. With ancillary data, we determined that the eating response of the bulimic-tending woman was a defense mediated by the fantasy that she doesn't need Mommy; she can feed herself. Each of us has developed a particular defense against abandonment. These women, as infants, had reacted by coming to believe that they didn't need Mommy. I felt I had a handle on an important phenomenon related to the early feeding situation and was eager to pursue the problem further, which I did. So the Patton replication became a stepping-stone for me. Before describing the subsequent research, I want to back up a bit in order to set the stage for presenting that research.

The Transference and Social Perception

What used to be referred to in the social psychological literature as social perception has been a major focus of research for some time (Asch, 1946; Jones and Davis, 1965; Kelley, 1967). Since social psychologists are concerned with the causes and effects of social interaction, how the parties to a social exchange perceive one another naturally emerges as a central issue. Questions of interest concern how the perceiver attributes intentions to someone else and how information about the other is organized. The traditional approach has been to regard the person as a more or less rational processor of information input about the other. Certain distorting biases have been acknowledged and identified but merely as penchants for skewing the information in one or another direction so that the inference or social percept about the other is shifted somewhat from the inference the person would have made had he or she been completely rational in putting together the information about the other. Complete rationality, with the person processing information much as a computer would, were it programmed to form percepts, is taken as the baseline ideal. Much of the cognitive revolution in social psychology has approached social perception from this perspective.

It is my contention that there is another set of determinants that influences social perception, which has not been studied by social psychologists. Freud described that part of the perceiver's mind that imbues the other and aspects of the external world with what are assumed to be residues of infancy and early childhood, referring to it as the dynamic unconscious. He called these residues imagos, which are in effect distorted versions of early caretakers and are inaccessible to consciousness. The "good" and "bad" breast imagos created in the early feeding situation would be examples. In spite of their inaccessibility, these imagos nevertheless influence how we perceive others through a process by which they are projected into the external world and experienced typically as characteristics possessed by others or by objects. The interplay between unconscious fantasy and reality creates our view of the world and hence how we function as persons. This interplay leads to various kinds of misattributions of the intentions of others, which Freud (1914/1966) considered under the general rubric of the transference.

Imagos exist in the mind as either the subject or object of an unconscious internal script. In a given script, the parental imago may be doing something to or having something done to it of a loving or aggressive nature by another imago. Scripts may also include versions in which the infant is doing something, typically of an omnipotent nature, to an internal parental or sibling imago. These scripts are formed very early on in psychological development. Many psychoanalytic writers, including Freud, would argue that we are born with potential templates for creating these scripts. Roger Money-Kyrle (1961) presents a compelling argument along these lines. The Oedipus complex is one of these scripts. Mental patterns or schemas seem to be in the mind in primitive form at birth, as outlines, and are filled in as a result of the infant's experience with early caretakers, especially the mother. Nature and nurture thus interact to form the dynamic unconsciousness.

I would argue that there is some finite number of such scripts that, in contrast to the cool attributional processes typically studied by social psychologists, are heavily laden with affect. The nature and relative strength of these scripts are what determine character structure, which expresses itself in the way we perceive and relate to others. These fantasy scripts typically occur in sequence. The initial fantasy, triggered by some felt need, may be a wish-fulfillment script, typically of an omnipotent nature, involving the infant and the breast and nipple. Depending on subsequent transaction with the other, a gratification or abandonment fantasy may be engendered, as described above, which may then be followed by another fantasy. Whether or not a defensive fantasy occurs, like the one the bulimic-tending women had, will be contingent on the arousal of anxiety. These scripts are created primarily through the process of projective identification, a central notion in psychoanalytic theory.

Melanie Klein's major contribution to the understanding of psychological development, which was based on her analysis of very young children, was to spell out in much greater detail how this process, in which projection and introjection are intertwined, takes place and to trace it back to a much earlier time in development, the first months of life. She was concerned with early superego development, which is the precursor of the later resolution of the Oedipal conflict at about age five, as described by Freud. Freud had left the pre-Oedipal period nearly blank and located the introjective-projective sequence at a late point in development, in the three- to five-year-age period.

Klein's ideas were forming in a series of important papers and a book she wrote in the 1930s (Klein, 1932), but it was not until 1946 that she was able to put it all together in her seminal paper bearing the disarming title, "Notes on Some Schizoid Mechanisms." She traces "projective identification," the name she gave to the projective-introjective sequence, to the very beginning of extrauterine life, when the helpless infant attempts to adapt to overwhelming anxiety by omnipotently splitting its world into good and bad as a way of protecting the good from the bad. Negative feelings, which derive from the innate aggression postulated by Freud (1920/1966), are projected into the breast, transforming it into both a persecutory internal part-object as well as a persecuting external one.

Klein argues that during moments of gratification the baby projects its love into the breast and then internalizes it as a transformed, "loving" breast. Similarly, when the breast is not available, it becomes hateful and attacking by virtue of the baby's having projected its hate into the breast and then internalizing it as cruel and aggressive. In contrast to the more passive Freudian secondary reinforcement view, the Kleinian baby animates the breast, transforming it, through projective identification, into a breast that is very much alive, at times to be worshiped and adored and at other times to be terrified of, retaliated against, and vilified.

Research on Unconscious Psychodynamics

In recent years cognitive psychologists have been hard at work studying information processing below awareness. Two features characterize that research: Scant attention has been paid to affective processes, and it purports to demonstrate that the effects of information processed below awareness parallels those found in conscious processing (e.g., Bargh and Pietromonaco, 1982; Higgins, King, & Mavin, 1982; Higgins, Rholes, & Jones, 1977; Marcel, 1983a, 1983b). Workers who have offered evidence supporting the latter proposition argue that information entering the sensorium, by whatever route, engages the cognitive apparatus in much the same way, except that subliminal information enters in an impoverished form. Work on category accessibility in the selection and interpretation of information about another person has shown that the accessibility of a category can be similarly primed by prior conscious or out of awareness exposure to category-relevant information. Even work by Zajonc (Kunst-Wilson & Zajonc, 1980; Moreland & Zajonc, 1979; Zajonc, 1980, 1984), in which he has studied affective responses to below-awareness information, is cast within the same parallel process framework in which, for example, liking for a stimulus increases with frequency of exposure regardless of whether the exposure is above or below the subject's awareness. The thrust of that work regards cognitive structures as being passively modified by new information, whether above or below threshold, which in turn changes subsequent response probabilities.

As Donald Spence (1987) points out, this kind of mind model does not include active transformational processes in which strong affects are engaged, which, of course, characterizes psychoanalytic formulations of unconscious dynamics. In contradistinction to the assumption by cognitive psychologists that above- and below-awareness information processing are more or less identical (which at times they can be), a major tenet of psychoanalysis is that much of the time there exists a discontinuity between the two levels. Conscious information processing, or what Freud (1911/1966) referred to as secondary process thinking, respects such constraints as transitivity, negation, time sequence, and that two objects cannot be in the same place at the same time, whereas information processing occurring below awareness by the dynamic unconscious, which Freud called primary process, respects no such constraints. Primary-process thinking is much more fluid, is timeless, and lacks other logical constraints such as transitivity and negation. It also tends to be omnipotent and omniscient.

The Restricting Effect of Awareness

Thus far we have carried out six studies on unconscious processes. I have already described the Patton replication, which strongly suggests that one can induce unconscious fantasy experimentally. In some research dating back to the 1960s, Spence (1964, 1966; Spence & Holland, 1962) reported a startling counterintuitive finding, namely, that when a word is presented subliminally, it induces a greater number of associations to that word than when it is presented above the awareness threshold. He argued that when the word is presented above awareness, associations to it are linear, one word leading to another, and so on. When the prime is presented below awareness, it enters the association network and triggers associations simultaneously. This parallels Freud's distinction between secondary and primary process. Spence referred to his paradoxical finding as the "restricting effect of awareness." His findings support the notion that the two levels of mental functioning are discontinuous.

Spence used as the stimulus prime the word "cheese," a relatively neutral term. We reasoned that the restricting effect of awareness ought to be greater for affectively charged words than neutral ones, since such words would tend to have richer association networks. Devah Pager carried out a study in order to test this notion. In a pretest she carefully generated association norms to three each of positive, negative, and neutrally toned words. (She included "cheese" as one of the neutral words.) This was done by administering the nine words to a large number of UCLA students, asking them to write down, for each word, the first word that came to mind. She then made a count of the associations and was able to generate a list of ten common associates to each of the test words for UCLA undergraduates, the pool from which she eventually drew her subjects.

The results were not as expected. Pager found the "restricting effect of awareness" only for the negative words but not for either the positive or neutral ones. The results make some sense since subjects would tend to deny or defend against negative words (e.g., "death," "knife") when aware of them, whereas they could not do so when the words were not consciously perceived. I plan to redo this experiment with other positive, negative, and neutral words to determine if the effect for only negatively toned words is truly general.

The Perception of Interpersonal Configurations and Emotional Maturity

Through projective identification, the infant identifies with the parts of itself it has projected into the breast. The infant is thus in a state of fusion with the breast and its mother. As development proceeds, the infant begins to see its mother and itself as separate whole objects. There is also a dawning awareness of third parties: daddy and older siblings, if there are any. To the extent that the infant successfully negotiates this early phase of development, which Klein called the "depressive position," it will become aware of others beyond the two-person mommy-baby relationship. David Miranda attempted to examine the relationship between emotional maturity and the ability to see the world as differentiated. Utilizing the microgenetic technique developed by the group working in Lund, Sweden (Westerlundh & Smith, 1983), Miranda gradually increased the exposure of two interpersonal configurations, one of a baby with only its mommy and another with a baby, mommy, and daddy. We reasoned that the more primitive the subject, the lower would be his or her recognition threshold for the dyadic scene, whereas the more mature subjects would have a lower recognition threshold for the triadic scene. Each subject responded to both configurations with the order of presentation being counterbalanced. Utilizing measures of ego development, the threshold predictions were confirmed.

Shame and Self-Esteem Regulation

In an experiment by Daniel Kupper, narcissism was viewed as a defensive mode of self-esteem regulation, wherein a cluster of interdependent strategies are utilized to cope with painful feelings of incompetence and shame. Among those strategies are denial, projection, impulsivity, hostility, grandiosity, and externalization of blame. Kupper devised a laboratory experiment in which subjects were made to experience uncontrollable failure or not on two tasks. Premeasures of self-esteem and narcissism were administered yielding a tripartite classification into high narcissism–high self-esteem, genuine high self-esteem, and low narcissism–low self-esteem groups. During the tasks the face of the subject was videotaped in order to detect signs of shame.

The dependent measures indicated nonverbally expressed shame for the male but not for the female high narcissists. Both male and female high narcissists tended to deny shame and externalized blame for failure. High narcissists did not, as predicted, show increases in hostility, grandiosity, projection, devaluation, or impulsivity. On the contrary, as compared to the other groups, they showed less of an increase in hostility, greater liking for the experimenter, and greater accuracy on task performance subsequent to failure. These results suggest that those subjects were engaging in defensive idealization and responding to failure with reactance (Brehm & Brehm, 1981). It would seem, therefore, that high narcissists seem preoccupied with denying, avoiding, or otherwise ridding themselves of negative affect. The results are reminiscent of the familiar syndrome referred to as attention-deficit disorder in children. This omnipotent defense to a threatened loss of self-esteem, which adults may also fall prey to, carries with it various interpersonal difficulties attendant on a kind of psychological swagger.

Counterposing Freud and Klein on Early Emotional Development

In a recent experiment, which I will describe in some detail, I attempted to counterpose Freud's conditioning view of the early feeding situation with that of Klein in which she sees the baby actively creating its internal world through projective identification. In the Patton replication, we studied the bulimic-tending woman's response to separation. She eats to fill the void. The underlying fantasy is that she doesn't need Mommy; she can feed herself. Each of us tends to employ one or another defense to separation anxiety. Whatever defense we use, it is a response to an archaic residue of the early feeding situation. Whereas in the Patton replication we studied the response to the "bad" breast imago residue, in this experiment the focus was on both the "good" and "bad" breast residues.

Investigators who employ subliminal psychodynamic activation (SPA) typically do so utilizing a tachistoscope with which stimuli can be presented with exposures on the order of a few milliseconds. Instead of a tachistoscope, the experimental paradigm we used employed a dichoptic viewing tube in conjunction with a computer-based method of stimulus presentation and data collection. A dichoptic viewing tube is a device with which the same or different stimuli can be presented independently to each of the subject's eyes without the subject's being aware that is the case. The subject looks at a vertically split computer screen through rotatable prisms that are adjusted until the two images, presented on the right and left halves of the computer screen, fuse. In order to effectively create the illusion of a single image, a square tube approximately 1 meter long, split vertically down the middle by a partition, is interposed between the rotatable prisms and the split computer screen. Without the partition the subject would see that the computer screen was split into right and left halves. In order to minimize head movement and maintain the subject's eyes level with the prisms, he or she places his or her chin on a rest, the height of which is adjustable. Also, prior to the start of the experiment we utilize a simple test in order to determine which of the subject's eyes is dominant. The reason for that test will become clear in a moment.

The dichoptic viewing tube is an ideal device for inducing SPA. Stimulus presentation can be controlled automatically by a computer, and the stimulus prime presented to the nondominant eye can be masked with visual noise, a random visual pattern presented simultaneously to the dominant eye (forward or backward masking can also be accomplished). The subject is not consciously aware of the stimulus presented to the nondominant eye when it is masked. Furthermore, masking can be accomplished utilizing stimulus exposures as long as 500 milliseconds, allowing the prime ample time to enter the sensorium.

The stimuli used in the experiment were color photographs of an infant and a mother representing the two basic situations described by Freud (1895/1966) in the *Project,* the gratifying feeding situation (the baby at the breast) and the frustrating one in which it is being abandoned (the same baby crying with its mother receding in the background). We also used a blank screen as a neutral control stimulus. These three different stimuli, "feeding," "leaving," or blank were presented either masked or unmasked. In the unmasked condition, when the same "feeding" or "leaving" image is presented to both eyes, the subject can easily see the image since, because of the prism arrangement, the right and left images fuse.

In order to counterpose the Freudian and Kleinian hypotheses of early mental development, we utilized a lexical decision task in which the latency of a subject's response in deciding whether a string of letters is a word or a nonword is used as a criterion variable. The assumption behind the task is that the subject will identify a word more quickly the more accessible to him or her is the experience represented by the word—in our application, whether or not an experience of feeding or abandonment was primed and what sort of fantasy was induced. Immediately after each presentation of one of the primes ("feeding" or "leaving") or a blank screen, either masked or unmasked, a string of letters appeared on the screen and the subject pressed a "word" or "nonword" button indicating whether or not he or she judged that the string of letters was a word. Response latency was timed. The subject's response also keyed the start of the next trial, and so on.

Six target words were used, three tailored to the "feeding" prime and three to the "leaving" prime. The feeding target words were "milk," "nice," and "love." "Milk" represents the surface experience of feeding; "nice" represents the Freudian secondary reinforcement effect, the "good breast"; and "love" represents the effect of Kleinian projective identification, the "loving breast." For the "leaving" prime, the target words were "gone," "upset," and "attack," representing surface, the Freudian, and the Kleinian experiences, respectively. We were thus comparing a nice versus a loving breast and an upsetting versus an attacking one. In order to create the lexical decision task, for each of the target words we included a corresponding orthographically similar nonword that was a nonword anagram of the letters in the target word. In addition we used six neutral words like "chair" and "table" and orthographically similar nonwords as filler trials. The experimental design counterbalanced the two primes, and the blank presented either masked or unmasked with each of the target words and nonwords and nontarget words and nontarget nonwords, all presented in a fixed random sequence of 144 trials (3 stimuli × 2 masked vs. unmasked × 24 letter strings). Thus all of the letter strings, both words and nonwords, were paired with each of the three stimuli, both masked and unmasked. The subject responded on a total of 288 trials in which the same random sequence was presented twice.

The lexical decision data enable us to determine which view of early emotional development, the Freudian or Kleinian, is more tenable. On the one hand, if the primes triggered the assumed Freudian fantasy residue of the early feeding situation based on secondary reinforcement, lexical decision time to "nice" in response to the "feeding" prime should be shorter than the lexical decision time to both "milk" and "love," since "nice" ought to be more accessible. By the same token, the lexical decision time for "upset" to the abandonment prime should be shorter than for "gone" and "attack." On the other hand, if the lexical decision time for "love" in response to the "feeding" prime and to "attack" for the "leaving" prime should be shorter than to the other corresponding target words, the Kleinian view based on projective identification would be supported. The above predictions should obtain in the "masked" but not in the "unmasked" condition because it is only in the "masked" subliminal condition that the prime is presumably able to enter the deeper layers of the mind to activate early fantasy residues. In the "unmasked" condition, the effect of the prime is blunted by either the mustering of conscious defenses or by efforts on the part of the subject to see details of the stimulus or both.

The subjects used in the experiment were drawn from introductory psychology classes. All were native speakers of English since we wished to equate for all subjects the recognizability of the target words. The subject, who was run individually, was ushered into the laboratory and was told that his or her task was to decide as quickly as possible whether a string of letters presented on the computer screen was a word or a nonword. He or she was further told that prior to seeing the string of letters, he or she might see something on the computer screen (remember that in the unmasked blank condition there was no prior stimulus); its nature would be explained after the experiment was over. As indicated above, we then determined, by a simple test, which of the subject's eyes was dominant. The subject then placed his or her chin on the chin rest and the prisms were rotated for image fusion utilizing the same test stimulus presented to both eyes. After inputting the eye dominance information into the computer, the experimenter started the computer, and the experiment ran automatically, with the lexical decision latency data on each trial recorded on the computer disk. The unmasked and masked primes were exposed on the computer screen for 250 milliseconds. At that exposure duration, the unmasked prime is easily seen, but the masked one is not consciously identifiable.

In analyzing the data, we selected the critical comparisons only. The nonword trials were not included in the analysis for obvious reasons. Those trials served to create the lexical decision task in the first place. Also, data for the neutral nontarget word trials are not presented since they were included as filler words in order to distract the subject from possibly guessing the purpose of the experiment. Response latency overall was about a half-second, which is typical, but it was moderated by word accessibility, which in turn was affected by which of the primes had been projected on a given trial and whether it was masked or unmasked.

The data clearly support the Kleinian model of early development, since the latency to "love" and "attack" in the masked "feeding" and "leaving" conditions is significantly shorter than the latencies to the other corresponding target words in the masked condition for each of the primes. That is, in the "feeding" treatment the differences between "love" and "nice" and between "love" and "milk" are significant, whereas the difference between "milk" and "nice" (the Freudian-level comparison) is not significant. Similarly, in the "leaving" treatment the differences between "attack" and "upset" and between "attack" and "gone" are significant, whereas the difference between "gone" and "upset" (the Freudian comparison) is not significant. The critical differences do not reach significance when the primes were not masked. When the "feeding" or "leaving" prime is visible in the unmasked treatment, its effect on the mind is presumably blunted by the subject's conscious attempt to determine what it is or by consciously defending against it. These findings are reminiscent of Spence's "restricting effects of awareness," which I discussed earlier. Evidently, when the prime is presented above awareness, it is somehow blunted from entering the deeper layers of the mind, whereas when the subject cannot consciously see the stimulus, its access to the mind is enhanced. Spence's findings and ours speak to the undoubted myriad of subtle influences that occur during most social interaction.

The common thread in the six studies I've described is the examination of the work of the dynamic unconscious, which we explored with techniques that attempt to get beneath the surface of conscious experience. I argued that unconscious processes are continually operative, coloring all of our conscious experience of the world around us. My purpose is to shine a light on this level of mind in order to direct attention to where I believe future social psychological research should be focused. The problems that have been of central concern to our field, such as how we come to perceive others as we do, the determinants of cooperation versus competition, the nature of close relationships, the underlying basis of altruistic versus aggressive behavior, the dynamics of prejudice, and so on, can, I firmly believe, all be illuminated by exploring their below-awareness underpinnings. As I said at the beginning of this chapter, I want to bring the gut, which is what psychoanalysis is concerned with, to the cognitive processes that social psychologists study, since it is the gut that drives those processes.

Reflections and Projections

Writing this chapter has made me aware of how happenstance determined, at various points, the direction of my career. I didn't start out, as some do, with a burning desire to do a particular thing and doggedly stay the course. Rather, I kept getting sidetracked. If Dorothy, my first wife, had shared my enthusiasm about my doing graduate work in economics at the University of Chicago or my taking Margaret Mead up on her offer to be my mentor, my career would have been quite different. Or if Cornell had been able to offer me financial support, I may have worked with William Foote Whyte and become an industrial anthropologist of sorts. If my studies at Columbia and the work I did with Robert Merton had been less fraught with anxiety, I might have stayed with sociology. If Elliot Aronson had not convinced me to attend the Interamerican Congress of Psychology with him in Mexico City in 1967, where we had such a good time, I never would have been at the next congress in Montevideo, where I met Desy, who eventually became a major influence in my becoming a psychoanalyst.

Back even further—to the beginning. When I was born, I was slated to become a doctor like my mother's oldest brother, Jacob. Unfortunately, my mother died when I was very young. I am quite certain that had she lived, I would have ended up in medical school. She was a very determined lady. As a matter of fact, when my mother's three brothers found out that I had decided against medical school, I had a lot of explaining to do. They felt responsible for seeing that their sister's wish be fulfilled. They called a meeting where I was on the carpet, having to justify my decision. They really put on the pressure. I eventually prevailed, but just barely. I suspect that my decision to enroll in the University of Buffalo Medical School was in part motivated by guilt at not having fulfilled my mother's wish.

All this makes me wonder whether my career experience is atypical, or do others take this kind of random walk through life? In any event, my career has had its frustrations, but by and large, it has been quite satisfying. Would I exchange it for one of those missed opportunities? I'm not sure.

I know that many of my friends, including some of the contributors to this volume, believe that I had dropped out of social psychology to become a psychoanalyst. After all, I had stopped publishing in mainstream journals. Nothing could be further from the truth. I had reached a point at which I had lost the old excitement about my research. The journals were being filled with more and more methodologically sophisticated research with less and less real meaning for me. I was disturbed by a sense of ennui that I had begun to feel. Fortunately, at that moment I rediscovered psychoanalysis and, this time around, the work of Melanie Klein. I could see the potential in it for illuminating the problems we social psychologists study. I was determined to learn more about the recent developments in psychoanalysis. In order to immerse myself in psychoanalysis, I had to declare a time out to be retrained. But rest assured, I am as committed to social psychology as I ever was, probably more so.

I shared the misconceptions of psychoanalysis held by most psychologists and promulgated in most introductory textbooks, that psychoanalysis was a useless and lengthy intellectual exercise focused on reconstructing the patient's past and had little effect on the patient's current behavior. In fact, psychoanalysis can be a form of treatment that focuses on the patient's behavior toward the analyst in the here and now, and it is anything but a purely intellectual exercise. It is also essentially a social psychological enterprise.

Up through the 1950s, psychoanalysis had been the dominant theory of personality and the preferred method of treatment. Since then, psychoanalysis has lost its currency in academic psychology. Graduate training in clinical psychology shifted to the cognitive and behavioral approaches. So my decision to go into psychoanalytic training in 1982 was swimming against the tide.

Psychoanalysis itself has been very short on research, one of the reasons it has fallen under a cloud. There is a growing realization that good research is needed. By research, the psychoanalytic establishment means clinical outcome studies in order to assess the efficacy of psychoanalytic treatment. It is therefore surprising to me that both the American Psychoanalytic and the International Psychoanalytic Associations have partially funded my research, which is completely theoretical.

When psychologists' interest in psychoanalysis was cresting in the 1940s and 1950s, a great deal of cross-fertilization between personality and social psychology took place. In our textbook Jones and I detailed the fruits of the infusion that took place, which culminated in the so-called New Look studies of Jerome Bruner, Leo Postman, George Klein, and others. That work demonstrated the effects of unconscious motivation on perception. In the late 1930s and early 1940s, a number of the faculty in the Yale Psychology Department were psychoanalyzed. That immersion led to the work on frustration-aggression hypothesis, spearheaded by Neal Miller (1941). Psychoanalysis was part of the zeitgeist in those days. Unfortunately, it never got a firm, permanent foothold in psychology, partly because of the difficulty of translating the theory into hypotheses that were testable in the laboratory. Also, the sense was that studies of psychological development in children were necessary to test psychoanalytic hypotheses. These are difficult and costly to do. Since the residues of infancy and childhood are very much alive in us in the present and can be activated experimentally, as I hope I've demonstrated in my research, it is not really necessary to limit oneself to developmental studies. I believe we are now on the threshold of returning to that natural connection between personality and social behavior with a much more sophisticated theory of the unconscious and its effects as well as a more highly developed research armamentarium. This has the potential for creating a new "New Look." I hope that young social psychologists will rise to the challenge and usher in a new millennium for a social psychology that is grounded in the emotional substratum of mind Freud discovered.

References

Allport, F. H. (1924) *Social psychology*. Cambridge, MA: Riverside Press.

Asch, S. E. (1946). Forming impressions of personality. *Journal of Abnormal and Social Psychology, 41*, 258–290.

_____. (1952). *Social psychology*. Englewood Cliffs, NJ: Prentice Hall.

_____. (1956). Studies of independence and conformity: A minority of one against a unanimous majority. *Psychological Monographs, 70*, 416.

Bargh, J. A., & Pietromonaco, P. (1982). Automatic information processing and social perception: The influence of trait information presented outside of conscious awareness on impression formation. *Journal of Personality and Social Psychology, 43*, 437–449.

Brehm, J. W., & Cohen, A. R. (1962). *Explorations in cognitive dissonance.* New York: Wiley.

Brehm, S., & Brehm, J. (1981). *Psychological reactions: A theory of freedom and control.* New York: Academic Press.

Cialdini, R. B., Levy, A., Herman, C. P., Kozlowski, L., & Petty, R. E. (1976). Elastic shifts of opinion: Determinants of direction and durability. *Journal of Personality and Social Psychology, 34,* 663–672.

Cohen, M. (1949). *A dreamer's journey.* Boston: Beacon Press.

Cohen, M., & Nagel, E. (1934). *An introduction to logic and scientific method.* New York: Harcourt.

Coren, S., & Festinger, L. (1967). An alternative view of the "Gibson normalizing effect." *Perception and Psychophysics, 2,* 621–626.

Durkheim, E. (1951). Suicide (J. Spaulding & G. Simpson, Trans.). Glencoe, IL: Free Press.

Festinger, L. (1947). The role of group belongingness in a voting situation. *Human Relations, 1,* 184–200.

_____. (1950). Informal social communication. *Psychological Review, 57,* 271–282.

_____. (1954). A theory of social comparison processes. *Human Relations, 7,* 117–140.

_____. (1957). *A theory of cognitive dissonance.* Evanston, IL: Row, Peterson.

_____. (1964). *Conflict, decision, and dissonance.* Stanford, CA: Stanford University Press.

_____. (1983). *The human legacy.* New York: Columbia University Press.

Festinger, L., & Carlsmith, J. M. (1959). Cognitive consequences of forced compliance. *Journal of Abnormal and Social Psychology, 58,* 203–211.

Festinger, L., Gerard, H. B., Hymovitch, B., Kelley, H. H., & Raven, B. H. (1952). The influence process in the presence of extreme deviates. *Human Relations, 5,* 327–346.

Festinger, L., Schachter, S., & Back, K. (1950). *Social pressures in informal groups: A study of human factors in housing.* New York: Harper.

Freud, S. (1895/1966). Project for a scientific psychology. In J. Strachey (Ed. and Trans.), *The complete works of Sigmund Freud* (Vol. 1). London: Hogarth Press.

_____. (1911/1966). Formulations on the two principles of mental functioning. In J. Strachey (Ed. and Trans.), *The complete works of Sigmund Freud* (Vol. 12). London: Hogarth Press.

_____. (1914/1966). On transference: An introduction. In J. Strachey (Ed. and Trans.), *The complete works of Sigmund Freud* (Vol. 14). London: Hogarth Press.

_____. (1920/1966). Beyond the pleasure principle. In J. Strachey (Ed. and Trans.), *The complete works of Sigmund Freud* (Vol. 18). London: Hogarth Press.

_____. (1923/1966). The ego and the id. In J. Strachey (Ed. and Trans.), *The complete works of Sigmund Freud* (Vol. 14). London: Hogarth Press.

Gerard, H. B. (1953). The effect of different dimensions of disagreement on the communication process in small groups. *Human Relations, 6,* 249–271.

_____. (1954). The anchorage of opinions in face-to-face groups. *Human Relations, 7,* 313–326.

Gerard, H. B., Conolley, E. S., & Wilhelmy, R. A. (1974). Compliance, justification and cognitive change. In L. Berkowitz (Ed.), *Advance in experimental social psychology* (Vol. 7). New York: Academic Press.

Gerard, H. B., Kupper, D. A., & Nguyen, L. (1993). The causal link between depression and bulimia: Counterposing two theories of mental development. In J. M. Masling and R. F. Bornstein (Eds.), *Psychoanalytic perspectives on psychopathology.* Washington, DC: American Psychological Association Books.

Gerard, H. B., & Miller, N. (1975). *School desegregation.* New York: Plenum.

Gerard, H. B., & Orive, R. (1987). The dynamics of opinion formation. In L. Berkowitz (Ed.), *Advance in experimental social psychology* (Vol. 20). New York: Academic Press.

Gerard, H. B., & White, G. L. (1983). Post-decisional reevaluation of choice alternatives. *Personality and Social Psychology Bulletin, 9,* 365–369.

Higgins, E. T., & Bargh, J. A. (1987). Social cognition and social perception. *Annual Review of Psychology, 38,* 369–425.

Higgins, E. T., Bargh, J. A., & Lombardi, W. (1985). Nature of priming effects on categorization. *Journal of Experimental Psychology, 11,* 59–69.

Higgins, E. T., King, G. A., & Mavin, G. H. (1982). Individual construct accessibility and subjective impression and recall. *Journal of Personality and Social Psychology, 43,* 35–42.

Higgins, E. T., Rholes, W. S., & Jones, C. R. (1977). Category accessibility and impression formation. *Journal of Experimental Social Psychology, 13,* 141–154.

Hull, C. L. (1938). The goal gradient hypothesis applied to some "field force" problems in the behavior of young children. *Psychological Review, 45,* 271–299.

Jones, E. E., & Davis, K. E. (1965). From acts to dispositions: The attribution process in social psychology. In L. Berkowitz (Ed.), *Advances in experimental social psychology* (Vol. 2). New York: Academic Press.

Jones, E. E., & Gerard, H. B. (1967). *Foundations of social psychology.* New York: Wiley.

Kelley, H. H. (1967). Attribution theory in social psychology. In D. Levine (Ed.), *Nebraska Symposium on Motivation* (Vol. 15). Lincoln: University of Nebraska Press.

Klein, M. (1932). *The psychoanalysis of children.* London: Hogarth Press.

_____. (1946) Notes on some schizoid mechanisms. *International Journal of Psychoanalysis, 27,* 9–110.

Kunst-Wilson, W. R., & Zajonc, R. B. (1980). Affective discrimination of stimuli that cannot be recognized. *Science, 207,* 557–558.

Lewin, K. (1931). Environmental forces in child behavior and development. In C. Murchison (Ed.), *A handbook of child psychology.* Worcester, MA: Clark University Press.

_____. (1935). *A dynamic theory of personality.* New York: McGraw-Hill.

_____. (1938). The conceptual representation and measurement of psychological forces. *Contributions to Psychological Theory, 1,* 4.

Lewin, K., & Lippitt, R. (1931). An approach to the study of autocracy and democracy: A preliminary note. *Sociometry, 1,* 292–300.

Marcel, A. J. (1983a). Conscious and unconscious perception: Experiments on visual masking and word recognition. *Cognitive Psychology, 15,* 197–237.

_____. (1983b). Conscious and unconscious perception: An approach to the relation between phenomenal experience and perceptual processes. *Cognitive Psychology, 15,* 238–300.

Miller, N. E. (1941) The frustration-aggression hypothesis. *Psychological Review, 48,* 337–342.

_____. (1944). Experimental studies of conflict. In J. M. Hunt (Ed.), *Personality and the behavioral disorders* (Vol. 1). New York: Ronald Press.

_____. (1959). Liberalization of basic S-R concepts: Extensions to conflict behavior, motivation, and social learning. In S. Koch (Ed.), *Psychology: A study of a science* (Vol. 3). New York: McGraw-Hill.

Miller, J., & Festinger, L. (1967). The effect of oculomotor restraining on the visual perception of curvature. *Journal of Experimental Psychology, 3,* 187–200.

Money-Kyrle, R. E. (1961). *Man's picture of his world.* New York: International Universities Press.

Moreland, R. L., & Zajonc, R. B. (1977). Is stimulus recognition a necessary condition for the occurrence of exposure effects? *Journal of Personality and Social Psychology, 35,* 191–199.

_____. (1979). Exposure effects may not depend on stimulus recognition. *Journal of Personality and Social Psychology, 37,* 1085–1089

Patton, C. J. (1992). Fear of abandonment and binge eating: A subliminal psychodynamic investigation. *Journal of Nervous and Mental Disease, 180*(6), 484–490.

Petty, R. E., & Cacioppo, J. T. (1981). *Attitudes and persuasion: Classic and contemporary approaches.* Dubuque, IA: Wm. C. Brown.

Petty, R. E., Cacioppo, J. T., & Goldman, R. (1981). Personal involvement as a determinant of argument-based persuasion. *Journal of Personality and Social Psychology, 41,* 847–855.

Rabbie, J. M., Brehm, J. W., & Cohen, A. R. (1959). Verbalization and reaction to cognitive dissonance. *Journal of Personality, 27,* 407–417.

Schachter, S. (1959). *The psychology of affiliation.* Stanford: Stanford University Press.

Spence, D. P. (1964). Conscious and preconscious influences on recall: Another example of the restricting effects of awareness. *Journal of Abnormal and Social Psychology, 68,* 92–99.

_____. (1966). How restricting are the restricting effects? *Journal of Personality and Social Psychology, 3,* 131–132.

_____. (1987). *The Freudian metaphor.* New York: W. W. Norton.

Spence, D. P., & Holland, B. (1962). The restricting effects of awareness: A paradox and an explanation. *Journal of Abnormal and Social Psychology, 64,* 163–174.

Suchman, E. A. (1950). The intensity component in attitude and opinion research. In S. A. Stouffer, L. Guttman, E. A. Suchman, P. F. Lazarsfeld, S. A. Star, & J. A. Clausen, *The American soldier: Vol. 4. Measurement and predication.* New York: Wiley.

Tesser, A. (1978). Self-generated attitude change. In L. Berkowitz (Ed.), *Advances in experimental social psychology* (Vol. 11). New York: Academic Press.

Westerlundh, B., & Smith, G. (1983). Perceptgenesis and the psychodynamics of perception. *Psychoanalysis and Contemporary Thought, 6,* 597–640.

White, G. L., & Gerard, H. B. (1981). Postdecision evaluation of choice alternatives as a function of valence of alternatives, choice, and expected delay of choice consequences. *Journal of Research in Personality, 15,* 371–382.

Whyte, W. F. (1955). *Street corner society* (2nd ed.). Chicago: University of Chicago Press.

Zajonc, R. B. (1980). Feeling and thinking: Preferences need no inferences. *American Psychologist, 35,* 151–175.

_____. (1984). On the primacy of affect. *American Psychologist, 39,* 117–124.

4 Adventures in Experimental Social Psychology: Roots, Branches, and Sticky New Leaves

Elliot Aronson

Elliot Aronson presents social psychology as a story of sin and redemption. He contends that although the field deals with "some of the least appetizing aspects of human behavior," it also provides "the tools and the understanding that encourage people to overcome" these unpleasant behaviors. In this chapter Aronson describes his copassions for doing rigorous research and focusing this research on issues of benefit to humanity. He traces these interests to the influence of two mentors, Leon Festinger and Abraham Maslow. Through reflections on his own life as a social psychologist, Aronson illustrates his firm belief in "an elliptical flow from theory back to theory." He believes that social psychology should rely heavily on experimentation, be capable of generating nonobvious hypotheses derived from theory and ingeniously testing them, and attempt to "do good" by applying the results of empirical research toward the solution of social problems. Oftentimes, he points out, it is in the process of applying knowledge to concrete situations that the original theory is refined, and with this the flow of theory-research-application-theory begins again. He concludes by emphasizing the importance of synthesis, when the role of "roots and branches" can be seen, and stressing the need for training students carefully to craft ingenious experimental designs.

The nature of this book is such that it virtually gives me an engraved invitation to engage in some flagrant self-indulgence. (Here I can hear the Greek chorus of my former students chortling and saying, "As if old Ellie ever needed an invitation for self-indulgence!") Be that as it may, in this essay I want to indulge my addiction as a chronic and habitual storyteller and tell you a little story about my forty-three-year love affair with experimental social psychology. Somewhere along the way, I will reveal my own biased, idiosyncratic vision of experimental social psychology "at its best." I put that last phrase in quotation marks to indicate that when I uttered it, my tongue was at least partway in my cheek. That is, I am, to some extent poking fun at myself because, in this essay, I will be talking primarily about my own research and my own values and feelings about the field. I think my way is a good way and perhaps the best way to go about doing research. This goes without saying (so, naturally, I'm just the man to say it). If I thought some other way of doing things was better or more exciting, I obviously would have spent my forty-three years doing it that other way. Moreover, I imagine that every practitioner of this highly artistic science of ours will have his or her own notion of what social psychology is like when it's at its best. I don't expect everyone to agree with me; I'm not sure I expect *any*one to agree with me. But let me warn you in advance: If you disagree with me, I am prepared to argue with you passionately—perhaps even wrestle you to the ground—for I believe that one of the defining aspects of social psychology "at its best" involves the passion of the researchers about the importance of the topics they are investigating and the methods they are using. As Hegel once said, "Nothing important was ever accomplished without passion."

My vision of social psychology is intimately imbedded in my professional autobiography, so it seems reasonable to begin with the story of how I entered this field and how I stumbled toward the beliefs I now have about social psychology. Along the way, my vision of social psychology will emerge—in much the same way as it emerged for me—unplanned, more or less by trial and error. I then proceed to spell it out more specifically and (I hope) with greater clarity at the end of this chapter.

A note of caution: A person always has to be careful in telling the story of his or her professional development. One can take the same events and tell the story in many different ways. At one extreme, it can seem like nothing but a series of accidents. At the other extreme, it can seem totally rational and deliberate—like a well-planned, integrated tapestry. My guess is that both of those extremes are false. As I stumbled through my own life, I managed to brush aside most of life's accidents, whereas a handful of other accidents inspired and guided my development. I guess what I am saying is that to some extent we get to pick and choose what we do with the pitfalls and pratfalls of our lives. And to quote Yogi Berra, "It ain't over till it's over"; that is, in synthesizing the important aspects of our professional lives, we increase the probability of gaining new insights and new directions for the continuing process.

The Nine-Year-Old Social Psychologist

It sometimes seems to me that I have been doing social psychology all of my life—and in a very real sense I have. Let me explain. I grew up in a very poor, working-class slum near Boston, Massachusetts. My father had an eighth-grade education and worked in a factory. We lived in a tough, rabidly anti-Semitic section of town; our family was the only Jewish family in the immediate neighborhood. When I was a child, I used to have to walk to the other side of town to go to Hebrew school late in the afternoon—and it meant walking through that hostile neighborhood carrying my Hebrew books. I was like a walking advertisement, a beacon to the anti-Semitic kids: "Hey, look at me—I'm Jewish!" Simply getting to and from Hebrew school every day was something of an adventure: I was forever trying to find creative routes, zigzag paths that would take me away from the greatest areas of danger. But in spite of my best efforts, I was frequently waylaid, pushed around, and occasionally roughed up by gangs of teenage tough guys shouting anti-Semitic slogans.

What is perhaps my most vivid childhood memory stems from one of those incidents. I was about nine years old, and I remember sitting on a curb, nursing a bloody nose and a split lip, feeling very sorry for myself—and wondering how it was that these kids could hate me so much when they didn't even know me. I wondered if they were born hating Jews or if that kind of hatred had to be taught. I wondered whether, if these kids got to know me better (and discovered what a sweet, generous, and charming little boy I was!), they would be able to like me a little more. And if they got to like me more, would they then begin to hate other Jews less?

Meeting Maslow and Wanting to Do Good

I didn't realize it at the time, of course, but these were profound social psychological questions. Ten years later, when I was a sophomore at Brandeis University, I happened to wander into a large classroom where the great humanistic psychologist Abraham Maslow was lecturing on introductory psychology. (I wasn't majoring in psychology; I wandered into his classroom quite by accident—because I was having a cup of coffee with a young woman I was attracted to, and she needed to leave to go to Maslow's class. I tagged along just to be able to sit next to her in the auditorium. The class might just as well have been about small-particle physics for all I cared).

What a fortunate accident! As it happened, Maslow was lecturing on prejudice that afternoon, and much to my astonishment he was raising the very same questions that I had raised when I was nine years old. That was the first time I became aware of the fact that there was actually a discipline—a science called social psychology—that attempted to deal with those kinds of question. What an epiphany! It was at that moment that I decided to switch my major to psychology. The next year I began working with Maslow, and eventually I became a protégé of his, sitting at the great man's feet, absorbing many of his ideas and values as if by osmosis. Maslow was brilliant—a visionary and a very warm person who cared about trying to improve the human condition. Not only did I learn a lot from him, but I was also inspired by him. I wanted to be like him. He thought I was fairly smart; he encouraged me to go on to graduate school. It was the first time I had any notion of going on with my education.

Meeting Festinger and Discovering
Dissonance Theory

As a first-year graduate school at Stanford, I was hell-bent to learn some things that would help me on my mission to do something toward improving the human condition. But I was feeling somewhat frustrated because, at the beginning, almost all of the courses were required and I found myself sitting in classes on statistics, animal learning, physiological psychology, and the like. In retrospect, I'm sure these were fine courses taught by competent professors, but I didn't see how they were going to help me in my quest to improve the human condition. In those days almost all of scientific psychology was dominated by reinforcement theory, which in essence presented a rather mechanistic and uninspired view of the world—a view suggesting that if you want a rat, a pigeon, or a person to do something, believe something, or value something, reward him for doing it, believing it, or valuing it. This was hardly an inspiring conception of human nature for someone who had cut his teeth on Maslow's brand of humanism. Moreover, as a student I wasn't doing all that well. My performance was well below the median of my cohort, and I felt in real danger of washing out at the end of my first year.

In the spring quarter I finally had room for an elective course on my schedule. There weren't a lot of courses to choose from, but there was a new professor in the department—some guy named Leon Festinger who was offering a seminary on a theory he was developing. Festinger had been on campus for only six months or so, but he had already established a reputation as a very bright and very angry young man. This is an understatement. Rumor had it that he was some sort of genius. He was also rumored to possess a rapierlike wit and apparently was fond of using it to slice up and devour tender young graduate students (like me) for breakfast. Needless to say, most of the graduate students were intimidated by him and tried to keep out of his way. I was well aware of this and was no less chary about dealing with this guy than was the typical graduate student. Nevertheless, I was curious. I considered the possibility of sitting in on his seminar for the first meeting (as a shopper) to see if this Festinger guy would be teaching something interesting—and to see if he was really as fierce as everyone said he was.

Because the course description in the catalogue was extremely vague, I wanted to find out more about the content of the seminar before I actually entered Festinger's lair. So it was with some trepidation that I walked into his office and indicated that I was thinking of enrolling in his seminar. I told him I didn't know anything about his work and asked him if there was anything I might read that might help me decide whether or not I wanted to enroll. He leaned back in his chair and looked me up and down. His eyes came to rest on my face, and he stared at me for a very long time; then he grunted, rolled his eyes toward the ceiling (as if to say, "Just look at the idiots they're sending me these days"), and with some reluctance reached into a desk drawer and handed me the carbon copy of a booklength manuscript he had just sent off to the publisher. He told me it was the only copy he had left, and he made me promise, under pain of death or dismemberment (whichever I preferred), not to let my toddlers get blueberry jam all over it. Needless to say, I kept it well out of their reach.

The manuscript was called "A Theory of Cognitive Dissonance." Although I am a very slow reader (I tend to move my lips when I read), I read the damn thing in one sitting—finishing it around 3 A.M.). It knocked me out. It was the most exciting thing I had ever read in psychology. That was over forty years ago; it's *still* the most exciting thing I've ever read in psychology.

In his book Festinger started with a very simple proposition: If a person held two cognitions that were psychologically inconsistent, he or she would experience dissonance and would attempt to reduce dissonance much as he or she would attempt to reduce hunger, thirst, or any drive. What Leon realized, in 1957, was the importance of forging a marriage between the cognitive and the motivational. Dissonance theory is essentially a theory about sense-making—how people try to make sense out of their environment and their behavior, resolve discrepancies, and thus try to lead lives that are (at least in their own minds) sensible and meaningful. The book contained very little original experimentation. But it contained some rich and wonderful ideas, as well as the seeds of some fascinating research that was to flood the journals for the next ten to fifteen years—and that revitalized social psychology.

But I'm getting ahead of my story; this was 1957. To me, what was most exciting about reading the book, what kept me awake into the wee hours of the morning, was not the research but the challenge. Leon's little book threw down the gauntlet and offered a serious vehicle for challenging the smug dominance of reinforcement theory. It did this not in a vague, philosophical manner, but in a powerful, concrete, and specific confrontation, exposing reinforcement theory's limiting conditions as well as its inability to predict some of the more subtle and more interesting nuances of human behavior.

For example, reinforcement theory would suggest that if you reward individuals for saying something, they might become infatuated with that statement (through secondary reinforcement). But Leon's book suggested something much more interesting, and just two years after the publication of his book, Festinger and Merrill Carlsmith performed an experiment that exploded that simplistic notion by showing that you believe lies that you tell only if you are *insufficiently* rewarded for telling them. That same year, Jud Mills and I designed and conducted an experiment demonstrating that people who go through a severe initiation in order to gain admission to a group come to like that group better than people who go through a mild initiation or no initiation at all. Reinforcement theory would suggest that we like people and groups that are associated with reward; Mills and I showed that we come to like things for which we suffer.

The publication of those two experiments generated a lot of excitement and a lot of controversy over the next several years. But eventually the notion and major findings of cognitive dissonance became part of the vernacular, not only of the social psychologist but of the layperson as well. It is a tribute to how thoroughly dissonance theory captured the imagination of social psychology that when I talk about this research to first-year graduate students these days they easily accept it as an obvious established fact—and sometimes even with a look of boredom on their faces. But let me tell you that in 1958 the simple mechanistic assumptions of reinforcement theory were so dominant that when Jud Mills and I first floated our hypothesis and procedure past our fellow graduate students, they laughed derisively. They thought our experiment was absurd. They knew that things become attractive through association with pleasure—certainly not through association with suffering. Their thinking was to change dramatically, but it didn't happen overnight. Old habits and old beliefs die hard.

But by the mid-1960s research inspired by dissonance theory brought about a sea change in the way we think about human behavior. The theory was like a clarion call—a powerful argument for taking cognition and motivation seriously in social psychology. The theory inspired experimental research that demonstrated convincingly, like no other theory before it, that people think; we are not simple reinforcement machines. And because we think, we frequently get ourselves into a tangled muddle of self-justification, denial, and distortion. The excitement and heated debate generated by the early research is not easy to describe. It's not an exaggeration to say that it revitalized social psychology.

Falling in Love with the Experimental Method

When I first sat in on Leon's seminar (and in a sense I've been figuratively sitting in on his seminar ever since), I was immediately struck by the fact that, unlike Maslow, Leon was not interested in improving the human condition. Not in the least. His motivation for doing research was intense curiosity. He approached research in social psychology as a puzzle to be solved, the way a chess master approaches a chess problem: Trying to understand human behavior and doing good research (not doing good) were more than enough to keep him excited.

As a methodologist, he had no peers. Not only was he brilliant, creative, and meticulous in designing and conducting experiments, but he also had a boldness that bordered on audacity. Indeed, in my judgment it was his audacity that was most impressive. Leon had the audacity to believe that with sufficient ingenuity, social psychologists could capture just about *any* conceptual variable and find a way to bring it into the laboratory—thus freeing all of us from what was in the 1940s and 1950s an overreliance on personality variables in our experiments. Like his own mentor, Kurt Lewin, Leon realized that in order truly to have a science of social psychology, we need to understand what causes what; and in order to fully understand what causes what, it is the experimenter (not the participant's mother) who must be responsible for creating the first "what"—that is, the independent variable.

The most important aspect of Leon's audacity is contained in the phrase "with sufficient ingenuity." That is, the belief that virtually all variables are manipulable in the laboratory becomes an idle boast unless it is coupled with great craftsmanship—even artistry—in the design and construction of an experiment. Festinger realized that in order to pull off some projects, the researcher must be able to invent and run the experiment with such skill that the participant gets caught up in a powerful scenario that is compelling, believable, and fully involving. Every detail of the construction and the performance is terribly important.

Anyone who ever worked with Leon will remember (almost certainly with a groan) the seemingly endless time and energy spent fine-tuning the procedure and rehearsing the script until we got it right. For example, let's look again at the Festinger-Carlsmith experiment. In this experiment the researcher enlists the participant's help, asking her if she would agree to substitute for the stooge (who apparently had failed to show up on time to interact with the incoming participant) and induce her to lie to that incoming participant—to tell him (for either $1 or $20) that a dull task was actually interesting. In this procedure you don't simply *tell* the participant that the stooge didn't show up and you'd like her to play that role and tell the next participant that packing spools is an interesting and enjoyable task. Oh, no. You must convince her that you are deeply distressed that your accomplice didn't show up. You sweat, you pace up and down, and you wring your hands; you convey to the participant that you are in real trouble here, that the next participant is waiting and the goddamn stooge hasn't shown up yet. You then appeal to the participant to do you a favor.

I have a vivid memory of the hours and hours Leon and I spent, prior to the experiment, coaching and directing the performance of a very precocious Stanford undergraduate named Merrill Carlsmith so that he could run the experiment in a convincing manner. Merrill was extraordinarily bright but, in those days, was shy and stiff to the point of being wooden. Leon and I worked very hard with him until he mastered his role and learned to play it effectively—day after day after day. In these situations Leon was a regular Lee Strasberg, and we graduate students felt that we were a part of Actors Studio. Art and craftsmanship in the service of science: It was an exciting process. It was very hard work, but we considered it a vital part of doing research. And it almost always paid off.

When I think about those years, I think of it as a difficult but unbelievably valuable apprenticeship. In those days, for better or for worse, there were no standard, cut-and-dried, cookbook ways of instantiating the conceptual variable in the laboratory. Each new experiment presented an entire new set of challenges that needed to be met with hard thinking, an enormous amount of effort, and even some occasional flashes of ingenuity. There were no shortcuts. It is customary to say of one's mentor that "he taught me everything I know." But Leon taught me much more than that: He taught me the process by which I could try to *find out* the things that neither he nor I nor anyone else knew before. He taught me how to think like an experimentalist. And he taught me to love the process for its own sake. I should also say that everything I had heard about Leon was true. And the longer I knew him the truer these things became. He *was* extremely tough, he could be difficult, he could be devastating, and he was brilliant. In addition he was capable of enormous warmth and great personal loyalty. We became close friends. Perhaps it was because of that friendship that we were able to disagree so vehemently about important substantive issues.

Modifying Dissonance Theory

One of the earliest and most important substantive disagreements Leon and I had was about the basic nature of dissonance theory itself, and it came early, in my third year of graduate school. After working with the theory for a while, I began to feel that it was a little too vague. Several situations arose where it wasn't entirely clear what dissonance theory would predict or, indeed, whether or not dissonance theory even made a prediction. Most specifically, Festinger and I argued strenuously about two of his classic examples. The first involved a person stepping out of doors in a rainstorm and not getting wet. Leon was convinced this would arouse a great deal of dissonance; I had difficulty seeing it. My disagreement went something like this: "What's that got to do with *him*? It's a strange phenomenon, all right, but unless he feared he was losing his mind, I don't see the dissonance."

The second was Festinger's classic example of a situation where dissonance theory *didn't* apply. This was the case of a man driving, late at night, on a lonely country road and getting a flat tire (Festinger, 1957, pp. 277–278). Lo and behold, when he opened the trunk of his car, he discovered he didn't have a jack. Leon maintained that although the person would experience frustration, disappointment, perhaps even fear, there are no dissonant cognitions in that situation. My argument was succinct: "Of course there is dissonance! What kind of idiot would go driving late at night on a lonely country road without a jack in his car?" "But," Leon countered, "where are the dissonant cognitions?"

It took me a while, but it gradually dawned on me that what was at the heart of my argument in both of those situations was the self-concept. In the raindrop situation, the self was not involved. In the flat tire situation, for me, what was dissonant was (1) the driver's cognition about his "idiotic" behavior (driving at night on a lonely country road without a jack) with (2) his self-concept of being a reasonably smart guy. I initially spelled this out in my very first grant proposal (Aronson, 1960), where I argued that dissonance theory makes its strongest predictions when an important element of the self-concept is threatened—typically, when an individual performs a behavior that is inconsistent with his or her sense of self. I then proposed and subsequently performed a couple of experiments to test this notion (Aronson & Carlsmith, 1962; Aronson, Carlsmith, & Darley, 1963). Initially, I did not intend this to be a major modification of the theory but only an attempt to clarify the predictions a bit to make the theory a little tighter. In my opinion this "tightening" retained the core notion of inconsistency but shifted the emphasis to the self-concept, thus specifying more precisely when the theory did or did not apply. I believe that this minor modification of dissonance theory turned out to have important ramifications inasmuch as it increased the predictive power of the theory without seriously limiting its scope.

In addition, this modification uncovered a hidden assumption contained in the original theory. Festinger's original statement—and all of the early experiments—rested on the implicit assumption that individuals have a reasonably positive self-concept. But if an individual considered himself to be a schnook, he might expect himself to do schnooky things—like go through a severe initiation in order to get into a boring group or say things that he didn't quite believe. For such individuals, dissonance would not be aroused under the same conditions as for persons with a favorable view of themselves. Rather, dissonance would occur when negative self-expectancies were violated—that is, when the person with a poor self-concept engaged in a behavior that reflected positively on the self.

To test this hidden assumption, Merrill Carlsmith and I conducted a simple little experiment that demonstrated that under certain conditions college students would be made uncomfortable with success, that they would prefer to be accurate in predicting and confirming their own behavior, even if it meant setting themselves up for failure. Specifically, we found that students who had developed negative self-expectancies regarding their performance on a task showed evidence of dissonance arousal when subsequently faced with success on that task. That is, after repeated failure at the task, participants who later achieved a successful performance, when provided an opportunity to repeat that performance, intentionally changed their responses from accurate to inaccurate ones in order to preserve a consistent, though negative, self-concept (Aronson & Carlsmith, 1962). Mort Deutsch and Lenny Solomon (1959) performed an experiment in which they made a similar prediction, starting from a different set of premises. Indeed, there was clearly something in the air at that time, because, independently, similar results soon followed from Hal Gerard and his students (1964) as well as from Andrej Malewski (1962) in Poland. In recent years William Swann (1991) seems to have rediscovered that phenomenon.

Over the next several years, I carried this line of thinking a step further (Aronson & Carlsmith, 1968; Aronson, Chase, Helmreich, & Ruhnke, 1974), elaborating on the centrality of the self-concept/dissonance processes and suggesting that in this regard people generally strive to maintain a sense of self that is both consistent *and* positive. That is, because most people have relatively favorable views of themselves, they want to see themselves as (1) competent, (2) moral, and (3) able to predict their own behavior.

Briefly, my reasoning goes something like this: Efforts to reduce dissonance involve a process of self-justification because dissonance is almost always experienced after engaging in an action that leaves one feeling stupid or immoral (see Aronson, Chase, Helmreich, & Ruhnke, 1974). Moreover, the greater the personal commitment or self-involvement implied by the action and the smaller the *external* justification for that action, the greater the dissonance and therefore the more powerful the attitude change. Thus in the Festinger-Carlsmith experiment what was dissonant was not the cognition "I believe the task is dull and I said the task is interesting" (as Festinger suggested). What was *really* dissonant was my self-concept as a decent, moral person with my knowledge that I have acted immorally by deceiving another person. In order to reduce that dissonance, one must convince oneself that little or no deception was involved—in other words, that the task *was*, in fact, a rather interesting activity. By justifying one's actions in this fashion, one is able to restore a sense of self as morally good.

What Ever Became of Doing Good?

After reading the above section, you might be wondering what had become of my initial intentions. Recall that I entered graduate school as a Maslovian, eager to improve the human condition. I left graduate school heavily influenced by Festinger—excited about doing basic research. My excitement was twofold: First, I was intrigued by the new and dramatically different predictions that dissonance theory had opened for me. They were not the usual obvious predictions that the late Bob Cohen referred to as "bubbe psychology"—predictions that your grandmother (in Yiddish your "bubbe") could have made—for example, that we like things because they are rewarded; that we conform because we want to avoid trouble; that we believe credible communicators more than noncredible communicators. We were exploring new ground. The questions were different. And I was passionately interested in finding out the answers. A lot has been written about whether or not nonobvious predictions advance the field more than obvious predictions. I'm not sure whether or not that is the case. What I *do* know is that it's a hell of a lot more exciting and fun to be predicting something that my bubbe would never have imagined. Doing an experiment is hard work, so anything that sustains my interest in a long and difficult research project and keeps me functioning is not to be sneezed at. And if the results of the experiment are not obvious, they usually arouse interest and skepticism from other scientists and therefore are more likely to inspire follow-up research from the scientific community.

Second, I was intrigued by the methodological challenge posed by the requirements of the hypotheses we were testing. These hypotheses required high-impact procedures where participants must be imbedded in a powerful and credible scenario that we, the experimenters, needed to invent from scratch each time we tried to tackle a new hypothesis. This was an exciting combination of science and art that electrified my interest and brought out abilities in me that I never knew I had. The challenge always left me tingling. Moreover, I gradually came to realize that this style of experimental social psychology was not arbitrary, not simply a matter of taste, but essential because in our research we are investigating the behavior of intelligent, curious, sophisticated adults who have been living in a social world for their entire lives. It goes without saying that like the experimenters who are studying them, the participants in our experiments have developed their own ideas and theories about what causes their feelings and behavior as well as the feelings and behavior of the people around them. This is not the case (or at least not to the same degree) when you are performing experiments with chemicals, with laboratory animals, or even with humans in nonsocial situations, as in cognitive psychology. So a few paragraphs ago, when I described the meticulous care that went into designing the typical high-impact experiment (like the Festinger-Carlsmith study), I hope it was clear that we exerted all that energy to run the experiment with a great deal of care and drama not because it's fun and not because our aunt Mathilda always wanted us to be an actor, director, and playwright. We ran it this way for one simple reason: If we failed to get the participant fully involved in the situation, she would sleepwalk through the procedure and the manipulation simply would not take.

This was a dual challenge: The excitement generated by testing interesting, novel hypotheses and using a methodology that continually pushed to its limits whatever meager creativity I might possess. This was enough to get me to put aside my initial interest in trying to do something directly useful to society, something toward improving the human condition. I use the word "directly" so as not to imply that basic research is not useful for society. And that's a point I want to ride on for a few sentences. I never really gave up my desire to do something useful. When I did a piece of basic research and wrote it up, I always tried to frame my account in ways that might be applicable to social problems. In addition, when I wrote *The Social Animal,* I almost always described laboratory experiments in ways that might help readers understand what was going on around them. I am well aware that the reader might regard the last few sentences as nothing but dissonance reduction on my part. All I can say about that is, "Maybe so!"

I cannot leave this section without going back to my two mentors for just a moment. Maslow and Festinger did not like each other very much. That's a bit of an understatement. As a matter of fact, when I first informed Maslow that I had decided to work closely with Festinger, he said, "How can you stand working with that bastard?" Maslow felt Festinger was cold, detached, inhumane. Festinger felt Maslow was too soft—a dreamer, a man given to making broad statements about human nature in the absence of data. He once said to me, "That guy's ideas are so bad that they aren't even wrong!"

Needless to say, this state of affairs caused me to experience considerable dissonance. I liked, respected, and admired them both. Indeed, I think it's fair to say that I *loved* both of those guys. Naturally, I wanted them to like and respect each other. But this was not to be. As I look back on my own research and thinking, I can now see that without being fully aware of it, I might have been trying in some small way to combine Maslow with Festinger—to forge a marriage, if you will, between my two mentors who hated each other. I tried to do experiments as rigorously as possible about issues that might be of benefit to humanity.

This was not readily apparent near the beginning. After leaving graduate school, I spent about a dozen years firmly in the mainstream of basic research. During that time I designed and conducted several experiments testing and expanding derivations from dissonance theory as well as exploring a great many aspects of social influence, persuasion, and interpersonal attraction. At the same time I was training some extraordinarily gifted graduate students to do the same kind of research I was doing. I would like to feel that during those years I contributed something to our discipline's core knowledge. I hasten to reiterate that this "career path" was not a conscious decision on my part. I didn't sit down and say, "I guess I will put aside my interest in doing good and become a basic researcher." It just sort of happened because I got excited about the beauty of the experimental method and I followed my nose toward testing hypotheses that intrigued me. And as indicated above, although I might have put aside my interest in doing something directly to improve the human condition, the impulse never totally left me. I always had this nagging feeling that I (and perhaps "we") would eventually want to spend some time and effort trying to apply some of our basic findings to a societal useful purpose. Again, if I was experiencing any dissonance about this nondecision, I think I convinced myself that I was uncovering important basic knowledge and that some day either I or somebody else would find a good application for that knowledge.

Desegregation Comes to Austin

That day came, without warning, in the autumn of 1971 when the schools of Austin, Texas, were ordered to desegregate and all hell broke loose. Within a few weeks the schools were in turmoil. African American, white, and Mexican American youngsters were in open conflict; fistfights broke out between the various racial groups in the corridors and school yards throughout the city. At the time I was teaching at the University of Texas at Austin, and ironically, while all of this racial hatred was being vented in the public schools of my city, I was busily and happily doing laboratory experiments on interpersonal attraction—trying to find out what made people like each other and hate each other.

As it turned out, the assistant superintendent of schools was a former graduate student at the University of Texas who had become a friend of mine—and he invited me to enter the system with the mandate to do anything within reason to create a more harmonious environment. He suggested that we begin in elementary school, where the situation was tense but less volatile than in the high schools.

My students and I entered a newly desegregated elementary school and spent several days systematically observing the classroom process to see if we could get any clues as to what was going on and how we might best intervene. We tried to do this with fresh eyes—as if we were anthropologists entering an exotic culture for the first time. This mind-set was invaluable. The one thing that leapt out at us was, of course, something that anyone who has ever attended traditional public schools simply takes for granted: The typical classroom is a highly competitive place. Here is a brief summary of our observation, our interpretation, and our diagnosis:

The most typical process we observed was this: The teacher stands in front of the class, asks a question, and waits for the children to indicate that they know the answer. Most frequently, six to ten youngsters strain in their seats and wave their hands to attract the teacher's attention. They seem eager to be called on. Several other students sit quietly with their eyes averted, as if trying to make themselves invisible. When the teacher calls on one of the students, there are looks of disappointment, dismay, and unhappiness on the faces of those students who were eagerly raising their hands but were not called on. If the student who is called on comes up with the right answer, the teacher smiles, nods approvingly, and goes on to the next question. This is a great reward for the child who happens to be called on. At the same time the fortunate student is coming up with the right answer and being smiled upon by the teacher, an audible groan can be heard coming from the children who were striving to be called on but were ignored. It is obvious they are disappointed because they missed an opportunity to show the teacher how smart and quick they are. In Austin the minority kids were underprepared for this competition. The schools they had been attending were substandard. When we tested them, we found that on average their reading skills were approximately one full grade level behind the white kids in their classroom. Thus they were engaged in a highly competitive activity where they were virtually guaranteed to lose. Moreover, the minority kids were not accustomed to the freewheeling competitiveness of the new classroom they had entered. They tended to sit quietly and not raise their hands. From what we could gather from interviews we conducted with the students, some of the existing stereotypes were confirmed and magnified: The white kids tended to conclude that the minority kids were stupid and lazy; the minority kids were of the opinion that the white kids were arrogant show-offs.

This was disappointing to say the least. In 1954, when the U.S. Supreme Court outlawed school segregation, hopes ran high that we might be on our way to a better society. At that time many of us believed that if only youngsters from various ethnic and racial backgrounds could share the same classroom, negative stereotypes would eventually fade, racial and ethnic prejudice would diminish, and cross-ethnic friendships would develop under the glow of increased contact. Moreover, because on the basis of testimony by social psychologists the Supreme Court held segregation partly responsible for the low self-esteem of African American children, it was believed that desegregation would also result in increases in self-esteem. These predictions proved to be naive to say the least. The events that took place in Austin were not an aberration but were a rather extreme exemplification of the fact that across the nation school desegregation was not progressing smoothly and was not having the salutary effects on behavior and attitudes that had been anticipated. In his review of the research literature, Walter Stephan (1978) found that following school desegregation the self-esteem of minority children underwent a further decrease—and there was virtually no clear evidence indicating even the slightest decrease in prejudice or stereotyping. In short, desegregation was not having the anticipated positive effects, but we didn't know why.

After observing classrooms and interviewing children, my students and I had one pretty good clue as to what might be going wrong. We surmised that it might be the highly competitive nature of the classroom that was preventing desegregation from working in the way it was intended to work. Accordingly, our intervention consisted of restructuring the dynamics of the classroom; we changed the atmosphere from a competitive one to a cooperative one. This involved inventing, developing, and implementing a technique that created small interdependent groups, designed to place the students of various racial and ethnic groups in a situation where they needed to cooperate with one another in order to attain their personal goals. We called it the jigsaw classroom because it resembled the assembling of a jigsaw puzzle (Aronson, 1975, 1992; Aronson & Bridgeman, 1979; Aronson & Gonzalez, 1988; Aronson et al., 1978; Aronson & Patnoe, 1997).

Here is how the jigsaw classroom works: Students are placed in diverse six-person learning groups. The day's lesson is divided into six paragraphs, so that each student has one segment of the written material. For example, if the students are to learn the life of Eleanor Roosevelt, her biography is arranged in six parts. Each student has possession of a unique and vital part of the information, which, like the pieces of a jigsaw puzzle, must be put together before anyone can learn the whole picture. The individual must learn his or her own section and teach it to the other members of the group—who do not have any other access to that material. If Debbie wants to do well on the ensuing exam about the life of Eleanor Roosevelt, she must pay close attention to Carlos (who is reciting on Roosevelt's girlhood years), to Natalie (who is reciting on Roosevelt's years in the White House), and so on.

Unlike the traditional classroom, where students are competing against each other, the jigsaw classroom requires students to depend on each other. To illustrate, let's look closely at "Carlos," one of the students in the first classroom in which we intervened. English was his second language, and although he spoke it well, he felt a bit insecure in this newly integrated classroom and spoke hesitantly and self-consciously. He was reluctant to speak up in class and was quiet unless specifically called on. In the traditional classroom, when Carlos, because of anxiety and discomfort, was having difficulty reciting, the other students could easily ignore him (or even make fun of him) in their zeal to show the teacher how smart they were. But in the jigsaw classroom, if Carlos was having difficulty reciting, it was in the best interests of the other students to be patient, to make encouraging comments, and even to ask friendly, probing questions to make it easier for Carlos to bring forth the knowledge within him.

Through the jigsaw process, the children began to pay more attention to each other and to show respect for each other. Children like Carlos tended to respond to this treatment by simultaneously becoming more relaxed and more engaged; this inevitably produced an improvement in their ability to communicate. In this instance after a couple of weeks the other students were struck by their realization that Carlos was a lot smarter than they had thought he was. As they began to like him more and treat him with more respect, Carlos became still more comfortable, more secure, and more effective. Carlos began to enjoy school more and began to see the Anglo students in his group not as tormentors but as helpful and responsible teammates.

Moreover, as he began to feel increasingly comfortable in class and started to gain more confidence in himself, Carlos's academic performance began to improve. As his academic performance improved, so did his self-esteem. The vicious circle had been broken; the elements that had been causing a downward spiral were changed. The spiral moved dramatically upward.

The formal data that we gathered from the jigsaw experiments were clear and striking. Compared to students in traditional classrooms, students in jigsaw groups showed a decrease in their general prejudice and stereotyping, as well as an increase in their liking for their group mates, both within and across ethnic boundaries. In addition, children in the jigsaw classrooms performed better on objective exams and showed a significantly greater increase in self-esteem than children in traditional classrooms. Children in the jigsaw classrooms also showed far greater liking for school. Absenteeism was significantly lower in jigsaw classrooms than in traditional classrooms in the same school. Moreover, children in schools where the jigsaw technique was practiced showed substantial evidence of true integration—that is, in the school yard there was far more intermingling among the various races and ethnic groups than on the playgrounds of schools using more traditional classroom techniques. Finally, children in the jigsaw classrooms developed a greater ability to empathize with others and to see the world through the perspective of others than children in traditional classrooms did (Aronson & Bridgeman, 1979).

We invented this technique within a few days of our first entry into the classroom. I am frequently asked how we were able to diagnose the problem and invent a solution as quickly as we did. Occasionally, the question is asked a bit more aggressively: "What made *you guys* so smart? How come the teachers weren't able to see that competition was the problem and cooperation the solution?" We weren't that smart, but we *were* outsiders. In 1971 the competitive structure of the typical classroom was more or less taken for granted. At that time most teachers were immersed in that structure and seemed implicitly to accept it as the way things had to be. I think that our coming from outside the system (and setting

ourselves to observe the classroom as if we were anthropologists observing an exotic culture) gave us an enormous advantage. With that mind-set, the destructive
aspects of competition fairly leapt out at us.

In addition to being outsiders, we were also social psychologists. It's true that
the idea for this cooperative technique came quickly and seemed almost intuitive.
But our so-called intuition was rooted in the work of our predecessors—most
specifically in Morton Deutsch's (1949) theorizing on cooperation and Muzafer
Sherif's (1966) research on conflict resolution at a Boy Scout camp. As I recall,
my students and I didn't say at the time: "Hey, that reminds me of Sherif's work
with the Eagles and Rattlers." Or, "Didn't Mort Deutsch have something to say
about competition and cooperation way back in 1949?" Nothing like it. But this
was part of our general orientation and informed our thinking.

I was so excited by the success of the jigsaw technique that I spent the next few
years going from school to school, trying to give it away and offering to train
teachers to use it. Although I was invited into a handful of schools, to my surprise
and disappointment during those first few years most school administrators were
not at all interested in what I had to offer. They expressed a desire to avoid rock-
ing the boat: As long as their schools were not in crisis, they seemed reluctant to
introduce so radical a technique that might lead some Anglo parents to complain.

For me personally, those years were frustrating and disheartening. I was confident that we had a technique that would make desegregation work, and I had collected convincing experimental data to prove it. In addition to publishing the
data in the usual journals, I had intentionally published in popular places (like
Psychology Today) to make the data more accessible to laypeople and school administrators. I had sent letters and clippings from *Psychology Today* to dozens of
school districts only to get a lukewarm response from the vast majority of school
administrators.

I now realize that my expectations were far too high. What I learned was that
ideas sometimes need time to marinate. And in addition sometimes the ideas
need a little help via formal recognition. Such recognition came in 1979, when, in
commemoration of the twenty-fifth anniversary of *Brown v. Board of Education,*
the U.S. Civil Rights Commission named Austin as a model city in which school
desegregation worked in the manner intended. Much of the credit went to jigsaw.
Interest in jigsaw immediately picked up, and I subsequently received a great
many invitations to enter school systems and train teachers to use the technique.
Moreover, several similar cooperative techniques have been developed (see Cook,
1984; Johnson & Johnson, 1987, 1989; Meier, 1995; Sharan, 1980; Slavin, 1980,
1996). The striking results described above have been successfully replicated in
thousands of classrooms in all regions of the country and abroad. What began as
a simple experiment in one school system in 1971 has spread dramatically. Cooperative learning has become a major force within the field of public education.
Indeed, John McConahay (1981), a leading expert in race relations has called the

cooperative learning revolution the single most effective practice for improving race relations in desegregated schools.

Energy Conservation and Condom Use

Following my first venture into applied social psychology, instead of returning to the laboratory I found myself looking around for other societal problems that I might try to tackle. The first issue that came up was energy conservation. In the late 1970s and early 1980s, our nation was in the midst of a serious energy crisis. At that time my colleagues and I did a number of studies aimed at finding ways to persuade people to conserve energy and reflected on ways to affect public policy. I lack the space to discuss that work here and refer you to a smattering of these articles (see, for example, Aronson, 1982; Aronson & O'Leary, 1982; Yates & Aronson, 1983; Stern & Aronson, 1984; Coltrane, Archer, & Aronson, 1986; Aronson & Gonzales, 1990; Archer, Pettigrew, & Aronson, 1992; Condelli et al., 1984; Costanzo et al., 1986).

In the mid-1980s a still more dramatic and dangerous problem confronted our nation and the world—the AIDS epidemic. AIDS has been referred to as the plague of the twentieth century. Unfortunately, that plague is still very much with us as we enter the twenty-first century and shows no signs of abating. There is no cure or vaccine on the horizon. Worldwide, over 30 million people are now HIV positive. It is estimated that 2.3 million people will die of AIDS in 1998. There are 16,000 new cases per day. Although it is most prevalent in the developing countries, even in highly developed countries like the United States it is a monumentally serious problem. In the United States there are currently 1 million people who are HIV positive, with 40,000 new cases every year. Our nation's public health officials have spent vast sums of money to educate the public about the hazards of unsafe sexual practices and intravenous drug use. In high schools and colleges, serious attempts have been made to teach sexually active young people about the causes of AIDS and to convince them that the threat to life is real. Such information has been accompanied by specific recommendations for preventive action— such as celibacy, monogamy, or the use of condoms. Although celibacy and monogamy may be worthwhile goals, it has proved to be unrealistic to expect the great majority of teenagers and young adults to exercise these options. Even politically and religiously conservative experts like former surgeon general C. Everett Koop eventually came to believe that for most sexually active young adults the proper use of condoms may be the most realistic mode of AIDS prevention.

Thus a major path to AIDS prevention among sexually active young adults would appear to be to persuade them to use condoms. This seems to be a straightforward task for a social psychologist. After all, communication and persuasion is at the heart of our discipline; we have had a great deal of experience convincing people to do all kinds of things that are good for them. Why not condom use?

Alas, that has proven to be a difficult and elusive problem. In spite of numerous attempts at persuasion, surveys on college campuses across the country indicate that the majority of sexually active college students are not engaging in safe sex, are not discussing sexually transmitted diseases with their partners, and have never even purchased a condom (Keller, 1993). Most college students take a dim view of condoms and are in a state of denial, convincing themselves that they could spot someone with AIDS a mile away. So in their minds it would seem that AIDS is a serious problem—but not for them. In my own research, I had tried a number of more or less traditional communication/persuasion techniques with very limited success. I had also tried some not so traditional techniques. For example, because my interviews with college students revealed a deep-seated prejudice against condoms as "antiseptic," unromantic devices that ruin the joy and spontaneity of the sexual encounter, I produced a soft-porn video in an attempt to convince sexually active students that the condom can be used in an erotic manner—as an exciting part of foreplay. The results were disappointing. Although the erotic video produced a significant positive change in their attitudes toward condoms, the effect faded within a few weeks. Subsequent interviews revealed that our participants would try condoms once or twice and then stop using them.

I had run into a stone wall. In pondering these data, I began to speculate about how we might bring about a more permanent change. My thoughts came back to my roots, to dissonance theory. After all, some of the research on dissonance theory (because it involved *self*-persuasion rather than attempts at direct persuasion) had succeeded in producing long-term effects (see, for example, Freedman, 1965).

I thought about ways of using the counterattitudinal attitude paradigm. That is, why not try to get people to argue against their own attitudes—as in the Festinger-Carlsmith experiment? On the surface it seemed like a great idea. After all, we had found that this strategy was powerful and, when judiciously applied, had long-term effects on attitude and behavior—exactly what was needed in this societal situation. But wait a minute: In the condom use situation, there were no counterattitudinal attitudes to address. That is, our surveys and interviews had demonstrated that sexually active young adults were in favor of people's using condoms to prevent AIDS. They simply weren't using them. They were clearly in a state of personal denial when it came to their own immediate danger, but they were in perfect agreement with the belief that using condoms was a very good idea. How could we invoke the counterattitudinal attitude paradigm if there was no counterattitude to invoke?

After giving the matter a great deal of thought, it occurred to me that the solution had to come from the self-concept—because being in denial is not an attractive thing to be doing. The problem was to find a way to place the individual in a situation where the act of denial would be unfeasible because it would conflict with his or her positive self-image. And then it struck me—in the form of a scenario. This should not be surprising in view of the fact that, as an experimenter, I had learned to think of research problems and design experiments in terms of scenarios. Here's the scenario that came to mind:

Suppose you are a sexually active college student and, like most, (1) you do not use condoms regularly and (2) have managed to blind yourself to the dangers inherent in having unprotected sex. Suppose, on going home for Christmas vacation, you find that Charlie, your sixteen-year-old kid brother has just discovered sex and is in the process of boasting to you about his many and varied sexual encounters. What do you say to him? Chances are, as a caring, responsible older sibling, you will dampen his enthusiasm a bit by warning him about the dangers of AIDS and other sexually transmitted diseases and urge him at least to take proper precautions—to use condoms.

Suppose that I am a friend of the family who was invited to dinner and happens to overhear this exchange between you and your kid brother. What if I were to pull you aside and say, "That was very good advice you gave Charlie—I'm very proud of you for being so responsible. By the way, how frequently do *you* use condoms?"

What I am doing here is confronting you with your own hypocrisy—I am making you mindful of the fact that you are not practicing what you preach. Almost all of us want to see ourselves as people of integrity. People of integrity practice what they preach. Your self-concept as a person of integrity is threatened by your own behavior—behavior that suggests you might lack integrity, that you might be behaving hypocritically. How might you reestablish your self-concept as a person of high integrity? There is only one surefire way: By beginning forthwith to put into practice what you have just finished preaching. In short, to start using condoms immediately.

In a series of experiments, my students and I constructed a procedure very much like the example mentioned above (Aronson, Fried, & Stone, 1991; Stone, Aronson, Crain, Winslow, & Fried, 1994). Specifically, we induced college students to deliver a convincing speech, talking about the dangers of AIDS and imploring the audience to use condoms. The speech was videotaped, and the speakers were led to believe that the tape was going to be shown to high school students as part of a sex education class. We then asked the speakers to talk about all of the situations in their day-to-day lives when they found it difficult or impossible to use condoms themselves, thus making them aware that they were preaching what they were not practicing. Confronted with their own hypocrisy, how could they reduce dissonance and reestablish their belief in their own integrity? Exactly as in the hypothetical example: by resolving to change their behavior to bring it into line with their own preaching.

How do we measure our success? The most direct way would be to see if the subjects in our hypocrisy condition are using condoms more than subjects in our control conditions. Needless to say, ethics and good taste preclude us from getting a direct behavioral measure of this behavior. I (or perhaps I should say *even*

I) must stop short of crawling into bed with the participants and observing whether or not they are using condoms. We could always ask them. Self-report data are a sensible option and usually the best a researcher can do in such a delicate situation. But we also wanted a more behavioral measure. We hit on the following: We had paid the participants $5 for their time and effort. On their way out of the experiment room and in the absence of the experimenter, they were allowed to purchase as many condoms as they wanted for the bargain price of 10 cents each. Number of condoms purchased became our immediate dependent variable. We also collected self-report data over the telephone three months after the experiment.

The results of these experiments are powerful. Compared to control conditions, college students in the hypocrisy condition purchased substantially more condoms immediately after the experiment. Even more impressive is that some three months later, when interviewed on the telephone about their sexual behavior, 92 percent reported that they were using condoms regularly. This percentage is almost twice as high as that of participants in the control condition who were not confronted with their own hypocrisy. Because of social desirability, we suspect that these long-term data may be inflated. It is reasonable to assume that the actual effect is somewhat less impressive than 92 percent. We will never know for sure. Be that as it may, there is no reason to assume that if there were inflation, it would be any greater in the hypocrisy condition than in the control conditions. Therefore we are confident of the differences and elated by their practical importance.

In a subsequent experiment, we increased our confidence in the efficacy of the "induction of hypocrisy" paradigm by testing the paradigm in a different situation—a situation where we could get a more direct behavioral measure. The venue for this field experiment was the shower room of our campus field house. In central California we suffer from periodic, chronic water shortages. On our campus the administration is constantly trying to find ways to induce students to conserve water. So we decided to test our hypothesis by using dissonance theory and the induction of hypocrisy to convince students to take shorter showers. What we discovered is that although it is impossible, within the bounds of propriety, to follow people into their bedrooms to observe their condom-using behavior, in our society one can easily follow them into the shower room and watch them take showers.

In this experiment (Dickerson, Thibodeau, Aronson, & Miller, 1992) we intercepted college women who had just finished swimming in a highly chlorinated pool and were on their way to take a shower at the university field house. Just like the condom experiment, it was a two-by-two design in which we varied commitment and mindfulness. In the commitment condition each student was asked if she would be willing to sign a flyer encouraging people to conserve water at the field house. The students were told that the flyers would be displayed on posters; each was shown a sample poster—a large, colorful, very public display. The flyer read: "Take shorter showers. Turn off water while soaping up. If I can do it, so can you!" After she signed the flyer, we thanked her for her time, and she proceeded to the shower room, where our undergraduate research assistant (blind to condition) was unobtrusively waiting (with hidden waterproof stopwatch) to time the student's shower.

In the hypocrisy condition, in addition, we asked the students to respond to a water conservation "survey," which consisted of items designed to make them aware of their proconservation attitudes and the fact that their showering behavior was sometimes wasteful.

The results are consistent with those in the condom experiment: We found dissonance effects only in the hypocrisy condition—that is, where the participants were induced to advocate short showers and were made mindful of their own past behavior, they took very short showers. The results were striking: In the hypocrisy condition the length of the shower averaged just over three and a half minutes (that's short!) and was significantly shorter than in the control condition.

Back to the Theory

The initial reason for the development of the hypocrisy paradigm was couched in my attempt to apply dissonance theory to the solution of a societal problem. There was an additional bonus to these experiments: Our results also shed some light on an interesting theoretical controversy among dissonance theorists. This involves the development of the "new look" in dissonance theory developed several years ago by Cooper and Fazio (1984). In examining the early forced compliance experiments, like the Festinger-Carlsmith experiment, Cooper and Fazio made an interesting discovery: In these experiments not only was inconsistency present, but aversive consequences were also present; that is, lying to another person is usually aversive because it does that person harm. Cooper and Fazio then asserted that dissonance is not due to inconsistent cognitions at all but rather is aroused only when an individual feels personally responsible for bringing about an aversive or unwanted event. Or to put it in my terms, dissonance is caused solely by harming another person—which is a threat to the perpetrator's self-concept as a morally good human being. At the time, although I always appreciated the boldness implicit in Cooper and Fazio's theorizing, I could never bring myself to buy into the notion that aversive consequences are essential for the existence of dissonance. But at the time I had no way of trying to refute their assertion.

The ultimate solution to a theoretical dispute is to do an experiment. How do you test this difference empirically? I was at a loss as to how to produce inconsistency in the Festinger-Carlsmith type of experiment without also producing aversive consequences for the recipient of one's message. After all, if you are misleading another person by telling him something you believe is false, then you are always bringing about aversive consequences, aren't you? But without quite realizing it, my students and I seem to have stumbled onto the solution with the hypocrisy experiments. In this procedure the participant is preaching what he is not practicing (and is therefore experiencing dissonance), but where are the aversive consequences for the audience in the condom experiment? There are none. Indeed, to the extent that the participant succeeds in being persuasive, far from producing aversive consequences for the recipient the "hypocrite" may well be saving someone's life. And still, it is clear from the data that our participants were experiencing dissonance.

An Idiosyncratic Vision

Okay, that's the end of my story—the context for my vision of experimental social psychology. So now I will sum up what I have learned in forty-three years by presenting this vision as simply as I can.

Sin and Redemption

First and foremost, I think the story of social psychology is a story of sin and redemption. What I mean is this: If you read any textbook on social psychology, you will see that most of the classic, important experiments in the field reveal some of the least appetizing aspects of human behavior: Our classic experiments are about mindless conformity (as in the Asch experiments); destructive obedience to authority (as in the Milgram experiments); cruelty (as in the Zimbardo Stanford prison experiments); aggression (as in the Berkowitz experiments); intergroup conflict (as in the Sherif experiments); blaming the victim (as in the Davis and Jones experiment); and so on.

But social psychology is also about redemption, in the sense that, as mentioned above, experimental social psychologists have the tools and the understanding to create situations that encourage people to overcome mindless conformity, curtail destructive obedience, eliminate prejudice, reduce aggression, transcend our need to blame the victim of our own aggression, and so on. The tools are there.

Focusing on the Situation

How do we go about this? According to my vision, one of the great strengths of social psychology is that it focuses primarily on the power of the situation. That is, when someone commits an act of violence or extreme prejudice or destructive obedience, social psychologists usually resist the temptation to leap to the conclusion that the perpetrator is psychotic or evil or a criminal type. Rather, we focus on the power of the situation. We ask what is there about that situation that increases the likelihood of that unappetizing behavior.

To take one not-so-random example, let's go back to my own personal history—the nine-year-old who was gamely trying to get to and from Hebrew school in one piece. If we look at the tough guys who frequently roughed me up, it's tempting simply to think of them as evil and think about cops, courts, and prisons as a way of preventing them from hurting others. But as a social psychologist, I want to go beyond that. My inclination is to give them the benefit of the doubt by assuming that they were caught up in a powerful situation that produced that prejudice and the accompanying aggressive behavior. If I can figure out the dynamics of that situation, perhaps I could understand their behavior better and try to find ways to change that situation and thereby bring about a modification of their behavior. And this is what I love most about experimental social psychology: It affords us the possibility of redemption. It allows us to intervene in a situation, to change the situation and thereby change the behavior of the people in that situation. In that sense, social psychology is an optimistic science that suggests that we can find ways to reduce such destructive behavior as blind obedience, aggression, and prejudice. Some thirty years after sitting on the curbstone nursing my bloody nose and my cut lip, it was my special privilege, as an experimental social psychologist, to come up with a technique that succeeded in reducing prejudice and turning interethnic enmity into friendship across the country.

Because odious behavior ("sin") is at the heart of our most powerful research in social psychology, it is poetically pleasing that the field provides us with the possibility of redemption. But not all of our work needs to be concerned with redemption. We can be making interesting, important, and exciting interventions without specifically working on the reversal of specific dysfunctional behavior. At the same time, I think that all experimental social psychologists are potential interventionists. From a scientific perspective whether my reason for doing an experiment is purely theoretical, stemming from my curiosity (as in Festinger's case) or a desire to change destructive behavior (as in the example of the anti-Semitic bullies) is irrelevant. From a scientific perspective there is no reason why the process of intervention would be any different.

Let me give you an example. Let's take a highly desirable cluster of behaviors that, for lack of a better word, I will call "creativity." How do we go about trying to understand creativity? One way to study it is to bring a bunch of highly creative people into a room and give them a battery of personality tests to see how they might differ from us ordinary folks. We could interview them about their family lives, find out what their parents were like, what their teachers were like, what their siblings were like—and from that, try to come up with a pattern that leads to creativity. There is nothing wrong with approaching the issue that way. But if I, as a social psychologist, were interested in understanding creativity, what would excite me more would be to try to figure out how to establish a creative environment—a situation that breeds creativity, a situation where ordinary people like me would be more likely to behave creatively. This would require an intervention based on a theory of what causes people to behave creatively.

Although the notion of creativity as an example just seemed to pop into my head, I'm pretty sure it was not random. My guess is that it was inspired by the fact that in this book I am surrounded by some very creative people. Moreover, a hefty percentage of these folks have something special in common: They were part of the first small group of students admitted to Kurt Lewin's social psychology graduate program at MIT some fifty years ago. What a hit rate! One *might* say that Lewin was incredibly skillful or lucky at *selecting* such a creative group. But I doubt that very much. Rather, I am convinced that Lewin was *doing* something special—setting up an environment that brought out an enormous amount of creativity in an entire group of people. Implicitly, many of us have tried to recapture some aspects of that intervention in training our own students. This was illuminated beautifully by one of my own students, Shelley Patnoe (1988) who traveled the country interviewing several distinguished social psychologists who had been students of Lewin or students of students of Lewin. What Patnoe discovered was that virtually all of these people had similar attitudes toward the training of graduate students and (usually without quite realizing it) had been recreating some of the very devices that Lewin had used at MIT. Most notable among these was the *Quasselstrippe,* regular, informal, group research meetings in the relaxed atmosphere of a private home, where ideas and research designs in their formative stages were discussed over beer and pretzels. What Patnoe found is that most of the third-generation professors did not quite realize they were emulating Lewin—they did it this way because it seemed "natural."

The Elliptical Flow: From Theory Back to Theory

A vital aspect of my vision of experimental social psychology concerns itself with where ideas come from, how these ideas lead to experiments, and how the results of these experiments in turn impact our ideas. The way I see it, there is an elliptical flow from theory to an interesting (nonbubbe) hypothesis, to a tightly controlled laboratory experiment, to an attempt at application, to the evaluation of the effectiveness of that situation. It doesn't happen quite this way very often, but many aspects of this idealized form can be realized. When an experiment is theory driven (or at least theory influenced) and produces a testable hypothesis (that the researcher is excited about), which is confirmed in a tightly controlled experiment, that's good enough. If the data lead to a richer understanding of the theory or a modification of the theory, so much the better. If the hypothesis is novel and therefore generates a great deal of interest and excitement in other people, so much the better—but at the very least the *experimenter* should be excited about it. If the experiment produces a strategy for making a useful societal intervention that can be evaluated, that's even better. And if that in turn leads to a clarification of the theory? Nirvana! I have been part of the full sequence only a few times in my life, but for me it is the ultimate research experience.

It should be clear from the above discussion that I believe that theories, at their best, are growing, responsive entities, not carved in stone—far from it. They are *supposed* to change. Theories are wonderful inventions. They serve as road maps, clarifiers of a puzzling world, and synthesizers of what might appear on the surface to be wildly different events. In other words, a good theory shows us where to look, helps us understand complex phenomena, and enables us to see the relationship among apparently disparate events. But as my friend Paul Meehl was always fond of saying, "All theories are lies," by which he meant that they are mere approximations of the empirical world—not to be confused with "truth." As such, they are supposed to change in the face of new data. It is the duty of the theorist to be responsive to new data, to see how they might lead him or her to modify the theory, not to get so enamored of the original formulation that he or she will cling to it for dear life in spite of disconfirming data. In the best of situations, these changes make the theory into a better road map, clarifier, and synthesizer.

I want to elaborate on a point I slid by a couple of paragraphs ago. If you are doing an experiment, the specific hypothesis must excite you. Part of my idealized notion of social psychology at its best involves the passion of the experimenter in attempting to understand the phenomenon he or she is investigating. I have tried to impart this as firmly as I could to my own graduate students, imploring them not to bother designing and running an experiment unless they are passionately concerned about the issue under investigation. Doing a good experiment is hard work. Why would we want to put in all that work if we are not deeply interested in the question we are asking? When I pick up a journal these days, I would like to believe that each and every experiment I read was conducted by someone who was truly excited about testing the hypotheses involved. Alas, that belief is not always easy to maintain.

Roots, Branches, and Sticky New Leaves

I'm almost done here. The final item stresses the importance of synthesis. This seems like an appropriate way to end this chapter because it takes us to both the past and the future. In looking back at my forty-three years of research, I find it crystal clear where the roots and branches are. For example, take my theorizing about the importance of the self-concept. This theorizing has been evolving since 1960 and eventually resulted in the condom and water conservation experiments. Of course this theorizing was grounded in Festinger's theory, a very sturdy branch emanating from the roots of Kurt Lewin's general conceptual orientation around tension systems. My high-impact style of experimental methodology was inspired by Festinger's approach to research, which I'm sure he in turn acquired from Lewin. In addition, my initial interest in doing something useful for society had its roots in Abe Maslow's gentle if imprecise humanism. At the same time it was nourished (even in the absence of direct personal contact) by Lewin's intense interest as a citizen—stemming from his early field experiments in America (e.g., on democratic vs. autocratic leadership). This was part of my historical heritage, a heritage I embraced eagerly.

In my own case the root goes wider still. In the late 1960s, I went back to school, spending several summers in Bethel, Maine, attending classes as an intern, training to become a T-group leader. After ten years as a professor, going back to school was not easy. I did it so that I could learn, firsthand and in raw form, as much about group dynamics as I possibly could. It also stemmed from my desire to be directly useful to people. The T-group method gave me the tools that enabled me to show people how their behavior influences others and to teach them more effective communication skills. Subsequently, I spent several intense summers at Bethel leading T-groups—just for the joy of it. T-groups were of course an invention of Lewin and his students—one of the most interesting accidental discoveries in the history of social psychology. In the process of leading these groups, I learned a lot of respect for the method, and I loved the intimacy they produced.

The T-group experience also provided a concrete serendipitous payoff for some of my research. Most specifically, the experiments on cooperative learning and prejudice reduction required me to train a great many teachers to use the jigsaw method effectively. This method provided me with the tools and experience to design workshops that were both efficient and thorough.

Speaking of jigsaw, it is doubtful whether I would have been able to invent that strategy if I hadn't been familiar with its rootedness in Mort Deutsch's theorizing on cooperation, which from my days as a graduate student had become part of my general, underlying knowledge as a social psychologist. When I entered the Austin school system, Mort's work provided an implicit road map for my observations and subsequent experiments. It isn't that I set out to test Deutsch's theory. I wasn't even thinking about it. But my knowledge of Mort's work formed part of the way I thought about the issue. This is a particularly salient example of what I am talking about in this section, and I am delighted to acknowledge my indebtedness to that particular root and branch. But this is only one of a number of instances where I thought I was entering a "new" area only to realize that a talented theorist or researcher had been there before me and had left behind important guidelines for my edification. Don't get me wrong. I always get a great kick out of breaking new ground, and when I discover that someone has been there before me, my initial feeling is one of disappointment at the realization that I'm not quite as original as I had thought. At the same time there is something gratifying about being constantly reminded that I am part of a family of scientists and the beneficiary of the thinking and research of those who preceded me.

To broaden this point, we all benefit to the extent that we are fully cognizant of the roots and branches of our discipline. Our science is only 100 years old. It shouldn't be too hard to make ourselves aware of the important research done in those 100 years. If we are ever to have something approaching a unified science, we must immerse ourselves in the "ancient" research of our infant science and make an honest attempt to see the connectivity that is out there. Otherwise the entire field becomes far more disjointed than it *can* be when it is at its best (see Berkowitz & Devine, 1989; Aronson, 1989, 1992; Campbell, 1988; Rosenthal, 1991, for a richer discussion of this issue). I'm not merely talking about including earlier, relevant research in the list of references at the end of an article. The problem runs much deeper than that. As Gerard (1992) has pointed out, many of our younger scientists seem to be ignorant of much of the research done prior to, say, 1975. He likens this to a reinventing of the wheel. Our discipline would be much more of an integrated whole if we made an honest attempt at thoroughly understanding our roots and branches, not simply as more or less interesting artifacts of an ancient civilization but as guideposts as well as a root system of ideas and data to be synthesized into contemporary thinking and research.

And the problem runs deeper still. The problem extends to choice of what methodology we employ, which in turn dictates the kinds of problems we explore. That statement requires some explanation. Throughout this essay I have discussed a style of experimentation that, for lack of a better term, I have called high-impact methodology. This involves creating a piece of drama, where participants are embedded in a scenario that forces them to take the events very seriously. The beauty and value of this kind of procedure is that it allows us to transform the sterile and artificial atmosphere of the laboratory into a real situation where important events are happening to the participants. Perhaps the best example of high-impact methodology is Milgram's obedience procedure. The ethics of that experiment are shaky to say the least. Yet at the same time no one can doubt that the participants were deeply involved in the events that were taking place. Moreover, although the procedure is now generally considered "too much" some thirty-five years later, there is no indication that any of Milgram's subjects was at all harmed by the experience. I am not recommending that we resurrect the Milgram procedure. That probably *was* over the top. What I *am* suggesting is that most of us may have given up much too easily on the use of procedures that are far less drastic than Milgram's. Let me state this as clearly as I can: There are some hypotheses that cannot be tested "cheaply." That is, there is no reasonable way to investigate some important social psychological phenomena (like destructive obedience) merely by showing the participants a videotape. The data would be meaningless. It would be wise to direct some of our energy to finding meaningful and ethical ways of testing these hypotheses.

Don't get me wrong. I am not suggesting that high-impact methodology should always be used. Not at all. I myself have departed from such methodology on many occasions, depending upon the question I was asking. Indeed in my essays on experimental methodology, I stressed my belief that the method must always suit the problem (see, for example, Aronson & Carlsmith, 1968; Aronson, Ellsworth, Carlsmith, & Gonzales, 1990; Aronson, Wilson, & Brewer, 1998). For example, suppose you are investigating stereotyping. It may be appropriate to use reaction time to various combinations of words or images as your basic procedure and dependent variable. In essence, the hypothesis allows for this kind of "judgment" procedure, and as such there is no need to embed the participant in a scenario. It's perfectly reasonable for the participant to be standing outside the scenario and to be stating his or her judgment as to what he or she is observing. But if you are investigating phenomena like obedience, conformity, bystander intervention, counterattitudinal advocacy, or a myriad of other important phenomena, you must use a high-impact methodology to generate data if you want those data to be valid and meaningful.

So what's the problem? During the 1980s and 1990s, experimental social psychology concerned itself primarily with hypotheses that could easily be investigated by judgment-type experiments. This in and of itself is no problem—unless, of course, the main reason for choosing the issue is the methodology. Let me explain. High-impact methodology is labor intensive; almost by definition it typically requires a lot more time, energy, and effort to perform a high-impact experiment than a judgment experiment. Moreover, high-impact methodology often involves deception and/or intense procedures. As such, as I have indicated, this methodology is ethically sensitive and without special precautions and perhaps even special pleading might not be approved by human subjects committees. This is not an insurmountable problem. I staunchly maintain, as did Festinger before me, that there is virtually no hypothesis that, with sufficient ingenuity (*and* with sufficient attention to ethical requirements), cannot be brought into the laboratory. But this would require additional time and effort on the part of the researcher. Accordingly, it is understandable that, all other things being equal, researchers might want to dodge this extra work and choose issues that can be easily investigated using judgment-type procedures. My concern is that interest in investigating certain areas of social psychology may be waning not because they are uninteresting or unimportant but simply because it's too much hassle to set up a high-impact experiment. Moreover, because, as I indicated early in this essay, high-impact methodology requires a great amount of hands-on training— an intense apprenticeship under the guidance of a master—I am concerned that students may be going through graduate school without having conducted a single high-impact experiment under appropriate supervision. This means they will begin their teaching careers without having learned how to do this kind of research.

So when they have students of their own, and their students are looking for a hypothesis to test, the probability is that they will be limited to areas that can be investigated using judgment-type procedures. How will *those* students learn to master high-impact procedures? Unless we are vigilant, entire domains of important social psychological inquiry may eventually become lost to us. The first 100 years of experimental social psychology have been an exciting adventure. Our graduate students are our hope for the future of our field. They are what Fyodor Dostoyevsky lovingly referred to as the sticky new leaves that indicate new growth and new adventures. The way we train them will determine what happens in social psychology over the *next* 100 years.

Is high-impact methodology really in danger of becoming a lost art, like Egyptian embalming techniques? Perhaps not. It is possible that my concern is unwarranted. I don't want to exaggerate. I simply want to sound an early warning signal. The truth is that although the frequency of high-impact experimentation has diminished sharply since the 1970s, it has not totally disappeared from the scene. Moreover, its use is not confined to us old fogies. Indeed, on occasion even I experience a surge of encouragement when, at conferences or upon picking up a journal, I see that a bright young scientist has investigated a difficult problem using the appropriate, time-consuming, ethically sensitive, high-impact methodology. It gives me hope that this methodology will survive. My hope for the future of our discipline is that this training will do more than survive, that it will expand. In my judgment, it is vital that we train all our graduate students to employ a wide range of methodologies so that they will never be dissuaded from investigating any problem because of lack of expertise.

References

Archer, D., Pettigrew, T., & Aronson, A. (1992). Making research apply: High stakes public policy in a regulatory environment. *American Psychologist, 47,* 1233–1236.

Aronson, E. (1960). The cognitive and behavioral consequences of the confirmation and disconfirmation of expectancies. Grant proposal submitted to the National Science Foundation.

_____. (1969). A theory of cognitive dissonance: A current perspective. In L. Berkowitz (Ed.), *Advances in experimental social psychology* (Vol. 4, pp. 1–34). New York: Academic Press.

_____. (1975). Busing and racial tension: The jigsaw route to learning and liking. *Psychology Today, 8,* 43–50.

_____. (1982). Energy conservation as a social science problem. In J. Harris & J. Hollander (Eds.), *Improving energy efficiency in buildings.* Berkeley: University of California Press.

_____. (1989). Analysis, synthesis, and the treasuring of the old. *Personality and Social Psychology Bulletin, 15,* 508–512.

_____. (1992). The return of the repressed: Dissonance theory makes a comeback. *Psychological Inquiry, 3,* 303–311.

Aronson, E., & Bridgeman, D. (1979). Jigsaw groups and the desegregated classroom: In pursuit of common goals. *Personality and Social Psychology Bulletin, 5,* 438–446.

Aronson, E., & Carlsmith, J. M. (1962). Performance expectancy as a determinant of actual performance. *Journal of Abnormal and Social Psychology, 65,* 178–182.

_____. (1968). Experimentation in social psychology. In G. Lindzey & E. Aronson (Eds.), *Handbook of social psychology* (2nd ed.). Reading, MA: Addison-Wesley.

Aronson, E., Carlsmith, J. M., & Darley, J. (1963). The effects of expectancy on volunteering for an unpleasant experience. *Journal of Abnormal and Social Psychology, 66,* 220–224.

Aronson, E., Chase, T., Helmreich, R., & Ruhnke, R. (1974). A two-factor theory of dissonance reduction: The effect of feeling stupid or feeling awful on opinion change. *International Journal for Research and Communication, 3,* 59–74.

Aronson, E., Ellsworth, P., Carlsmith, J. M., & Gonzales, M. H. (1990). *Methods of research
in social psychology.* New York: McGraw-Hill.

Aronson, E., Fried, C., & Stone, J. (1991). AIDS prevention and dissonance: A new twist on
an old theory. *American Journal of Public Health, 81,* 1636–1638.

Aronson, E., & Gonzales, M. (1990). The social psychology of energy conservation. In J.
Edwards (Ed.), *Social influence processes and prevention.* New York: Plenum .

Aronson, E., & Gonzalez, A. (1988). Desegregation, jigsaw and the Mexican-American experience. In P. Katz & D. Taylor (Eds.), *Eliminating racism.* New York: Plenum.

Aronson, E., & Mills, J. (1959). The effect of severity of initiation on liking for a group.
Journal of Abnormal and Social Psychology, 59, 177–181.

Aronson, E., & O'Leary, M. (1982). The relative effectiveness of models and prompts on
energy conservation: A field experiment in a shower room. *Journal of Environmental
Systems,* 219–224.

Aronson, E., & Patnoe, S. (1997). *Cooperation in the classroom: The jigsaw method.* New
York: Longman.

Aronson, E., Stephan, C., Sikes, J., Blaney, N., & Snapp, M. (1978). *The jigsaw classroom.*
Beverly Hills, CA: Sage.

Aronson, E., Wilson, T., & Brewer, M. (1998). The experimental method in social psychology. In G. Lindzey, D. Gilbert, & S. Fiske (Eds.), *Handbook of social psychology.* New
York: Random House.

Berkowitz, L., & Devine, P. G. (1989). Research tradition, analysis, and synthesis in social
psychological theories: The case of dissonance theory. *Personality and Social Psychology
Bulletin, 15,* 493–507.

Campbell, D. T. (1988). *Methodology and epistemology for social science: Selected papers* (E.
S. Overman, Ed.). Chicago: University of Chicago Press.

Coltrane, S., Archer, D., & Aronson, E. (1986). The social-psychological foundations of
successful energy conservation programmes. *Energy Policy, 14,* 133–148.

Condelli, L., Archer, D., Aronson, E., & Pettigrew, T. (1984). Improving utility conservation programs: Outcomes, interventions, and evaluations. *Energy, 9,* 485–494.

Cook, S. W. (1984). Cooperative interaction in multiethnic contexts. In N. Miller & M.
Brewer (Eds.), *Groups in contact: The psychology of desegregation.* New York: Academic
Press.

Cooper, J., & Fazio, R. H. (1984). A new look at dissonance theory. In L. Berkowitz (Ed.),
Advances in experimental social psychology (Vol. 17, pp. 229–266). Orlando, FL: Academic Press.

Costanzo, M., Archer, D., & Aronson, E. (1986). The behavior of energy conservation: The
difficult path from information to action. *American Psychologist.*

Davis, K. E., & Jones, E. E. (1960). Changes in interpersonal perception as a means of reducing cognitive dissonance. *Journal of Abnormal and Social Psychology, 61,* 402–410.

Deutsch, M. (1949). A theory of cooperation and competition. *Human Relations, 2,*
129–151.

Deutsch, M., & Solomon, L. (1959). Reactions to evaluations by others as influenced by
self-evaluations. *Sociometry, 22,* 93–112.

Dickerson, C., Thibodeau, R., Aronson, E., & Miller, D. (1992). Using cognitive dissonance to encourage water conservation. *Journal of Applied Social Psychology, 22,* 841–854.

Festinger, L. (1957). *A theory of cognitive dissonance.* Evanston, IL.: Row, Peterson.

Festinger, L., & Carlsmith, J. M. (1959). Cognitive consequences of forced compliance. *Journal of Abnormal and Social Psychology, 58,* 203–211.

Freedman, J. (1965). Long-term behavioral effects of cognitive dissonance. *Journal of Experimental and Social Psychology, 1,* 145–155.

Gerard, H. (1992). Dissonance theory: Cognitive psychology with an engine. *Psychological Inquiry, 3,* 323–327.

Gerard, H., Blevans, S. A., & Malcolm, T. (1964). Self-evaluation and the evaluation of choice alternatives. *Journal of Personality, 32,* 395–410.

Haney, C., Banks, C., & Zimbardo, P. (1973). Interpersonal dynamics in a simulated prison. *International Journal of Criminology and Penology, 1,* 69–97.

Johnson, D., & Johnson, R. (1987). *Learning together and alone: Cooperative, competitive, and individualistic learning* (2nd ed.). Englewood Cliffs, NJ: Prentice Hall.

_____. (1989). *Cooperation and competition: Theory and research.* Edina, MN: Interaction Book Company.

Keller, M. (1993). Why don't young adults protect themselves against sexual transmission of HIV? Possible answers to a complex question. *AIDS Education and Prevention, 5,* 220–233.

Lewin, K., Lippitt, R., & White, R. K. (1939). Patterns of aggressive behavior in experimentally created "social climates." *Journal of Social Psychology, 10,* 271–299.

Malewski, A. (1962). Some limitations of the theory of cognitive dissonance. *Polish Sociological Bulletin, 3,* 39–49.

McConahay, J. B. (1981). Reducing racial prejudice in desegregated schools. In W. D. Hawley (Ed.), *Effective school desegregation.* Beverly Hills, CA: Sage.

Meier, D. (1995). *The power of their ideas.* New York: Beacon.

Milgram, S. (1965). Some conditions of obedience and disobedience to authority. *Human Relations, 18,* 57–76.

Patnoe, S. (1988). *A narrative history of experimental social psychology.* New York: Springer-Verlag.

Rosenthal, R. (1991). *Meta-analytic procedures for social research.* Newbury Park, CA: Sage.

Sharan, S. (1980). Cooperative learning in small groups. *Review of Educational Research, 50,* 241–272.

Sherif, M. (1966). *In common predicament: Social psychology of intergroup conflict and cooperation.* Boston: Houghton Mifflin.

Slavin, R. E. (1980). *Cooperative learning and desegregation.* Paper presented at the meeting of the American Psychological Association.

_____. (1996). Research on cooperative learning and achievement: What we know, what we need to know. *Contemporary Educational Psychology, 21*(1), 43–69.

Stephan, W. G. (1978). School desegregation: An evaluation of predictions made in *Brown vs. Board of Education. Psychological Bulletin, 85,* 217–238.

Stern, P., & Aronson, E. (1984). *Energy use: The human dimension.* New York: W. H. Freeman.

Stone, J., Aronson, E., Crain, A., Winslow, M., & Fried, C. (1994). Inducing hypocrisy as a means of encouraging young adults to use condoms. *Personality and Social Psychology Bulletin, 20,* 116–128.

Swann, W. B., Jr. (1991). To be adored or to be known? The interplay of self-enhancement and self-verification. In R. M. Sorrentino & E. T. Higgins (Eds.), *Motivation and cognition.* New York: Guilford.

White, L., Archer, D., Aronson, E., & Pettigrew, T. (1984). Energy conservation research of California's utilities: A meta-evaluation. *Evaluation Review, 8,* 167–186.

Yates, S., & Aronson, E. (1983). A social psychological perspective on energy conservation in residential buildings. *American Psychologist, 38,* 435–444.

5 Reflections on Interpersonal Influence and Social Power in Experimental Social Psychology

Bertram H. Raven

After describing how he became involved in social psychology, Bertram Raven recounts the excitement of the years after World War II among young, democratic-minded social psychologists. The value orientation of many of the leaders within this new and fascinating discipline was impressed upon their students. Before French and Raven published their well-known taxonomy of power bases in 1959, many studies highlighted the importance of reward, coercion, reference, legitimacy, expertise, and information in interpersonal influence. In the second part of his essay, Raven describes the integration of a number of social psychological phenomena within the framework of his power/interaction model.

The Second Half Century from a Personal Perspective

As we celebrate a century of theory and research in social psychology, it is startling for me to realize that I have been involved in our field for exactly half of its life span. In January 1947 I began my university studies at Ohio State, fresh out of my World War II military service. Those were heady times. The long war was finally over. Nazism was destroyed, and we looked toward an era of peace, prosperity, and democracy. There was new interest in eliminating prejudice and discrimination on the basis of race, religion, and nationality. The United Nations was established to further international understanding and cooperation, and there was a determination that never again would we need to settle international differences through wars.

My last year in the army seemed like a meaningless waste of time. I had been trained as a medium tank crewman, prepared for the final battles in the Far East. But by the time our replacement units were at sea in the Pacific, the war was over.

For my remaining days in the army, I felt that I was just waiting to begin my studies in the university and to participate in all the exciting things that were happening at home. Now I could really begin my life, and as I thumbed through the university catalogue I felt like a kid in a candy store. I had already decided that I was interested in psychology, though I wasn't clear exactly what that meant. My first courses in psychology were firmly anchored in Hullian learning theory. Though I was intrigued by the careful formal theory of human behavior, somehow this did not do it for me. I was very eager to deal with "real-world" problems, and as I studied psychology more, it seemed to me that I was moving away from my real interests.

It was my courses in sociology that first captured my interests, since they seemed more focused on current social problems than were my courses with the learning theorists. When I found there was a course called "*social* psychology," it seemed made to order. The course in social psychology in which I enrolled in the Department of Psychology was taught by Donald Campbell, and it was not long before it was clear that that was my true direction. Campbell told me later that this was also his first course in social psychology—strange that he had never taken a social psychology course at Berkeley. Of course, we learned a lot about cultural factors in human behavior, about how social behavior is in part determined by personality. We looked at individual and group identity and marginality. As a son of Russian Jewish immigrants, I found that this hit home particularly. It was also in that course that I first learned about Kurt Lewin, whose writings were to have a special impact on my future. Shortly after it was published, I eagerly read his *Resolving Social Conflicts* (Lewin, 1948), edited by Dorwin Cartwright. Lewin's articles in psychosocial problems of minority groups and Jewish self-hatred opened up new vistas for me. In fact my first term paper, which I wrote for Don Campbell, was a psychosocial analysis of Jewish identity, drawing heavily on writings of Kurt Lewin and *The Marginal Man* by the sociologist Everett Stonequist (1961).

Studying Socially Relevant Issues with
Laboratory Experiments

The studies on group decision and social change also fit in with my democratic ideology. Then I read Lewin, Lippitt, and White (Lewin & Lippitt, 1938; Lewin, Lippitt, & White, 1939) and learned that democratic leadership was demonstrated to be superior, unequivocally and scientifically. I was impressed not only by the ideology but that it was possible to study in a scientific laboratory a phenomenon that was so complex and socially significant. I was hooked. Interesting that that study is still widely cited, though it would never pass muster today in our current respected social psychological journals.

In Ohio State's Arps Hall library, I eagerly studied the first issues of *Human Relations* and the *Journal of Social Issues*. The first two issues of *Journal of Social Issues* were on "racial and religious prejudice in everyday life," beginning with a series of case studies. One presented by Ronald Lippitt was titled "To Be or Not to Be—a Jew." There was a historical introduction by Goodwin Watson and a commentary by Rabbi Mordechai Kaplan, the founder of the Reconstructionist movement in Judaism. Other contributors were Kurt Lewin, Daniel Katz, Gardner Murphy, Goodwin Watson, and Gordon Allport. There followed a series of issues on problems of reeducation, problems of bureaucracy, conflict and cooperation in industry, and military occupation as a test of democracy. I began to look forward to each issue. In the first volume of *Human Relations,* I found the fascinating article "The Role of Group Belongingness in a Voting Situation," the title of which was so close to my personal concerns. Here it was unequivocally demonstrated, in a carefully designed laboratory experiment, with statistical tests of significance, that the tendency of Jewish and Catholic female students to vote for a leadership candidate of their religious persuasion would be increased if the candidate's religious identification was made salient.[1] Amazing! The author of that article was someone I had not heard of before—a fellow named Leon Festinger (1947).

I later learned more about this fascinating group of midcentury social psychologists. Before the war a number of them had been concerned about poverty and the depression and were active in the labor movement. During the war many had been actively involved as psychologists or social researchers in the war effort. In some cases they had begun as traditional laboratory experimental psychologists but had retooled to meet the nation's needs as social psychological researchers. With the war over, they were clearly dedicated to creating a better world from the ashes of a horrible conflict. Several of them had come from a liberal religious background, with a strong sense of social purpose (Hilgard, 1986). Goodwin Watson had been ordained as a deacon in the Methodist Church and later was a student at the Union Theological Seminary at Columbia, along with Theodore Newcomb and Rensis Likert. Likert, Dorwin Cartwright, and Angus Campbell had studied under Kent Fellowships from the National Council on Religion in Higher Education (Eisenstadt, 1986; Nicholson, 1997). Liberal, social activist religion also played a role in the next generation of social psychologists. John Thibaut at one time was planning to become a worker priest and applied and was accepted as a seminary student (Patnoe, 1988, p. 48). During and after World War II, a number of the postwar pioneers in social psychology became involved in action research, particularly on intergroup relations. Here, again, there was liberal religious support, most notably by such organizations as the American Jewish Congress and its research wing the Commission on Community Interrelations (guided by Lewin), where a number of social psychologists, such as Stuart Cook and Kenneth Clark, played important roles.

Many of us who entered the university at that time were excited about prospects for the future. Things were about to change, and for the better. With the United Nations, war and conflict would become a thing of the past. Peace and prosperity lay ahead. Intergroup prejudice could finally be overcome. And we were privileged to become part of that. I rushed through the undergraduate program in two fiscal years and applied for graduate work—to only one place, the University of Michigan. That was where they had an interdisciplinary program in social psychology, the Research Center for Group Dynamics, and included in the faculty were many of the people whose work I admired. When I was accepted into the program and was offered a research assistantship working with Leon Festinger, it was a dream come true.

In Ann Arbor the social psychology program had a get-together of the new students and faculty. We felt we were in the forefront of something important, and there was a sense of great excitement and anticipation. The evening was capped with folk songs, led and accompanied on the guitar by Milton Rosenberg, one of the incoming students. The songs characterized the group: socialist worker songs, Spanish civil war songs (in English, German, and Spanish), Jewish and Israeli folk songs (in Hebrew and Yiddish), union songs, Afro-American liberation songs. Under the direction of Theodore Newcomb, the program was determined to turn students into hybrid social psychologists, so that some came with a sociological and some with a psychological background. The faculty generally had appointments in both departments, and the courses were similarly represented. It is impressive how many students in that group became important leaders in the field. There were not many social psychology departments, and eventually we had to make a choice: sociology or psychology. There were a number of cases in which students ended up in a discipline different from the one they entered—sociologists became psychologists and psychologists became sociologists—but most maintained their identity as social psychologists. After a number of years, the interdisciplinary program collapsed, to the sadness of most of the alumni. Why? I am not sure, but I have heard that some members of the Sociology Department felt that a disproportionate proportion of the promising graduate students from sociology ended up identified as psychologists. Unfortunately, other social psychology programs, such as the Harvard Social Relations Program, suffered similar fates.

Military Support for Social Psychological Research

At the Research Center for Group Dynamics, some of the newly entering assistants were in for a bit of a shock: Much of our research, and indeed our very salaries, came from research grants with the Group Psychology Branch of the Office of Naval Research. Why were we involved in military-supported research? Hadn't we finished the war and headed toward peace? We were told that for the time being, at least, it would be necessary to maintain some armed forces, and so it was important for the military to understand such social psychological things as the nature of leadership, effects of cohesiveness on performance of groups, communication processes and rumor transmission, cooperation and competition, pressures toward uniformity, and so on. But, we were reassured, the findings from our research would not be classified as secret, would be available to everyone, and would have implications for all social behavior, not just the military. Those who would take the trouble to review research from that era would be amazed at the amount of significant social psychological research that was in fact supported by military funds, particularly from the Office of Naval Research, as well as the army and the air force. That funding continued, though somewhat reduced, for decades thereafter.[2] It took the Vietnam War, which many social psychologists actively opposed, finally to reduce that money to a mere trickle. In the meantime, following the lead of the military, other agencies such as the National Science Foundation and the National Institute of Mental Health and, later, private foundations such as the Ford Foundation and Rockefeller Foundation picked up support for basic research in social psychology.

A Model for Reviewing Research on Social Influence

In reviewing literature in that area for this chapter, I was impressed that a number of the experiments dealt with questions about similar and related phenomena, to which the investigators attached different names, depending on their orientation. It would be fair to say that there is substantial waste of precious time and energy as a result. I think this is especially true in recent publications, where younger investigators are not inclined to review the older literature and thus in effect tend to reinvent the wheel. Sometimes an overarching model is helpful in pointing out how these concepts and findings overlap (see Chapter 9 by Robert Zajonc for a more detailed discussion of the cumulative nature of social psychology). It is my contention that looking back with the benefit of our more modern theoretical tools, we may benefit from earlier developments in ways we cannot always anticipate. As some readers might suspect, my focus in this essay is on research related to interpersonal influence and social power relationships.

Within this model, I include research carried out under the following labels: social facilitation, social contagion, group effects, group norms, pressures toward uniformity, leadership, resistance to change, modeling, frame of reference (and reference groups), obedience, compliance, authority, imitation, suggestion, persuasion, consensual validation, and helping behavior. As if that weren't enough, I also attempt to point out below how the direction of experimental social psychology reflected social and political developments of its time.

The Bases of Social Power

I begin, then, with the original typology of the six bases of social power first presented by John R. P. French and myself (1959) and shown in Table 5.1

The bases of power are grouped in terms of two important dimensions: the extent to which influenced change is socially dependent on the influencing agent and the importance of surveillance by the agent in order for that change to be ef-

TABLE 5.1   The Six Bases of Social Power

Basis of Power	Social Dependence of Change	Importance of Surveillance
Coercion	Socially dependent	Important
Reward	Socially dependent	Important
Legitimacy	Socially dependent	Unimportant
Expertise	Socially dependent	Unimportant
Reference	Socially dependent	Unimportant
Information	Socially independent	Unimportant

fected. Coercion (threat of punishment) and reward are socially dependent and, at least initially, require surveillance. Legitimate, expert, and referent power do not require surveillance but are socially dependent. It is only informational power (perhaps we could have called it persuasion) that leads to cognitive change in the target, such that it immediately becomes independent of the influencing agent.[3]

Coercive Power and Reward Power

Now here already it seems that French and I could have benefited from a more careful consideration of earlier works in experimental social psychology. When we developed our system, we were thinking particularly of an organizational setting where a supervisor or manager was attempting to influence a subordinate. We defined reward power in terms of the offer of potential tangible rewards for compliance (e.g., offering an increase in pay or promotion); similarly, we defined coercive power in terms of threats of tangible punishments (e.g., threat of being fined, demoted, or fired). Later we found it necessary to differentiate such tangible, impersonal rewards and punishments from more personal rewards and punishments (see Table 5.2)

Murphy, Murphy, and Newcomb (1937), in their encyclopedic review of experimental social psychology up to that point, included a number of experimental studies on children, their performance, and experience of success and failure. In the 1920s and 1930s, a significant factor in such performance was the "praise" and "reproof" from the parent and teacher. It was clear that the promise of personal approval and the threat of personal disapproval or rejection could significantly affect a child's performance (e.g., Briggs, 1927). As the studies of level of aspiration indicated, children (and adults as well) also get a sense of adequacy of their performance by comparing it to that of peers. We thus see the significant roles of both what we later call referent power and personal reward and coercive power.

Referent Power and Group Norms

Referent power, using others as a frame of reference for evaluation of one's attitudes, beliefs, and behavior (Sherif, 1936), though not yet defined at the time of

TABLE 5.2   Further Differentiating the Bases of Social Power

Basis of Power	Further Differentiation
Coercion	Impersonal coercion
	Personal coercion
Reward	Impersonal reward
	Personal reward
Legitimacy	Formal; legitimacy
	Legitimacy of reciprocity
	Legitimacy of equity
	Legitimacy of dependence (powerless)
Expertise	Positive expertise
	Negative expertise
Reference	Positive reference
	Negative reference
Information	Direct information
	Indirect information

the early praise/reproof studies, also appeared to play an important role in children's performance. Referent power generally suggests a tendency toward similarity with the comparison person. This point is also stressed by Festinger (1954) in his theory of social comparison processes. But Murphy, Murphy, and Newcomb introduced an interesting further notion: that, in our terms, referent power, combined with personal reward (praise) and personal coercion (reproof), could lead children to try to exceed the performance of others.

Pressures to Exceed the Norm.   Figure 5.1 shows how Murphy, Murphy, and Newcomb begin by pointing out that initially a child learns the importance of approval and disapproval by the parent. This value of personal reward/coercive power is then transferred to the teacher, who praises a child for doing well and reproves a child for not doing so well. But in the classroom the praise and reproof is also offered in comparison to other children—it isn't just that "you did well" but "you did better than anyone else" or "you did worse than anyone else." The child, affected by the personal reward and coercive power of the teacher, thus learns to respond to referent power of other children in the classroom—not just to be *similar* but to *surpass* them in performance. And with that we can now look back with new insight to the Triplett (1898) experiment (which grew from his interest in bicycle racers). Triplett wanted to test what was called a "dynamogenic effect," a psychophysiological notion that a bicycle racer, sensing the physical activity of another bicycle racer, released nervous energy enabling him to bicycle more rapidly. With our current perspective, we can look at that phenomenon as both

FIGURE 5.1   Authority-Competition Process

Individualistic society implies importance of individual child and individual parent-child relation.	→	Creates dependence of child upon parents' exclusive approval or preference.

$\downarrow$

Child transfers to
teacher the relation
of dependence upon
adult approval.

→

Teacher gives approval
for being "good," doing
best work; this stimulates
competition with other
children.

$\downarrow$

Child transfers to other
group situations the
competitive attitude
developed in the
teacher-child relation.

The process is intensified the more the child feels he or she must "earn" parents' approval and love.

SOURCE: From G. Murphy, L. B. Murphy, and T. M. Newcomb, *Experimental Social Psychology: An Interpretation of Research upon the Socialization of the Individual,* rev. ed. (New York: Harper, 1937), p. 446.

referent power of the other (the racer's using the other to evaluate himself) and as personal reward (it is not sufficient simply to race at the same speed of the other; the racer is pressed to exceed that speed). This, then, is one way in which competition is fostered. Yes, I know that Floyd Allport (1924) had also referred to this explanation of Triplett's results as a "desire to win"—he called it "rivalry." But I think the conception here is a bit different, emphasizing a form of referent power in that a person looks above the other as a point toward which to evaluate him- or herself. Festinger described a similar notion in his work on social comparison in abilities (Festinger, 1954). I discuss this phenomenon later.

Now back to Sherif and his early demonstration of what we can call referent power of the group: Sherif found that when asked to judge the ambiguous "movement" of a pinpoint of light in a completely dark room, individuals might initially vary considerably in their estimate of the distances moved, but on subsequent judgments the more extreme estimates would move toward the middle, eventually tending toward a consensus. Individual members with very high or very low estimates were using the group as a frame of reference for their respective estimates (Sherif, 1936).

That study led to the now classic studies by Solomon Asch (1951, 1952, 1956) wherein a subject, part of a group of eight who were asked to judge which of three lines was the same length as a standard line, would hear the others in the group all pick a line that seemed clearly either much shorter or much longer than the standard. Would the subject then answer "correctly" or answer as did the others in the group (who, of course, were paid participants told to answer incorrectly)? Personal communications with those who knew Asch well suggest that Asch carried out that study because he felt that the Sherif experiment was trivial: When judging something as ambiguous as the movement of a light in a dark room, how else could a subject respond but to go along with the members of the group? But in a clearly demonstrated, unambiguous judgment of line lengths, certainly a subject would not conform to the group. From what we have heard, Asch was astounded, perhaps even angered, at the number of subjects who went along with the group and gave clearly incorrect answers. In his monograph he referred to them as "yielders" (suggesting spinelessness) as compared to the "independents" who had enough backbone to resist pressures from the group.

Asch did interview his subjects afterward (something that should be done more often) and asked why they would conform to the group. I reviewed those responses (quoted in the monograph) and found them especially enlightening, since I could see instances of the various bases of social power of the group. Many subjects showed what Asch called "distortion of judgment," believing that the group response was appropriate even if they didn't see it that way. Most of these seemed to be influenced by the collective expert power of the group: "There's a greater probability of eight being right" (p. 28) or "I think that a majority is usually right." Some suggested that perhaps there was an optical illusion that they could not see through or that their perspective, seated at the far end of the group, might have distorted their perceptions. Some appeared to recognize the power of the group as legitimate: The group collectively has a right to determine the behavior of the individual (isn't that the democratic way?). As one said, "After all, majority rules" (p. 28). Others seemed to cite referent power: "I felt the need to conform"; "It is hard to be in the minority"; "You always like to go along and be like everybody else" (p. 48). There were some subjects who, Asch felt, showed distortion of behavior—they answered incorrectly even though they *knew* that they were answering incorrectly. Why? Because the approval (reward power) of the group was important to them, as was their concern that the group's disapproval would be painful (personal coercive power). Asch seemed to be particularly disappointed by this group of people. The importance of coercive and reward power is evident in later studies using the basic Asch approach, where the amount of conformity reduced dramatically when the critical subject's response would not be seen by the other members of the group (e.g., Deutsch & Gerard, 1955; Milgram, 1961).

The realism of coercive power of the group in the Asch experiment is evident in one form of the experiment that Asch conducted with sixteen naive subjects and one paid participant, who answered incorrectly, as the majority had in the original experiment (Asch, 1952). He described the majority's incredulity, followed by their ridicule and uproarious laughter. One member of the majority described "a pitying contempt for a person who . . . was comparing the wrong lines."

Group Decisions, Democratic Ideology, and the Power of the Group. Further evidence for the referent power of the group in the Asch-type conformity study was provided years later in a cross-national study by Stanley Milgram (1961). Milgram carried out a variation of the Asch experiment in Norway and France. He found that conformity to the group norm was substantially greater in Norway than in France. In effect, he argued that people in Norway are more likely to look toward others as a basis for evaluating themselves and their judgments, to emphasize referent power. This he attributed to the high degree of homogeneity of Norwegians among all sorts of dimensions, fostered in part by Norway's isolation from other cultures. France, by contrast, was a nation of continual change, with waves of migration and contacts with people from other nations, such that others provided a less certain and less stable frame of reference.

The tremendous power of the group to affect the beliefs, attitudes, and behaviors of an individual member played an important role in the series of experiments carried out by Lewin and his followers. Here, I think, it is important to consider the social and ideological factors that led to these studies. In the late 1930s American social psychologists were caught up in the threat of Nazism and fascism. The forthcoming World War II was seen as a struggle of humanistic democratic forces against authoritarianism. The Lewin, Lippitt, and White experiments (Lewin & Lippitt, 1938; Lewin, Lippitt, & White, 1939) demonstrated the advantages of democratic leadership (with patterns of behavior that we would now see as using informational, expert, and referent power) over autocratic leadership (with its emphasis on coercive and unquestioned legitimate position power). These experiments were exhilarating to many young social psychologists, both in terms of their ideological implications and in demonstrating that complex phenomena like this could be studied in laboratory experiments.

The group decision studies (Coch & French, 1948; Lewin, 1943, 1947; Marrow, 1969) were, it seems clear to me, developed with such democratic ideology in mind. In an era where it was most common for the boss or supervisor to tell others what they had to do, these experiments tested the notion that group participation and group decisions regarding some aspects of the work situation would lead to more effective change and higher morale. When a time/motion consultant tells workers the appropriate level of production, the consultant's expert power and informational power are countered by the referent power, and even the coercive power, of the work group. For Lewin and his co-workers, group discussion and decision, in keeping with good democratic expectations, would lead the work group to change its work norms collectively, which would then be reflected in pressures on the individual worker to change and to accept change. The expert power of the consultant was insufficient or even rejected by the workers as lacking credibility. After participation, discussion, and democratic group decision, the workers more readily accepted the referent power of the work group. This was demonstrated dramatically in a series of field experiments by Lewin, Alex Bavelas, John R. P. French, and others at the Harwood Manufacturing Company in North Carolina (Marrow, 1969).[4]

Group Decisions as Manipulative?   Those social psychologists and others who felt exultant both by such effective use of experimental social psychology in group dynamics and by its support for a democratic ideology that most of them cherished were startled by an article that suggested that group dynamics and group decisionmaking was a hoax rather than a hope (Gunderson, 1950). Management, the article alleged, was really using group dynamics to engineer group decisions to accept a higher work rate, thus getting employees to work harder with no increase in pay and adding to the coffers of the company. To the distress of the group dynamics advocates, that argument was then echoed by Walter Reuther, president of the United Auto Workers. A young social psychologist named Herbert Kelman (1950) responded and put the issue into perspective. Group dynamics, he said was neither a hope nor a hoax. The group decision experiments helped point out the value of having workers and others participate in discussion and decisions as to what they were required to do. Like many scientific findings, such techniques might be manipulated and misused by unscrupulous power holders. One would hope that workers or others involved would accept the virtues of participation and be able to respond accordingly if these devices are used manipulatively.

Valuing Independence over Group Referent Power.   More recently, the experiments indicating the power of the group to influence the dissenting individual came under attack from a quite different quarter. To see this phenomenon in context, we must recall that during and after World War II experimental social psychology went through a very rapid growth in the United States. We were exhilarated by the victory of democracy over totalitarianism and by our ability to carry out what we felt was careful experimental research on socially relevant topics. Europe was still devastated and struggling to recover economically, politically, and academically. The United States was eager to assist and direct reconstruction, and social psychologists (among others) descended on Europe with the zeal, and perhaps the condescension, of missionaries.

Eventually, Europe was to assert its independence in all of these spheres, and in social psychology, as in other areas, new questions were raised as to the propriety of American dominance. It is interesting that this quest for independence showed itself particularly in questioning our research on the power of the group over the individual. Among the leaders of this movement was Serge Moscovici at the School of Higher Education in the Social Sciences in Paris (Moscovici, 1976). He felt that American social psychologists overly valued the power of the group on the individual. In fact, he pointed out, their experiments (for example, the classic Asch experiment) were so designed as to preclude the possibility of the lone dissenting subject's influencing the majority. If given a proper opportunity, the lone individual, or minority, could indeed overcome the majority. And one might also expect that the minority of social psychologists in Europe might then influence the more powerful majority in the United States. Essentially, in his experimental design, a lone deviant member in a group would be instructed to behave in a predetermined manner so as to influence the large majority. This could be done by behaving in a consistent, self-confident, certain manner. In this way the dissident would appear to reinforce his or her expert power.

We must give credit to Moscovici and his co-workers for the clever design of their experiments, their indicating the possible negative effects of unthinking surrender to referent power, and their demonstrating the possibility of minority influence and the value of independence in the face of the majority. In that sense, they even seem to echo Asch's personal feelings toward the "yielders" who succumbed to the majority view in judging lengths of lines. However, I must say that at times their position is overstated and perhaps too laden with political overtones. In their writings they suggest that for American social psychologists conformity to group pressure and uniformity is a desirable state, that they thus represent a conservative position that is opposed to change (Paicheler, 1988). Those of us who were familiar with people such as Lewin and those who followed his line of research would be more understanding of the underlying democratic ideology that permeated their theories and research (Marrow, 1969). These included studies that pointed out the values of having a group facilitator who encouraged minority expression (e.g., Maier, 1950; Maier & Solem, 1952).

The Dangers of Pressures to Exceed the Group Norm. In my earlier discussion I examined the ways in which the social power of the group may press the members not only to adhere to the norm but to exceed it. Such an analysis may help us to account for the phenomenon known as the risky shift (Stoner, 1961), in which individuals in groups tend to take more risky positions than they would individually. The assumption, with some support, is that when you are with a group where it is desirable to be risky, the social rewards come from taking a position at least moderately more risky than that of your peers, a phenomenon that extended to other social judgments and behavior as well (Moscovici & Zavaloni, 1969). This process, which was demonstrated by Triplett in a simple motor task and with children in classrooms, could even be extended to much more complex situations, including some that can have grave national and international implications.[5]

Guarding Against Groupthink.   The dangers of group pressures in important decisionmaking processes were demonstrated especially effectively by Irving Janis in his influential analysis of "groupthink" (Janis, 1972, 1982). Janis's long career might be seen as a model for blending experimental social psychology, field research, and applications to important social issues and problems. He was fascinated by the Bay of Pigs fiasco, in which the advisers to President John F. Kennedy, a brilliant group characterized as the best and the brightest, participated in the development of a disastrous invasion of Cuba. Janis proceeded to review that event, drawing heavily on social psychological research literature. Much of his analysis focused on group norms, group effects, and the referent power of the group, including pressures to adhere to or even exceed the norm in taking strong action against an "enemy." In his study we can see traces of findings about the risky shift, the normative pressures of groups, group coercion against deviant members, and even the group pressure to exceed that was first demonstrated in Triplett (1898). Janis's work has had an important impact nationally and internationally not only in theories in social and political psychology but on policymakers (Hart, 1990).

Legitimate Position Power

In the French and Raven (1959) bases of power model, the concept of "legitimate power" was taken from the works of Max Weber (1922/1957). It was Weber who pointed out the strong pressures on an individual to follow the orders of someone in a higher position of authority. He discussed particularly the legitimate power of higher rank in a political structure or an industrial organization, what later organizational theorists would refer to as "position power." For me, that concept had particular salience based on my experience in the army, where the legitimate power of officers of higher rank was given such weight. An important part of our basic training consisted of encouraging automatic and unthinking obedience to such orders. Trainees were ordered by superior officers to do meaningless acts, which they had to obey without question—with coercive and reward power supporting such compliance until legitimate power could be firmly established. It later became more clear why the establishment of legitimate position power would be necessary. In the heat of battle, the soldier could not be allowed to insist on complete explanations (informational power), and though coercive power and reward power might be effective in some circumstances, they required observability, something that was not possible on the battlefield. In our first experiments we examined how legitimate power of supervisors compared to expert power and coercive/reward power, which had not been examined previously in the experimental social psychology literature (Raven & French, 1958).

The understanding of such legitimate position power has received considerable attention in the experimental and nonexperimental literature, both in social psychology and organization psychology. Industrial surveys have replicated earlier studies in which workers, when asked why they comply with a request from their supervisor, most frequently answer that "it is my duty" (Tannenbaum, 1974). Perhaps this finding is not so surprising, but what is surprising is the extent to which such legitimate power carries over into other settings.

Legitimate Power of the Experimenter. In most social psychological experiments, the experimenter who directs the study is seen as outside of the system. Robert Rosenthal (1966) should be credited with making us more aware that there is in fact a social psychological relationship between the experimenter and the subject in the experiment, with various forms of influence operating, sometimes resulting in the subject's being subtly influenced to support the experimental predictions. After all, subjects in an experiment develop an implicit or explicit contractual relationship, ceding to the experimenter the legitimate power, obliging the subjects to do what the experimenter requests within broad limits (Orne, 1962). How far does this legitimate power go? Quite far, it seems. Subjects on command from the experimenter would eat huge numbers of dry soda crackers (Frank, 1944); add numerous columns of meaningless numbers, tearing up each sheet as they finished (Orne, 1962); spend ages turning pegs on boards one-quarter turn (Festinger & Carlsmith, 1959)—many silly, boring, senseless behaviors.

It remained for Stanley Milgram to demonstrate further limits of the experimenter's legitimate position power. Milgram carried out this experiment following the post–World War II revelations—particularly in the trial of the notorious Adolf Eichmann—that soldiers in Nazi death camps killed and tortured innocent inmates on orders from their superiors. His classic study demonstrated the surprising and frightening potency of legitimate power to lead a "teacher"/subject to obey the experimenter in administering painful and possibly even life-threatening electric shocks to another subject (Milgram, 1974). Moving from laboratory experiments back to real life, Kelman and Hamilton (1989), analyzing the dynamics of the My Lai incident, in which American troops followed orders from a superior in a brutal massacre of Vietnamese villagers, showed how responsibility for such a crime might be mitigated depending on one's attitudes toward legitimacy of authority in a military situation.

Other Forms of Legitimate Power. Basic to legitimate power is the acceptance of an obligation to adhere to a social norm. For legitimate position power, the norm requires that you comply with the requests of someone in a particular position. This would most obviously be a supervisor or a military officer, but other positions also acquire such power: A parent has a right to determine behavior for a child, a doctor sometimes has the right to prescribe behavior for a patient, and, as I noted above, an experimenter has a right to request certain forms of compliance from a subject.

But work in experimental social psychology has suggested several other more subtle social norms that serve as bases for legitimate power: (1) the legitimate power of *reciprocity*—"I did that for you, so you should feel obliged to do to this for me" (Goranson & Berkowitz, 1966; Gouldner, 1960; Regan, 1971); (2) *equity*—"I have worked hard and suffered, so I have a right to ask you to do something to make up for it" (Walster, Walster, & Berscheid, 1978); (3) *compensation*—"You have harmed me in the past, so you should feel obliged to make up for this by complying with my request now" (Walster, Walster, & Berscheid, 1978); and (4) *responsibility* or *dependence* (sometimes referred to as the "power of the powerless"), a norm that says that we have some obligation to help others who cannot help themselves, who are dependent upon us (Berkowitz & Daniels, 1963).

Though these mechanisms of influence were not framed by the investigators in terms of legitimate power, it is one of the values of a model that they can fit in this context, with similar dynamic properties. Each of them in turn has its underpinnings in a sense of normative obligation to comply to a legitimate influencing agent.

Expert Power

Early in history of experimental social psychology, H. T. Moore (1921) carried out several studies on expert influence. The experiments typically consisted of getting subjects' judgments on matters of ethics, music, or speech; presenting them with the judgments of experts in these areas; and then measuring the extent to which the subjects changed their judgments. He then compared the influence of experts versus the influence of the majority (referent power). Both experts and majorities affected reported judgments, but overall majority effects were greater. The problem with such a comparison, of course, is that Moore did not assess what form of expert is equivalent to how large a majority, a problem that has still not been solved in more recent investigations. But the experimental demonstration of these phenomena was in itself an advance.

Informational Power

Influencing people's behaviors by changing their attitudes and beliefs has long been central to experimental social psychology—long before it was given a formal name. Early experiments used the classroom curriculum to change the attitudes and beliefs of students toward "Negroes" and other races, war, and prohibition of alcohol. The changes following a planned curriculum often led to more positive racial attitudes (Campbell & Stover, 1933), opposition to war (Gardiner, 1935), and positive attitudes toward prohibition (Gardiner, 1935)—but not always. It would be reasonable to assume that a substantial proportion of research aimed at intervention, getting people to change their attitudes and behaviors, focuses particularly on what we are calling information power. This includes consumer behavior and advertising (getting people to change their attitudes toward a product), political interventions, human relations (changing prejudicial attitudes and behaviors), health interventions (getting people to change their diets and lifestyles), and so on.

An example of an elaborated model that essentially emphasizes informational power would be the widely utilized Ajzen and Fishbein (1980) model: the behavior (e.g., smoking) is changed by an informational campaign in which the undesirable behavior is associated with negative outcomes (cancer, increased costs, inconvenience) or a desirable behavior is associated with positive outcomes.[6]

As I have suggested, informational power has definite advantages over other bases of power, since it is grounded in cognitive changes in the target, such that, as compared to coercive power and reward power, surveillance is not important and, as contrasted with other bases of power, the changed behavior or cognition is no longer dependent upon association with the influencing agent. Although some have questioned the need to distinguish between expert power and informational power, Petty and Cacioppo (1985) have demonstrated the need for this distinction in their elaboration likelihood model. In one study they found that expert power may be sufficient to change a person's beliefs, attitudes, and behavior, if the consequences of such change have no great effect on the target. But informational power becomes more necessary if the consequences of the change have important practical implications.

General Comments and Discussion

In this chapter I have attempted to review some significant developments in experimental social psychology, as viewed from my perspective and through a general model of interpersonal influence and social power. Others in this volume review these developments from their own perspectives.[7] Obviously, we cannot begin to cover a century of experimental social psychology in these brief pages; however, we cannot fail to be impressed with what our field has contributed to theory and to practice, and to try to understand it in terms of the many social events within which this body of research developed.

As part of my project sponsored by the Group Psychology Branch of the Office of Naval Research, I took it on myself to review the body of literature relevant to the social psychology of the small group, abstracting the many articles and books and categorizing them according to their theoretical content. When I completed the fourth edition of this review in 1969, I had listed 5,156 items (Raven, 1969). Given the exponential increase in such research, one can hardly imagine what that number would be today. A first reaction to this body of research might be pride—how active and productive we have been! But on second thought it left me with a sense of depression that led me to abandon further reviews of this literature: How much intellectual energy went into planning, carrying out, and writing up this research? How many hours from student participants? And of course we are not including the many studies that ultimately were not completed or, once completed, were never published. Did the total amount of energy and expense justify the new information that we obtained? The increasing emphasis on experimental research in social psychology, coupled with the general publish-or-perish standard, has led us to encourage undergraduates to carry out experimental research as soon as possible (lest they lose out in the competition for graduate or professional school admissions), to press our graduate students to carry out as many experiments as they can beginning in their first year, and of course for new faculty working with these undergraduates and graduates to publish as soon and as much as possible. There is further pressure to develop new journals and to expand the pages of current journals to publish many of these experiments. It seems to me that often these experiments are developed prematurely—before the experimenter has a good grounding in theory or a knowledge of past research. They are also carried out with the readily available college sophomore subjects, which raises questions of external validity (Sears, 1986). Furthermore, the emphasis on empirical quantitative research has led us to ignore nonexperimental research, including historical, biographical, and political analyses that do not lend themselves to our accepted format.[8] These are concerns that have also been raised by others (e.g., Gergen, 1982; Ring, 1967; Sampson, 1991). Brewster Smith, an active nonexperimental social psychologist who contributed greatly to interrelating social psychological theory and social action, expressed concern that "experimental social psychology was at risk of becoming an increasingly arcane enterprise for the principle edification of social psychologists, existing for academic career advancement more than for the advancement of knowledge" (Smith, 1983, p. 175). Rather than insist that our students begin experimenting so soon, should we perhaps insist that they not be permitted to carry out research until they have developed a greater level of theoretical sophistication, an awareness of alternative approaches, and a greater appreciation of earlier social psychological publications?

When I raised such questions at the Yosemite conference, Robert Zajonc had an excellent response: Why not compare the productivity of social psychologists with that of people in other fields? How many works of art, music, literature, and so on have been produced and at what expense? How many of these ultimately survive and have value for our society? How about research in biology, physics, chemistry, philosophy? And with that I felt some sense of relief. Part of the expense of accomplishments in sciences, literature, and the arts includes the many products that led to blind alleys, that did not succeed, that ultimately faded out to be lost and forgotten. We can take great pride in what experimental social psychology has accomplished in its century of existence and the impact it has had on our society. But some measure of doubt still remains.

Notes

1. Actually, although both groups tended to favor their own religions, the group identification effect was significant only for the Catholic subjects. I was very impressed with this study, but I don't recall Festinger's ever citing it or referring to it, suggesting that perhaps it did not meet his later standards.

2. The social scientists on the staff of the Office of Naval Research and other military agencies were often hard-pressed to defend before their superiors the support for basic research in experimental social psychology. We are deeply indebted to people such as Luigi Petrullo of the Group Psychology Branch and others for their dedication in this regard. Though we had considerable freedom in selecting our areas of research, our contract officers would often give us the current buzzwords to use in the section of our proposals in which we were asked to indicate relevance for the military—for example, "These findings on social power are especially important for consideration by military officers in the manner in which they exercise their authority," or, "The research on group cohesiveness and group effectiveness has relevance for the operation of residents of naval facilities in isolated communities." Later the buzzwords became more ominous, such as justifying how the research might be relevant to counterinsurgency. Yet I do not believe that the social psychologists involved felt pressed to alter what we wished to study.

3. Note that we listed "information" only as a means of influence in our original paper (French & Raven, 1959) but I later logically included it as a basis of power (Raven, 1965).

4. The Harwood Manufacturing studies also represent one instance in which experimental social psychology was portrayed in a very popular Broadway musical, *The Pajama Game*. The basic theme of the musical parallels the discussion by Marrow (1969, pp. 141ff.), a struggle between the industrial advocates of the time/motion, work efficiency orientation of Frederick Taylor and the group participation, human relations approach of Kurt Lewin.

5. This process of escalation has been described as a "runaway norm." The analogy would be a thermostat in which the element was altered so that each increase in temperature resulted in a further increase, rather than a decrease, in the heat supply (Raven, 1974).

6. The model also includes referent and expert power as "subjective" norms.

7. In providing an overview of experimental social psychology, this collection of essays may be rather restricted in that all of the contributors are strongly identified and committed to the approach to social psychology. This brief section of my chapter is intended to give at least some recognition of alternative views.

8. I have found it personally exciting to apply basic theory and research developed through experimental social psychology to the analysis of nonquantitative historical data. See my analysis of the "Nixon group" (Raven, 1974), two publications applying the power/interaction model to the analysis confrontations between political figures (Gold & Raven, 1992; Raven, 1990), and my application of the model to an analysis of religion as a mechanism of social control (Raven, in press).

References

Ajzen, I., & Fishbein, M. (1980). *Understanding attitudes and predicting social behavior*. Englewood Cliffs, NJ: Prentice-Hall.

Allport, F. H. (1924). *Social psychology*. Boston: Houghton Mifflin.

Asch, S. E. (1951). Effect of group pressure upon the modification and distortion of judgments. In H. Guetzkow (Ed.), *Groups, leadership and men*. Pittsburgh: Carnegie Press.

———. (1952). *Social psychology*. Englewood Cliffs, NJ: Prentice-Hall.

———. (1956). Studies of independence and conformity: I. A minority of one against a unanimous majority. *Psychological Monographs, 70*(9, Whole No. 416).

Berkowitz, L., & Daniels, L. R. (1963). Responsibility and dependence. *Journal of Abnormal Psychology, 66,* 429–436.

Briggs, T. H. (1927). Praise and censure as incentives. *School and Society, 26,* 596–598.

Campbell, D. W., & Stover, G. F. (1933). Teaching international-mindedness in the social studies. *Journal of Educational Sociology, 7,* 244–248.

Coch, L., & French, J. R. P., Jr. (1948). Overcoming resistance to change. *Human Relations, 1,* 512–532.

Deutsch, M., & Gerard, H. B. (1955). A study of normative and informational social influences upon individual judgment. *Journal of Abnormal and Social Psychology, 51,* 629–636.

Eisenstadt, J. W. (1986). Remembering Goodwin Watson. *Journal of Social Issues, 42*(4), 49–52.

Festinger, L. (1947). The role of group belongingness in a voting situation. *Human Relations, 1,* 184–200.

———. (1954). Theory of social comparison processes. *Human Relations, 7,* 117–140.

Festinger, L., & Carlsmith, J. M. (1959). Cognitive consequences of forced compliance. *Journal of Abnormal and Social Psychology, 58,* 203–211.

Frank, J. D. (1944). Experimental studies of personal pressure and resistance: II. Methods of overcoming resistance. *Journal of General Psychology, 30,* 43–56.

French, J. R. P., Jr., & Raven, B. H. (1959). The bases of social power. In D. Cartwright (Ed.), *Studies in social power* (pp. 150–167). Ann Arbor, MI: Institute for Social Research.

Gardiner, I. C. (1935). Effect of a group of social stimuli upon attitudes. *Journal of Educational Psychology, 26,* 471–479.

Gergen, K. J. (1982). *Toward transformation in social knowledge*. New York: Springer-Verlag.

Gold, G. J., & Raven, B. H. (1992). Interpersonal influence strategies in the Churchill-Roosevelt bases-for-destroyers exchange. *Journal of Social Behavior and Personality, 7,* 245–272.

Goranson, R. E., & Berkowitz, L. (1966). Reciprocity and responsibility reactions to prior help. *Journal of Personality and Social Psychology, 3,* 227–232.

Gouldner, A. W. (1960). The norm of reciprocity: A preliminary statement. *American Sociological Review, 35,* 161–178.

Gunderson, R. G. (1950). Group dynamics—hope or hoax? *Quarterly Journal of Speech, 36,* 34–38.

Hart, P. (1990). *Groupthink in government: A study of small groups and policy failure*. Amsterdam: Swets & Zeitlinger.

Hilgard, E. R. (1986). From social gospel to the psychology of social issues: A reminiscence. *Journal of Social Issues, 42*(1), 107–110.

Janis, I. L. (1972). *Groupthink: A psychological study of foreign-policy decisions and fiascoes*. New York: Houghton Mifflin.

_____. (1982). *Groupthink: Psychological studies of policy decision fiascoes.* New York: Houghton Mifflin.

Kelman, H. C. (1950). Group dynamics—neither hope nor hoax. *Quarterly Journal of Speech, 36,* 371–377.

Kelman, H. C., & Hamilton V. L. (1989). *Crimes of obedience: Toward a social psychology of authority and responsibility.* New Haven, CT: Yale University Press.

Lewin, K. (1943). Forces behind food habits and methods of change. *Bulletin of the National Research Council, 108,* 35–65.

_____. (1947). Frontiers in group dynamics: I. Concept, method, and reality in social science: Social equilibria and social change. *Human Relations, 1,* 5–41.

_____. (1948). *Resolving social conflicts.* New York: Harper.

_____. (1952). Group decision and social change. In G. E. Swanson, T. M. Newcomb, & E. L. Hartley (Eds.), *Readings in social psychology* (2nd ed., pp. 459–473). New York: Holt, Rinehart, and Winston.

Lewin, K., & Lippitt, R. (1938). An approach to the study of autocracy and democracy: A preliminary note. *Sociometry, 1,* 292–300.

Lewin, K., Lippitt, R., & White, R. K. (1939). Patterns of aggressive behavior in experimentally created "social climates." *Journal of Social Psychology, 14,* 229–256.

Maier, N.R.F. (1950). The quality of group decisions as influenced by the discussion leader. *Human Relations, 3,* 155–174.

Maier, N.R.F., & Solem, A. R. (1952). The contribution of discussion leader to the quality of group thinking: The effective use of minority opinions. *Human Relations, 5,* 277–288.

Markus, H. R., & Kitayama, S. (1991). Culture and self: Implications for cognition, emotion, and motivation. *Psychological Review, 98,* 224–253.

Marrow, A. J. (1969). *The practical theorist: The life and work of Kurt Lewin.* New York: Basic Books.

Milgram, S. (1961). Nationality and conformity. *Scientific American, 205*(6), 45–51.

_____. (1974). *Obedience to authority: An experimental view.* New York: Harper & Row.

Moore, H. T. (1921). Comparative influence of majority and expert opinion. *American Journal of Psychology, 32,* 16–20.

Moscovici, S. (1976). *Social influence and social change.* London: Academic Press.

Moscovici, S., & Zavaloni, M. (1969). The group as a polarizer of attitudes. *Journal of Personality and Social Psychology, 16,* 125–135.

Murphy, G., Murphy, L. B., & Newcomb, T. M. (1937). *Experimental social psychology: An interpretation of research upon the socialization of the individual* (rev. ed.). New York: Harper.

Nicholson, I. (1997). The politics of social reform, 1936–1960: Goodwin Watson and the Society for the Psychological Study of Social Issues. *Journal of the History of the Behavioral Sciences, 33,* 39–60.

Orne, M. T. (1962). On the social psychology of the psychological experiment. *American Psychologist, 17,* 776–783.

Paicheler, G. (1988). *The psychology of social influence.* Cambridge: Cambridge University Press.

Patnoe, S. (1988). *A narrative history of experimental social psychology: The Lewinian tradition.* New York: Springer-Verlag.

Petty, R. E., & Cacioppo, J. T. (1985). *Communication and persuasion: Central and peripheral routes to attitude change.* New York: Springer-Verlag.

Raven, B. H. (1965). Social influence and power. In I. D. Steiner & M. Fishbein (Eds.), *Current studies in social psychology.* New York: Holt, Rinehart, and Winston.

_____. (1969). *A bibliography of publications relating to the small group* (4th ed., Tech. Rep. No. 24. Los Angeles: University of California.

_____. (1974). The Nixon group. *Journal of Social Issues, 29*(4), 297–320.

_____. (1990). Political applications of the psychology of interpersonal influence and social power. *Political Psychology, 11,* 493–520.

_____. (1992). A power/interaction model of interpersonal influence: French and Raven thirty years later. *Journal of Social Behavior and Personality, 7,* 217–244.

_____. (1993). The bases of social power: Origins and recent developments. *Journal of Social Issues, 49*(4), 227–252.

_____. (in press). Influence, power, religion, and the mechanisms of social control. *Journal of Social Issues.*

Raven, B. H., & French, J.R.P. French, Jr. (1958). Legitimate power, coercive power, and observability in social influence. *Sociometry, 21,* 83–97.

Regan, D. (1971). Effects of a favor and liking on compliance. *Journal of Experimental Social Psychology, 7,* 627–639.

Ring, K. (1967). Experimental social psychology: Some sober questions about frivolous values. *Journal of Experimental Social Psychology, 3,* 113–123.

Rosenthal, R. (1966). *Experimenter effects in behavioral research.* New York: Appleton-Century-Crofts.

Sampson, E. E. (1991). *Social worlds/personal lives: An introduction to social psychology.* New York: Harcourt Brace Jovanovich.

Sears, D. (1986). College sophomores in the laboratory: Influences of a narrow database on social psychology's view of human nature. *Journal of Personality and Social Psychology, 14,* 515–530.

Sherif, M. (1936). *The psychology of social norms.* New York: Harper & Row.

Smith, M. B. (1983). The shaping of American social psychology: A personal perspective from the periphery. *Personality and Social Psychology Bulletin, 9,* 165–180.

Stonequist, E. V. (1961). *The marginal man: A study in personality and culture conflict.* New York: Russell & Russell.

Stoner, J.A.F. (1961). A comparison of individual and group decisions involving risk (Master's thesis, Sloan School of Management, Massachusetts Institute of Technology).

Tannenbaum, A. S. (1974). *Hierarchy in organizations.* San Francisco: Jossey-Bass.

Triplett, N. (1898). The dynamogenic factors in pace-making and competition. *American Journal of Psychology, 9,* 507–533.

Walster (Hatfield), E., Walster, G. W., & Berscheid, E. (1978). *Equity theory and research.* Boston: Allyn & Bacon.

Weber, M. (1922/1957). *The theory of social and economic organization* (A. M. Henderson & T. Parsons, Trans.). Glencoe, IL: Free Press.

Zimbardo, P. G., Haney, C., Banks, W. C., & Jaffee, D. (1973, April 8). A Pirandellian prison: The mind is a formidable jailer. *New York Times Magazine,* pp. 33–60.

6 Experimental Social Psychology: Behaviorism with Minds and Matters

Philip G. Zimbardo

This chapter begins with Philip Zimbardo's reflections on being an experimental social psychologist. He describes the old paradigm that dominated experimental social psychology in the 1950s, 1960s, and early 1970s, characterized by ingenious stage settings in which the subject's behavior was observed. With the surge of ethical concerns regarding subjects' well-being, this paradigm has been replaced by the tendency to ask subjects to imagine situations and report how they would react to them. Zimbardo lists a number of factors responsible for the demise of the old and the advent of the new research paradigm. He then considers how his experiences growing up in the Bronx revealed to him the importance of situation, arousing in him an interest for social psychology. He reports on the golden years of social psychology at Yale and shows how he came to learn what matters in social psychology: situation, culture, content, methodology, behavior, people, and application. Zimbardo concludes by recognizing three outstanding social psychologists he interacted with: Hovland, Schachter, and Milgram.

It is an honor to be included among the distinguished social psychologists whose ideas enrich not only this volume but also the entire field of social psychology. Although I am now a registered member of the Medicare generation, nevertheless I am the "baby" of this group, along with my slightly older sibling, Elliot Aronson. As such, in this chapter, I play the role of the student, wide-eyed with enthusiasm and endless curiosity about the social nature of human nature. I begin by telling what it means to me to be an experimental social psychologist, then describe the "candy store" that I found and raided as a graduate student at Yale University in the mid-1950s and how I was influenced by the behaviorist orientation that ruled the day back then to take some of its best values into social psychology. I use this occasion to reflect on the boustrophedonic path my career has taken, its meandering nudged by random personal experiences and fortuitous circumstances, pushed along by puzzles to be solved and student questions to be answered, and always guided by the desire to make a difference in how we understand and work to enhance the human connection. In their Yosemite conference presentations and their chapters here, my colleagues have focused heavily on the vital influences of Kurt Lewin, Leon Festinger, and Fritz Heider, along with other theorists and researchers whom they studied under and worked with and who profoundly influenced them. So I conclude by singing the praises of three other seminal contributors to our field, Carl Hovland, Stanley Schachter, and Stanley Milgram, each of whom I knew well and whose talents I respected enormously.

What Does It Mean to Be an Experimental Social Psychologist?

The joy of being an experimental social psychologist is taking an idea, a hypothetical relationship, an informed hunch about the way things ought to be if your way of thinking is correct and then testing its validity in a highly controlled, elegantly orchestrated laboratory experiment. For me, that has involved arousing and directing a research participant's inner states of cognition, conation, and affect, as well as her or his perceptual orientation by means of carefully constructed scenarios, with special instructions, tasks, confederates, and stage props. Indeed I have always thought of my most interesting studies (of affiliation, dissonance, deindividuation, persuasion and attitude change, and the Stanford prison experiment) as dramatic renderings of intellectual issues. The instructions serve as dialogue for the experimenter, research assistants, and confederates; their appearance and dress as the costumes; and the physical arrangement of the laboratory space as the stage sets. What remains is the improvisation of the naive research participant. If the theory or underlying reasoning is correct, then that improvisation is the predictable event, the dependent outcome, the "data." Although most participants can rarely explain the true reason for acting as they did, the right theory, like the Shadow, knows.

What is critical in this approach is the focus on *behavior*, real on-line behavior: what people do, how they act, what they report feeling or thinking in response to the particular situation they have encountered. Sometimes they laugh, cry, get angry, bargain, cheat, defend their views, work to conceal or highlight their identity, strike out, aggress, get conditioned, and more. But it is not research that begins and ends with what people *say* they would do in a given situation; rather, it is about what they *do*, how they actually behave.

If one is a social psychologist who believes that many subtle features of the social environment function to shape how individuals perceive a given life space, construe its meaning, and respond to its challenges and demands, then it can never be satisfactory to settle for the proxy of what research subjects *report* about how they *imagine* they would behave in a setting that has been experienced secondhand, only in the verbal depictions of the researcher. It is only by being within the crucible of that situation, where its powerful social forces are acting to shape behavior, that people can truly know how they would behave by observing how they are behaving currently. All kinds of self-serving biases operate to distort our vision of what we would do or not do in an imaginary setting.

But more than that is at stake. The research participant cannot appreciate, nor is it likely the paper-and-pencil researcher would or could provide, the dynamic personal transactions that occur in some situations that are difficult or impossible to capture in its procedural descriptions. The experimenter's comforting pat on the shoulder, the discomfort of wanting to leave but facing the experimenter standing above you and between you and the exit, the feeling of camaraderie with the other subjects in your cohesive group, the desire to prove to the researcher that you can do better after failing a task (that was insoluble), and the exciting dynamic of being in an acting-out group where one's identity is submerged are but some of the situational phenomena that must be experienced firsthand to be fully appreciated.

In the bygone era when cognitive dissonance theory ruled the research roost of social psychology, such situational manipulations were the coin of the realm. Some researchers with street smarts knew intuitively how to design a setting to generate a certain internal state likely to trigger a particular reaction in their research "subjects" (now research "participants"). That is because in their everyday lives these "old-fashioned" researchers made it part of their profession to observe real people across many situations, to figure out what people are likely to do, when, and how, in response to various inputs and different scenarios in which they were naturally immersed. That set of skills was passed on in the informal apprenticeship training that took place inside research laboratories when the mentor was designing and pretesting the experiment and its alternative manipulations alongside his or her graduate student research assistants. It was never made fully explicit in the journal descriptions of the research or captured in the formal lectures these researchers gave at conventions and colloquia about how they accomplished what they did. I am sure that many failures to replicate came not from exposing theoretical weaknesses but rather from not recognizing experimenter "inadequacies" in re-creating the necessary conditions for testing specific predictions. These social skills were part and parcel of what it meant to be an effective experimental social psychologist, whose research bore the fruits of the experimenter's set of learned talents. Those skills were derived not from book learning but from people watching in the ordinary lives of these researchers. They looked at what people did in natural settings, in moving around in their life space, and wondered why they did those things or what would happen if some aspect of the social situation were changed. Their "what if" question was the first kiss that triggered a romantic involvement with an experimental significant other.

In a sense, that tradition is now dead and not mourned by those who hastened its demise, a cabal of some cognitive social psychologists, human subjects research committees, Protestants, and female social psychologists. For the new breed of cognitive social psychologists, the action is not in gross behavior but in subtle predictions, estimations, judgments, and decisions. A one-paragraph typed description of a scene or setting takes the place of the laboriously constructed stage sets of the old-time experimentalists. A check mark on a five-point scale fills in for the buttons on a shock generator or the amount of food or water consumed by the subject. It is so clean, concise, and effortless to construct, to analyze, and to publish that I imagine newcomers to our field wonder why anyone would waste so much time and effort with the old-line experimental approach that I nostalgically depicted above.

Human subject research committees (and institutional research boards) overreacted to the questionable ethics in some of the research by these oldies but goodies in experimental social psychology by throwing out the research along with the researchers. Imagining college students to be physically fragile and psychologically delicate, these groups have imposed increasingly stringent limitations on what could be done and said to research participants in order to minimize their potential distress—to the end of eliminating most of what could be called traditional experimental social psychology. They even limit wording in the now ubiquitous survey questionnaires so that they do not "arouse" respondents (from their passivity) or make them sensitive to certain domains that might in any imaginable way be upsetting to their precious natures. To be sure, it is indeed difficult and time consuming to do good experimental social psychology, so now many of my colleagues have given up even trying rather than deal with the ever escalating demands of the IRBs and yielding to the need for repeated submissions with yet another necessary procedural limitation. Others have taken the low road of trading in their white lab coats for the clipboard of the survey researcher. To get a sense of the fallibility of generalizations about human nature based on what respondents tell us instead of observing what they actually do, I recommend viewing the *Candid Camera* segment "Tampa TV Survey." Fannie Flagg, Alan Funt's brilliant confederate and later author of *Fried Green Tomatoes,* pretends to be a survey researcher interested in viewers' reactions to an alleged new TV program, *Space Doctor.* We see and hear person after person describing favorite episodes, making specific comparisons with other programs—about something that did not exist.

When I said it often took a kind of street smarts to do good experimental social psychology, I meant it literally: that these early social psychologists were often from big-city ghetto environments where survival was dependent on learning and practicing people skills. Many were from minority groups who learned much from careful observation and assessment of the power relationships they witnessed and by which they were often controlled. They also came from backgrounds where ethics were often situationally relative. Big, tough kids did not need them, nor did rich kids, but appropriate white lies, a bit of deception here and there, ingratiation tactics could go a long way in keeping someone from stealing your lunch money or hitting you upside the head. For the powerful (to me that always meant the Protestants), there were rules and regulations that formalized social interactions—and got them what they wanted. Because they did not have to rely on the tricks of the trade or duplicity, these righteous folks could deal with the world in a more formal, stylized fashion. They had the privilege of being up-front, able simply to say what they wanted and then to take it straight away. We always thought they were square and socially ungrammatical in not knowing the power of a compliment or how to play the dozens. Cognitive social psychology as practiced today is really a Protestant toy, clean like Protestants' nails, starched like their white shirts, straightforward like their Calvinist career paths, and abstract and top-down rather than empirical and bottom-up, like Catholic incense or Jewish guilt. The WASP contribution to modern social psychology is to the earlier, more ethnic, and streetwise contribution as a Big Mac is to a corned beef and pastrami sandwich.

The old breed of experimental social psychology was also doomed when many talented women started taking over the field of social psychology in the 1970s and 1980s. Implicit in much of that earlier work was a kind of surreptitious game playing in which the research subject was the pawn pitted against the intellectual might of the researcher armed with deception as his most powerful weapon. That was really a "man thing," something that does not resonate with most women social psychologists, neither the gaming and dominance nor the use of deception (which men have traditionally practiced against women). It may also have been the case that many of these outstanding women were not personally mentored by the men who practiced in this tradition— Festinger and Schachter being two exceptions, since they worked as well and closely with their female as male research assistants, as long as they were smart and tough enough to merit their respect. Finally, I could add that the issues or topics that have come to interest many of these female researchers are more focused on broader conceptual phenomena than in previous generations. This can be seen in the areas of relationships, attraction, health psychology, gender stereotyping, and equity issues, where it is the stuff of the phenomena—the dependent and intervening variables rather than the independent variables—that intrigues them, not merely using concepts in a domain to test causal hypotheses about inferred theoretical processes.

Life in the Living Lab of a New York Ghetto

Poverty is a relative thing; it is easier if you have relatives around to count on and if there are others who are poorer than you. (So downward social comparison was a fact of life for us generations before it became a published process.) I was fortunate to have both conditions in effect while I was growing up. Although affluence buys rich folks the luxury of creating physical distances from neighbors as well as selective exposure to others, if you're poor, others are always in your face. That's great if you're a kid living in a crowded urban area. For me, it meant that there were always other kids available for play, day and night, right outside my house on the streets and stoops. It also meant that there were always new social learning opportunities lurking out there in the real world when those others were not friends but enemies. The other thing about growing up poor, that helped me to become a social psychologist, is that it encourages situational breeding, since you want to blame the situations and not the persons for all the failures you see around you. The economically advantaged prefer to rely on dispositional attributions to account for their favored status in life, since they want to believe that their radiance comes from inherent natural differences favoring them and their kind.

Many lessons of social psychology I learned firsthand, from personal experience. Prejudice? I was chased and beaten daily for weeks by the neighborhood toughs until one day my mother asked the janitor's son to take me to church on Sunday, and he admitted that he and his buddies were making my life miserable because they thought I was a "dirty Jew boy"—big nose, slim, blue eyes, fragile. I was six years old and sickly. Group initiation rituals? To join the East 151st Street gang, first I had to fight the last kid who was admitted to the gang. I did that reluctantly, since I was so scrawny and did not like to be hurt and did not want to hurt anybody. The bloodthirsty kids formed a circular boxing ring, screaming constantly and urging us to hit harder. The fight officially ended when the older kid gave up or the new kid got a bloody nose, which I did as soon as possible. Next I had to climb to the top branches of a tall corner tree and bring down my sneaker, which had been thrown up there by the gang leader, "Popeye the Armenian." Scary, but not as much as having to crawl through the transom of the fruit store late at night and steal a bag full of fruit to be eaten by the gang. Finally came the strangest ritual of all to a six-year-old. Around the corner was the Stocking Man's Store, a small shop selling women's stockings and undergarments. In front of the store were his goods, laid out on a platform resting on orange crates and sawhorses—and above an iron grill that let air and light into the basement below the store. The final initiation task was to break into the basement and then look up the women's dresses as they shopped above, thereafter to tell tales of what you had seen to the assembled gang. You were notified in advance that you could not come back up until you saw someone who had no panties (we called them bloomers) and could regale the masses with the forbidden sexual sights that you had witnessed. These childish urban initiation rituals seem to tap into some of the same basic aspects of masculine identity as do adult cultural rituals reported in anthropological accounts of "primitive" tribes in exotic places. Ingratiation tactics? If you were frail, your survival depended on learning and effectively utilizing finely honed ingratiation tactics to ward off attacks and exploitation by the big, bad kids, to get some of them to take you under their mentoring wings.

The general level of poverty in the many neighborhoods I lived in (we had moved nineteen times before I commuted to college at age eighteen) also meant that play always revolved around group-centered, people-initiated games, not commercial toys or TV or solitary activities. And there was no overlap between the world of children and that of adults. They never intruded upon our world in the streets except to curtail it for dinner and daily tasks. There was no Little League or organized soccer; nothing was arranged by or watched by adults. We owned the streets; they owned their small tenement apartments. That meant that we learned and refined bargaining, negotiating, and conflict resolution strategies on the job without interference from our parents. To that extent, then, my earliest informal training as a naive social psychologist came directly from the streets in this neighborhood overflowing with diversity. In those days of the late 1930s and early 1940s, New York could be characterized as having many side-by-side mini ghettos: Most people living on one street were Irish; around the corner they were all Jewish; across the street were Italians; down the street were mostly blacks. Often a corner candy store or grocery store or bar was the central meeting place where these ethnic divisions would blend in the quest for that particular service. My friends were an amalgam of the whole American melting pot. World War II changed everything. Poor people had jobs and made money since the demand for workers was high and there was not much available on which to spend your money.

Shortly after the war, four simultaneous events changed the nature of the South Bronx from a poor but family-oriented neighborhood without serious crime where I loved living into a chaotic, burned-down place to avoid. Those who had saved money during the war were able to move up the ladder and out of the old neighborhood—most of these were the Jews who moved north to new housing developments. Into the vacuum they left came Puerto Ricans to the land of plenty, many migrating from rural areas and farms into the heart of the inner city. They were in conflict with blacks for the bottom rung of the economic ladder, and new tensions ran high and often exploded into violence. Returning soldiers and mafia contributed drugs to the South Bronx, and drugs created a new lifestyle for local gangs, so turf meant a business domain that was guarded by guns, threats, and action. Finally, as violence escalated and gangs took over, many of the other old-timers moved to safer places, leaving behind vacant apartments and tenements. Gangs torched the buildings to get rid of the remaining tenants so they could take them over as clubhouses. Landlords who were not making any money on their rent-controlled, dilapidated buildings also arranged to have them torched to collect the insurance. The South Bronx became a symbol of urban blight, resembling bombed-out European cities.

These dramatic ecological and sociological changes were exciting for me to observe firsthand. I was eager to go beyond mere personal concern to collecting data as these events were unfolding. As a senior at James Monroe High School, I discussed some of these situational upheavals and their consequences with one of my classmates, a very smart, skinny kid, Stanley Milgram. He came from a more affluent neighborhood in that school district; I attended "his" high school by falsely representing my address as being other than the South Bronx. But it was clear to me that I wanted to be either a journalist or a psychologist. I was cured of both desires freshman year at Brooklyn College by struggling to do well in English composition and getting a C (from Evelyn Raskin) in introductory psychology. That C was an unexpected, alien thorn in the side of my academic career—I ultimately graduated summa, with that one C blemish.

The superstar psychologist on our campus, Abe Maslow, who floated around with an ever-present entourage, was on his way to Brandeis University (to inspire Elliot Aronson) so would not be around to make up for the boring psychology texts, useless lectures, and silly little psychology experiments. I switched to sociology and dual majored in sociology and anthropology, where the professors were asking big questions about the ethics of the atomic bomb, the nature of mass movements, and the differences between bottom-up and top-down revolutions. I glommed on to a wonderful Polish sociologist, Felix Gross, a former colleague of Brunislav Malinowski, who took me under his wing after I had taken more than fifteen credits with him. He took me camping and always had a story about life in academia in Europe and the need to understand the deeper structure of social phenomena and not settle for the surface appearances. After I helped review his book on European mass movements, Felix recognized me in the preface; it was so exciting to be in print. I was also attracted to Charles Lawrence, a sociologist of enormous talent who specialized in race relations and the Negro family. Charlie's infectious smile and wit were a lovely counterpoint to Felix's serious demeanor. He also encouraged me to join the National Association for the Advancement of Colored People (NAACP) and to become more socially conscious, which I made efforts to do, but I was more interested in varsity track and fraternity socializing.

The sociological frame enabled me to channel my neighborhood observations into several interesting studies. The first examined the dynamics of prejudice between Puerto Ricans and Negroes in the South Bronx, using interviews and surveys. It was published in a sociological journal during my junior year. The second was an observational and archive data collection of the appeal of the political parties to the minority vote in the South Bronx during the 1952 national election. My third undergraduate foray into field research emerged from observing that despite the norm of tolerance and integration at Brooklyn College, a decidedly socialist stronghold in the 1950s (called by some "the Little Red Schoolhouse"), self-segregation was apparent in the student cafeteria. I set out to make systematic observations of the seating patterns of whites and blacks at each table across the term and over all hours—to reveal that indeed there were some race-exclusive tables. No white ever sat at certain tables even when they were empty, and the same was true of blacks, although of course tables were not marked "white" or "black." I replicated that study at CCNY ten years later, since *Brown v. Board of Education* had intervened between my undergraduate experiences and later experiences as an NYU professor. The pattern of self-segregation by race was as evident in 1963 as it had been in 1952.

In my senior year, my buddy Gerry Platt, a psychology major and fraternity brother, talked me into pairing with him in experimental psychology. Although reluctant to get involved with psychology at first, I was soon smitten by the precision of answering specific hypotheses with hard data. Sociologists asked the big questions but never quite had good enough answers, whereas it became evident that psychologists were asking low-level questions but were good at methodology and analysis. I liked that and realized it was up to me to pose more interesting questions and maybe do so by wedding my broad interests in the sociology of institutions with the psychology of individuals. After that course, I switched my major to psychology and Platt switched his to sociology (eventually becoming a postdoctoral scholar with Talcott Parsons at Harvard and now chair of sociology at the University of Massachusetts, Amherst). Although I was a psychology major for only a short while, the major influence on me came from Harold Proshansky, recently out of Ann Arbor, Michigan, and teaching personality theory. His intellectual enemies were something he called "rat behaviorists" at Yale. Later in the year, when I was accepted for graduate study at Yale, Hal was distressed since he wanted me to go either to Michigan or Minnesota. But he gave me valuable fatherly advice to help my transition, first about not letting those narrow stimulus-response (S-R) ideas get into my head and then to consider changing the way I dressed, since those Yalies would not appreciate the essence of my New York ghetto sartorial style and might reject me. Of course I said that I would not change, that they would have to adjust to me since the clothes were part of my basic self-expression—the blue suede shoes, the Billy Eckstein rolled-collar shirts, string ties, peg pants, and of course my Phi Beta Kappa key hanging proudly from my knee-length key chain.

On Almost Being the First Black Graduate Student at Yale

Jump ahead to 1959. I have graduated Yale and am in Bonn, Germany, at the International Congress of Psychology presenting my first big-time paper on differentiating between the concepts of fear and anxiety using Schachter's affiliation paradigm. While talking to Harold Kelley, who had been one of my teachers during my first year at Yale before he moved to UCLA, I mentioned how difficult it seemed for our Jewish colleagues to deal with being in Germany and relating to Germans, since the wounds of the Holocaust were still open. Hal floored me with his rejoinder, something like, "Well, it's probably similar to how you felt at Yale when the faculty assumed you were Negro." Say what? He then went on to recite the battery of circumstantial evidence that led to that reasonable assumption and a major split in the Yale Psychology Department faculty over whether I should be accepted given my record or rejected given my record. In fact, they did neither. I never received the accept, reject, or wait list letter from them—nothing at all. On April 14 I had prepared my letter of acceptance to the University of Minnesota to work in the famous social psychology laboratory under the direction of Stanley Schachter, who called me to say that he liked my interests in race relations and group dynamics and would encourage me to develop them. That night I got a call from a Yale professor asking if I was still interested in Yale graduate school because he was coming down to New York City the next day for the Eastern Psychological Association (EPA) convention and would like to interview me for a possible position as his paid research assistant. He asked me to hold off mailing my letter to Schachter until we had a chance to talk at the bar in the New Yorker Hotel, 10 A.M. sharp. I was excited because Yale was my first choice, since it was close to my home so I could visit often. And it was, after all, the Ivy League, and Yale and Harvard were the big *its* in the Bronx.

After he had two double martinis and I pretended to drink mine and made small talk, Professor K. C. Montgomery said that he was doing research on exploratory behavior in rats and needed a good research assistant to help him carry out the many studies for which he had just received a big NSF grant. Did I know anything about "running rats"? "Yes, sir" (we ran them out of our apartment regularly and deftly). Could I build equipment? "Certainly, sir, as long as there is a diagram to follow" (my father could be recruited to build anything with Renaissance eloquence, even rat cages, if need be). "OK, then, you've got the job, free tuition, and a $1,700 stipend for twenty hours of research assistance. Read these reprints of mine and come up to the lab before the term starts so we can begin breeding and building the cages." "Sure thing. You won't be sorry you chose me. I will be a good worker." I don't recall if he said, "See you later, *boy*." Maybe it was my imagination.

When I got to those hallowed halls of ivy, I quickly became a rat runner of the first degree. I bred hundreds of rats, nursed them, fed them, watered them, cleaned their shit and cages (after building untold number of special cages by hand), some to deprive them of behavioral freedom, others to encourage it in a free environment, and still others to deprive them of both behavioral and sensory stimulation. We graduate student rat runners worked around the clock, during holidays (we traded caretaking and rat-running duties to go home either Easter or Christmas). At first I felt like a slave laborer, working my research assistant butt off up to forty hours a week in addition to my studies (where I did not excel since I had a weak undergraduate psychology background). I complained to the chair, Claude Buxton, but to no avail. I called my mother just before Christmas to say I was going to quit and come home for good. Wisely she said I could do so but not until the summer, since my sister was using my old bedroom and it would not be right to disrupt her in the middle of her studies; by summer I was cutting the mustard and had no thoughts of leaving ugly New Haven. Montgomery would give me a long "to do" list and then disappear. What the department faculty concealed was that he was suffering from clinical depression and was in and out of local mental hospitals. The next year he committed suicide.

I'm not sure if it was guilt over Montgomery's death (caused in part by not getting tenure) or the dissonance of persuading myself that what I really wanted was to live my life in the animal basement wing of the Institute of Human Relations

(IHR), not doing human relations, which I thought I wanted when I was a no-nothing undergraduate in that Gestalt stronghold at Brooklyn College. But whichever it was, I became totally committed to my rats, their data, and publishing our findings. I convinced someone at NSF to sign over the remaining two years and $38,000 of Montgomery's grant to me, with professor Fred Sheffield serving as ex officio supervisor. I wrote and published four articles on this research enterprise and on the side a few more of my own. One was with Neal Miller, whom I think of as my behaviorist-experimentalist mentor supreme; the other was with another graduate student, Herbert Barry. Our faculty was shocked when—without their involvement—we got *Science* to accept an article about the effects of two drugs on inhibiting or enhancing sexual behavior in male rats.

I was in my third year, feeling like hot stuff, doing some reanalyses of our *Science* article data in the calculator room, when a faculty member, Bob Cohen, asked me what I was doing. I went into great detail about the merits of this rigorous experimental protocol. He then stopped me to ask if I would do him a favor and look out the window across to the street in front of the medical school and tell me what I saw. I did so assuming he wanted to know if his beautiful wife, Barbara, was there waiting for him. I said no one was there. He said, "Really? No one?" I then told him there were a bunch of people in one group and a couple in another, to which he asked me to try to figure out what the couple were discussing. I examined their body language and made some inferences, with the caveat that I could not be at all sure of the accuracy of my interpretation. Bob then threw the solar plexus punch: "Don't you think that it would be more interesting to spend your career as a psychologist trying to figure out what people mean by their behavior than what white laboratory rats do?" Needless to say, I was furious at being duped into this rather obvious "soft side" psychology trap. But when that emotion subsided, it made me think. I had betrayed my origins by giving up my love for observing people and trying to understand the complexities of human interactions for the accessibility of rat psychology.

The next term Bob Cohen and Jack Brehm cotaught a new course in advanced social psychology. I took it and persuaded my roommate, Gordon Bower, to join me. As independent reading under the guidance of Leonard Doob, I had taken a basic social psychology course that focused on the classics but stopped sharply at 1950. The main reading of the Cohen-Brehm course was Leon Festinger's manuscript "A Theory of Cognitive Dissonance." Brehm had been Festinger's student, and his thesis was one of the first experiments on dissonance theory. Cohen, who was a student of Michigan's Alvin Zander, was less a methodologist than Brehm and took more of a holistic approach to social psychology, even admitting personality interactions, and he promoted ideas such as the need for cognitive clarity. Together they were a dynamic duo that were delightful to study under and work with.

I was entranced by Festinger's chutzpah in drawing such wide-ranging derivations from such simple assumptions and premises. But more than that was fascinating to me and my peers. Dissonance theory went directly against the very rational, systematic, bottom-up empirical approach dominant in the Yale attitude change program and even in much of the animal behaviorist research since the heady theoretical days of Clark Hull, a few years before my arrival at Yale. We got caught up in the appeal of those nonobvious predictions that challenged the validity of "bubbe psychology," in which anyone's grandmother can predict the outcome of any psychological study described to her. For example, in Hovland's attitude change course one of our assignments was to construct a table of all existing results in a certain area by coding them first according to the categories of input, mediating, and output variables; then by whether they were stimulus (communication) factors, audience factors, or media or channel factors; and then according to processes borrowed from Hovland's earlier training as Hull's student: message learning or encoding, motivation to accept or resist, message retention, and action consequences. He believed that a comprehensive theory of communication, persuasion, and attitude change could be developed from such a taxonomic approach. But faced with Festinger's daring style of theory formation, this static approach immediately lost its appeal for many of us. However, I felt like a bit of a traitor since Hovland had been my first social psychology mentor and I learned much from this genius. I had worked with him on issues of judgmental distortion, did some research that was published on semantic ambiguity, and wrote my major area paper for him reviewing the literature on traditional psychophysical judgment and social psychological judgment. "Mr. Hovland," as everyone reverently called him, told me that he and Muzafer Sherif, his visiting collaborator, found some of it to be useful in their new formulation of latitudes of acceptance and rejection. My doctoral dissertation, jointly sponsored by Cohen and Brehm, pitted predictions from their rational formulation against dissonance theory's rationalizing formulation—and dissonance carried the day and my Ph.D. degree.

I withheld turning in my dissertation until 1959 to avoid the military draft, which I could escape by turning twenty-six years old. It helped also to be working at the West Haven Veteran's Hospital as social psychology postdoctoral trainee, under the supervision of Aaron Hershkowitz, who was steeped in the social ecological approach of Roger Barker and his teachers at the University of Kansas. It was different from anything I had ever studied, focusing on how aspects of the physical environment influenced individual and group response. I benefited more, though, from the opportunity to wander the wards, talk with patients, and attend clinical staff meetings. I had developed an interest in psychopathology from taking a fabulous course, taught by Irving Janis, which met for a full day a week at the Middletown State Mental Hospital. Janis's real genius was less in experimental social psychology than in experimental psychopathology. He would interview a patient before the class, generate hypotheses about his or her behavior in response to further stimuli, which were then invariably proved to be correct. We each were assigned our "own" patient on whom we did a complete psychological workup. Although I was auditing the course, I wrote a sixty-page report that I later used as material in an introductory psychology course as well as in my textbook *Psychology and Life*. That interest in psychopathology was encouraged by my contact with Irv Sarnoff, a wonderfully creative clinician, also just off that post–World War II train from Michigan to New Haven. He was a rare breed at Yale since he actually believed in Freudian theory and set out to show that some of Freud's ideas could be translated into ingeniously testable laboratory experiments. Together we did an elegant study to show that Schachter's association of high anxiety to social affiliation was not accurate since he was confusing anxiety with fear. We reasoned, following Freud, that fear, as the reaction to an objectively valid, external threat, would increase affiliation with others similarly aroused whereas anxiety, as an irrational evaluation of an objectively harmless stimulus, would lead instead to the desire for social isolation. We found this to be true in an interaction between two levels of fear and anxiety.

After I presented that study at the International Congress of Psychology, using a variety of colorful slides to depict the experimental setting and the research procedure, in addition to the usual slides of results, Ned Jones complimented me graciously and recommended we submit our study to the *Journal of Personality*, which we did. It was published in 1961. I was feeling a professional high when Hal Kelley and I had that exchange about my nearly not being admitted to Yale because I was thought to be black. His recollection of this strange tale was later validated by Seymour Sarason in his memoirs (I worked with Seymour for several years codirecting his project on anxiety in children as he began to move off into community psychology). So here is the gist of that story.

Hal said that my graduate school application was "tabled" because there was a split among the faculty on how to deal with it, with me. He went on to tell me that was the case because some were sure I was a black or mulatto ghetto kid; others were less sure, but that diagnosis would change the way they interpreted my grades, recommendations, and test scores. Once the circumstantial evidence in my file was framed as coming from a minority city kid, then everything seemed to fall into place naturally. "For instance?" I want to know.

Let me now briefly summarize that evidence contained in my Yale application:

Interests: listening to modern jazz—Charlie Parker, Lester Young, Dizzy
   Gillespie, Miles Davis, Lady Day
Favorite reading: *Downbeat* magazine
Activities: Captain of the track team
Major: sociology-anthropology (and also psychology), with top grades in
   courses on the Negro family in the United States and race relations
Extracurricular activities: Secretary of the local NAACP chapter
Primary recommender: Charles Bradford Lawrence, well-known Negro so-
   ciologist, who happened to send his letter on NAACP stationery because
   he was out of college stationery at home and his letter was late

Research evidence: two studies enclosed, one on a publication on the dynamics of intergroup prejudice between Puerto Ricans and Negroes in
the Bronx, the other on patterns of racial self-segregation in a college
dining facility

My Italian name: Roy Campanella, famous Brooklyn Dodger catcher at that
time, was surely Negro with an Italian name

And so it went. Even the GRE scores fit the stereotype: low math relative to
good verbal scores.

It was not unreasonable for the faculty to assume, "This dude is black." But
wait. Those days there was also a photograph glued to the application, and that
cemented the false identification. To save money on the cost of sending out photos with all my applications, I had one of my graduation photos duplicated
cheaply, ten for a dollar, and they were dark and grainy copies that showed off a
skinny, dark young man with a pencil mustache wearing some high-style Bronx
clothes that were not sold at New Haven's J. Press clothiers or the Yale Co-op.

Expert psychological reasoning from a false, if not unreasonable premise, went
like this: Good letters of recommendation need discounting since they obviously
reflect reverse biases. This young man will have difficulties adjusting to life at Yale
since there are none of his kind in the department or in the university, so it would
be a disservice to him to admit him. Some faculty may have difficulty adjusting to
him and his lifestyle, especially those from the South (like the professor who interviewed me in New York City). But the liberals in attendance argued that it
would be good to take this one black, even if a token one, since this one was not
too bad. But if he failed and had to be kicked out, how would that look for the department? In any case indecision ruled the day, and my application was shelved
with an intention of getting back to me later. On the next to the last day of the
student acceptances, Gordon Bower, the top admittee, deferred to get a master's
degree in philosophy of science at the University of Minnesota, and that southern
professor with the grant and the drive to explore was suddenly without a research
assistant. Maybe he called those on the waiting list who either did not want to
run rats or by that late date had made a prior commitment elsewhere. That left
only me in the null category. Montgomery called; I said I was eligible and eager to
come to Yale. But he did not offer me the position over the phone. Instead he
came to New York, asked a few simple questions that I lied to, sized me up, and
offered me the job on the spot. After Kelley told me the admission tale, I thought
back to that April 15, 1954, in the bar at the New Yorker Hotel and wondered why
Montgomery had to interview me in the flesh, since I could have answered those
same questions during his phone call. In those days no admitted student went
through an interview process, so why did he have to see me before he could offer
me a research assistantship on his grant money and thereby admission to Yale?

Upon my arrival at Yale, some of the faculty were indeed sorry to see that I
seemed white when they had hoped I would be their first black. But I doubt my

boss man saw it that way. In fact, I now think that had he believed before he met me that I was black, he would have given the job to a more qualified applicant the morning before the interview. Maybe I am going too far beyond the data. But the data that I can add in conclusion are that my mixed-message application and transcript also included the line items that I was summa cum laude, junior-year Phi Beta Kappa, fellowship winner, fraternity president, varsity athlete with a presidential award for distinguished scholarship, and some other nuggets thrown in for good measure. All of that was not sufficient to get me a seat on the first-run bus to New Haven, maybe because it was negated by all that circumstantial evidence that triggered negative stereotypical thinking even among some of the most brilliant scholars and honored psychological researchers in the land.

Although I was nearly the first black graduate student in the Psychology Department at Yale, James Jones was heir to that claim many years later. Jim has gone on to make important contributions to the study of racism and prejudice that mark him as one of Yale's important native sons.

Learning What Matters

It should be evident from this personal travelogue that I learned early many of the most vital lessons in social psychology. From my ghetto experiences, I learned that situations matter and also that culture matters in shaping human behavior and interpersonal relationships. I learned further that content matters, on the basis of my days as a sociology student and my field observations of prejudice in action and the persuasive appeals made (only) by the American Labor Party to get the minority vote in the 1952 election. At Yale I learned two more things that mattered a great deal to me and influenced the rest of my research career: methodology and behavior.

The latter are the two residuals of Yale behaviorism that are not given enough credit when we dismiss the rest of the behaviorist manifesto: Learning via principles of reinforcement follows species-universal principles that transcend content, situation, and of course culture. It was that misguided, arrogant ideology that sidetracked much of psychology for decades, just as Benton Underwood's mindless study of how memory retains nonsense syllables delayed the study of the dynamics of remembering narrative and personally significant events. As an apprentice to Neal Miller and Carl Hovland, I learned the importance of conducting research that is rigorous, operationally as precise as possible, and with sufficient preexperimental observation and considerable pretesting to assure you understood the phenomenon under investigation and can demonstrate the causal connections your hypothesis advances.

From my years of studying rats, I learned how to observe and record their behavior rather than infer what was going on inside their furry little bodies and small brains. So much of my research since then has focused on dependent variables that were observable gross behavior patterns and not just check marks on scales or elicited predictions about how research respondents imagine they would behave in a given situation. But I learned from Bob Cohen the message repeated over the years by my colleagues who are represented in this volume, most notably Elliot Aronson, Hal Kelley, Harold Gerard, and Morton Deutsch: people matter the most. Awareness of that axiom tempers the austerity of any social behaviorism with a compassion for human vulnerability, a respect for human dignity, and an appreciation of the complexities of the human mind. It has helped me to try to design research that is characterized by style with substance and given me an eye for applying what I have learned to improve some aspect of human functioning. I think that the research I reported in my 1969 book, *The Cognitive Control of Motivation,* is the best example of my attempt to wed the rigorous methodology of my Yale behaviorist training with the rich texture of social cognitive constructs.

The Yale Candy Store

I mentioned earlier the metaphor of Yale as my personal candy store that I raided as often as I could. The background for that image comes from the candy store run by the father of my friend Melvin Semmel (on the corner of my block at East 151stStreet and Prospect Avenue). During the first air raid drill and blackout of World War II, all the big kids waited outside the store patiently until, under the darkness, with sirens wailing, they raided the candy store of much of its delicious delights. When I arrived at Yale in 1954 until I left in 1960 to start my first full-time job at NYU, up in its Bronx campus, Yale was the most remarkable social psychology candy store in the entire land. Table 6.1 lists some of the faculty and students who were there during that time or arrived the next year (when I visited as a part-time teacher in the master of arts in education program)

IHR was directed by psychologist Mark May (of Hartshorne and May, whose failure to find cross-situational consistency among children gained them later fame among some social psychologists). It had been the center for an attempt to integrate experimental psychology, social psychology, psychoanalysis, sociology, and anthropology, but in the long run the experiment proved to be largely unsuccessful, except for the research and publication on frustration and aggression by Neal Miller and his colleagues. Anthropologist Alfred Whiting did some interesting interdisciplinary research with Irwin Child, and Hovland and others published a book on a hypothetico-deductive theory of rote learning. I understand, however, that its faculty seminar series was the center of some very lively interdisciplinary dialogues.

The Yale attitude change program had just published the landmark *Communication and Persuasion* in 1953 coauthored by Hovland, Janis, and Kelley. With several large grants and contracts from private foundations (Rockefeller and Sterling money), Hovland was able to bring to Yale a cadre of promising young

TABLE 6.1   The Golden Days of Yale Psychology, 1954–1960

Faculty
  Carl Hovland[a][b]
  Irving Janis[a]
  Harold Kelley[a]
  Leonard Doob[a]
  Irwin Child[a]
  Bob Abelson[a]
  Jack Brehm[a][b]
  Bob Cohen[a][b]
  Bill McGuire[a]
  Milton Rosenberg[b]
  Irving Sarnoff[b]
  John Dollard and Neal Miller[a][b]
  Seymour Sarason[a]

Later Arrivals
  Howard Leventhal
  Chuck Kiesler
  Stanley Milgram
  Norman Miller[b]
  Ed Ziegler

Visiting Professors
  Donald Campbell[a]
  Muzafer Sherif[b]

Bell Labs Research Link
  Morton Deutsch
  Harold Gerard
  Bob Krauss

Prominent Visitors
  Leon Festinger[a]
  Stanley Schachter

Some Notable Students
  Dave Sears, Tim Brock,
  Jon Freedman, Phyllis Katz,
  Dean Pruitt, Jaap Rabbie,
  Roger Shepard, Buzz Hunt,
  Gordon Bower, and Tony Greenwald
  (an honors undergraduate)

[a]Those from whom I took courses.
[b]My research colleagues.

social psychologists, recently graduated after having served in the war effort, to teach and conduct research, as well as visiting professors who were available to the graduate students. He also helped set up the social research laboratory at Bell Labs in Murray Hill, New Jersey, headed by Morton Deutsch and staffed by Hal Gerard, Bob Krauss, and later by other fine young social psychologists. I was fortunate enough to be included on one of Hovland's visiting team treks to Bell Labs that started friendships with each of the principals there.

Three Influences: Hovland, Schachter, and Milgram

Hovland's Nonobvious Impact on the
Field of Social Psychology

Of the three experimental social psychologists who had the greatest impact on my thinking (and surely that of many others), Carl Hovland is the least well known and cited among contemporary students. One of his enduring contributions is as a facilitator of the entire field of social psychology by promoting the development of experimentally focused social psychology programs at Yale, Bell Labs, and through his widespread personal influence at other universities and among granting agencies to support such programs. Hovland was considered a genius whose objectivity, sense of equity, and breadth of interests earned enormous respect from his peers. He functioned like a human computer, with a near photographic memory that was legendary, an ability to do complex analyses rapidly in his head, and the capacity to suspend emotion and personal biases when dealing with others and evaluating research. His approach to theory development was a lot like that designed by a computer programmer: It began with a categorization of all possible input, output, and intervening variables and processes, then a listing of subcategories within each of those conceptual classes, followed by a summary of all known evidence that fit within the resulting matrix. The theory was supposed to emerge from higher-order analysis of that conceptual-empirical matrix. But Hovland died before he could realize that dream, if indeed it could have been achieved by following that path.

Another contribution that he made to the field was the way he carved up the complex dynamics of persuasion and attitude change into bite-size chunks that could be reduced to experimentally testable parts of hypotheses. Hovland moved from the general survey of the impact of propaganda films and other forms of communication in the military during World War II to the first systematic analysis in controlled experimental paradigms that assessed the components of persuasion and attitude change. He also encouraged many of the bright young researchers of his time to become involved in the study of attitudes and persuasion.

On balance, though, there are three negatives that I must add to his slate. Curiously, his approach to social psychology did not follow the grander theoretical model building of his mentor, Clark Hull. Hovland had the talent to do so but elected to follow the more conservative categorical approach described above. Also surprising, since he was nurtured in the crucible of behaviorism, was that Hovland did not study behavior change that should have followed from attitude change. His research stopped at demonstrating the effects of an independent variable in changing a given attitude and did not go the next vital step. And finally, I objected even then to the assumption that those attitudes were content neutral. The Yale attitude change program typically studied attitudes with content that did *not matter*. They were selected because they were low ego-involving topics that should be easy to modify, thus get big effects, in order to study input-output variables and assumed mediating mechanisms. This was again curious given Hovland's earlier training in the military Office of Strategic Services (OSS), where all the research was based around issues, topics, and content of great social significance. Not incidentally, ego involvement was one of the key variables I included in my dissertation research.

Schachter's Gift of Tracking Down Categorical Differences to Theoretical Nuances

Just as the Festinger tsunami swept over the social psychology graduate students in 1957 when he visited Yale and we could appreciate his theoretical brilliance and game-playing, combative intellectual style, Stanley Schachter's visit the next year also galvanized students and faculty. He lectured to us on his first line of research on the psychology of affiliation. But he had no theory handy to explain his data. In a seminar that Hovland organized following his talk, the notion was hatched of extending social comparison theory to understand the social labeling of emotions. I was taken with Stanley's research style, and we developed a personal friendship after he left Minnesota and was a bachelor at Columbia University (we even went dancing with other friends at the Peppermint Lounge in the Village, doing the twist to Chubby Checker's urging).

Schachter's theory building typically started with an observation of some existing widespread difference among people in the real world: Some are joiners, some loners, some firstborn, others later born, some fat, some skinny. He then went on to isolate key variables that might account for that categorical difference and, finally, added a theoretical conception that tied it all together. His experiments were always fascinating in their dramatic design and wonderful to teach because of their vividness. Schachter's theoretical approach raised vital questions about the subject's interpretation of the situation as well as the underlying experiential processes, which led to new research on attribution and misattribution processes. I was fortunate enough during my yearlong visit to the social psychology program at Columbia (1967–1968) to work with two of Schachter's most talented graduate students, Lee Ross and Judy Rodin, on one of the first misattribution experiments. Incidentally, Judy went on to take my job at NYU when I moved on to Stanford the next year, and then I helped Lee join me on the West Coast soon after.

My admiration for Schachter's research led me to do several experiments to clarify some of the results he had found in the area of the psychology of affiliation—that misery loves miserable company; that those who are four or more years younger than their firstborn siblings behave much like firstborns; that fear, not anxiety, leads to affiliation; and the conditions under which people prefer affiliation with those with similar personalities versus similar current emotional states. What was very impressive in Schachter's research agenda was the facility with which he saw and extended the implications of one line of research into the next one. For example, consider how he moved gracefully from considerations relating emotion to affiliation to the social psychology of emotions. The field of emotion had fallen on barren times when he and Jerry Singer proposed their two-factor theory of emotion and conducted their classic study on unexplained arousal and the cue value of the overt behavior of others in the behavioral space.

Despite many methodological flaws and rather questionable treatment of their data, Schachter and Singer did a great service to resurrecting emotion from the doldrums of experimental psychology. They helped to integrate physiological, cognitive, and social processes as necessary for understanding the workings of emotion, and they demonstrated that emotion could be studied in experimentally manipulated laboratory settings. In the rush to the cognitive, psychologists had forgotten that people have an emotional side, just as the behaviorists put minds out of what mattered to them.

I set out to see how far their basic idea could be extended: Would an aroused but unaware subject act and feel depressed or paranoid if the only available social-labeling cues were from a confederate who was acting depressed or paranoid? Before beginning this study at Stanford, I needed to replicate Schachter and Singer's basic result and then build on it with the appropriate new conditions. But I was unable to do so despite several years of trying hard. Gary Marshall and I systematically varied the dosage of epinephrine and many of the experimental conditions, but we could not show that a happy confederate induced happy emotions in our subjects. Quite the contrary: When we reexamined the original data reported by Schachter and Singer, we realized that they had not found the significant effect differentiating their experimental and control condition and never directly contrasted in an ANOVA the positive and negative emotion conditions. Christina Maslach also failed in her replication attempt using hypnosis as the arousal induction with and without explanation, as did other investigators. So I believe that the data from that experiment are neither valid nor reliable; nevertheless, Schachter's views on emotions have been valuable in clarifying the roles of physiological arousal and social cuing as well as subjective appraisals of emotion. I have remained intrigued by those initial concerns about the pathological side of emotion and for the past twenty-five years have been conducting research on experimental psychopathology that blends cognitive and social variables in a posthypnotic paradigm of emotional arousal and source amnesia.

Milgram as the Master of Powerful Demonstrations

Stanley Milgram once startled me by confiding that he felt his work was not sufficiently recognized by his peers. Given the extensive coverage of his obedience studies in every social and introductory text, I questioned his assumption. However, upon reflection, I think I knew what he meant. His research did not inspire scores of dissertations as had Festinger's and Schachter's research and Kelley's revision of Heider's attributional notions because it was essentially atheoretical and primarily demonstrated a phenomenon. There were no control groups in his studies because the base rate was the readers' or viewers' personal assessment of how they would behave, and then those expectations would be violated by the research data.

In the best Lewinian tradition, Milgram demonstrated how socially and politically significant real-world issues could be brought into the social psychologist's laboratory and operationalized and miniaturized in well-controlled experiments. Milgram's obedience paradigm quantified "evil," and in doing so forced us all to reappraise how far we would go on that continuum before we changed our verbally easy dissidence into behaviorally difficult disobedience. His research created strong intrapsychic conflicts among his subjects' personal values, empathy, and need to obey authority. He showed us that intelligent people fail to distinguish between just and unjust authority when the first kind is transformed into the latter. In revealing the so-called darker side of human nature, Milgram's research put a torch to the superficial analyses of social behavior conducted by most of his colleagues at that time.

It also amazes me how many students and even professional social psychologists think that the obedience research is limited to one study and not the nineteen situational variations that Stanley conducted on more than 1,000 subjects from the widest array of backgrounds that I know of in any social psychological research. The size and diversity of his subject population along with the many variations in the stimulus situation make the results of his obedience program of research the most generalizable in all of psychology.

I should also call attention to Stanley's interest in film and video as media for promoting psychological ideas to the general public. His obedience film is still powerful and holds audience attention even thirty years after it was made. He also made several other films on social psychology that were quite effective. Stanley was very much interested in the *Candid Camera* shows as exemplars of social psychology demonstrations and wrote a fine paper with his student John Sabini extolling the creative genius of Alan Funt. (I have more to say about Funt in my epilogue to this chapter.) But Stanley's interest in real-world phenomena led him to study the "small-world phenomenon"—the few degrees of separation there are between apparent unrelated strangers—to develop the lost-letter technique for investigating social responsibility, to investigate urban overload long before social ecology was fashionable, and more. But through it all he championed the power of social situations in shaping our beliefs, values, and actions.

Applying Social Psychology Wisely and Well Also Matters

In my own research I have tried to move back and forth between studying real-world phenomena in field and lab settings and illustrating the applicability of my findings and those of my colleagues in a variety of ways. It is my strong belief that short of research done to test the conceptual adequacy of some theoretical formulation, social psychologists have an obligation to contribute to the enhancement of the human condition through research that applies what we know in sensitive and effective ways. Elliot Aronson has shown us how with the use of his jigsaw classroom technique for promoting cooperation among schoolchildren, an intervention that integrates minority children into the mainstream of class activity better than any other available educational tactic. I have used my various research programs as vehicles for promoting prison reform and judicial legislation, reducing urban vandalism, and overcoming shyness (the latter in my popular writing and media appearances and by establishing a clinic in the community to treat shyness in adults and adolescents). For me, application matters.

So my meandering path through social psychology finds me now studying both situational and dispositional variables and their interaction in research on the psychology of time perspective, the cognitive and social bases of the origins of psychopathology, and the effects of technology on shyness, along with the development of prosocial and antisocial behavior among schoolchildren. It has been my lifelong passion that those cuddly white rats could never quite fulfill, although it was easier to predict their behavior and publish their data than it is dealing with capricious people and the editors of the *Journal of Personality and Social Psychology.*

A *Candid Camera* Epilogue

I, too, have always considered *Candid Camera* a storehouse of ingeniously contrived social psychology manipulations and have used them in my teaching and training of research assistants. I wanted to make Funt's classic gems available to psychologists and set about to ingratiate myself with Funt in a host of ways, among them by interviewing him for *Psychology Today* when it was still read widely by psychologists. He later consented to making his old clips available, and a set of his classics are now on both VHS and laser disks for social psychologists and general psychologists to use (see the media section of my Web site).[1]

While interviewing Funt at his home, I sought to learn about his prior training in psychology, which I assumed would reveal the obvious background for his inventive manipulations. He assured me there was none, and in fact he had never taken a single psychology course when he was at Cornell. He did not read psychology texts, hardly even knew any of that breed. He majored in art and communication, and the idea for *Candid Camera* came from his days in the military, when he discovered that people responded differently depending on whether they were aware or unaware that they were being tape-recorded (the advent of portable wire recorders made it possible to conceal the recording apparatus for the first time).

Just as I was ready to give up on establishing any remote psychological association between Funt's career and his socialization into social psychology, I asked him if he ever had any connection whatsoever with psychologists.

"Come to think of it, I did, during my senior year in 1934 when I worked part time in the home economics program at Cornell."

"Tell me how, please."

"I was a research assistant for some German professor who studied eating behavior among foundlings and ordinary babies, when fed by nurses or sometimes the mother of the babies. I watched behind a one-way mirror and recorded the distance between the adult and the baby and what they did and said to get the infants to eat."

"Do you recall anything about that German professor?"

"Yes, his name was Kurt something or other."

"Could it have been Kurt Lewin, by any chance?"

"Yes, that's it; that was his name. Why? Is he important?"

"Yes, for the field of experimental social psychology and maybe for pointing you in a career direction of observing human nature surreptitiously."

"That's curious. What a small world it is!"

"And a wonderful world for social psychologists."

Notes

1. Available: http://www.zimbardo.com. My publications are listed at that site as well. Those of my colleagues appear in the latest edition of the *Handbook of Social Psychology* and in the reference listings in other chapters of this volume.

7 On the Changes in U.S. Social Psychology: Some Speculations

Leonard Berkowitz

In this chapter Leonard Berkowitz presents his "impressionistic" view of the field of social psychology. Although he has mixed feelings about whether social psychology is better or worse today than it was when he entered the field, Berkowitz asserts that it is now "dramatically different." He spells out what he believes are some of the most significant of these differences, particularly as social psychology is practiced in the United States. He also speculates upon conditions that might have been responsible for these changes, some of which he traces to the maturation of the field. One of the changes Berkowitz highlights is the effort to integrate social psychology with anthropology and sociology in the earlier days, compared to the contemporary emphasis on a psychological social psychology. Another change involves the greater identification of social psychologists with psychology as a whole. Today, he observes, social psychologists "are psychologists first and members of the social science fraternity second." He argues that this explains the current emphasis on social cognition and the abandonment of some themes more sociological in nature, such as that of reference groups, and the increasing interest in "within-the-skin" rather than "between-skins" phenomena. Berkowitz further addresses methodological idiosyncrasies, research funding, and publication policies.

A few years ago, at a small meeting sponsored by the American Psychological Association, when a distinguished senior member of the profession was asked to say a few words about himself, he replied that he was engaged in an "old academic's activity": writing a history of his discipline. Of course not every "old academic" writes a history, but many of them, it seems to me, do adopt a historical perspective in viewing their field. Very often they look at current developments through the glass of all the changes in the discipline they had experienced over their careers. And in doing this, not a few of them are likely to bemoan the current nature of their field, claiming that in many respects it and/or its practitioners have gone downhill since their day. I suspect a number of us in this book harbor these thoughts, even if they haven't expressed them openly.[1]

Whether or not social psychology is better in the late 1990s than it was in the 1940s or 1950s, there is little doubt that it now is dramatically different. Most obviously, contemporary U.S. social psychology no longer encompasses the same broad range of topics. Consider what was included in the first, 1947 edition of *Readings in Social Psychology* (Newcomb & Hartley, 1947), the collection of papers that was required reading in almost every general social psychology course: Although the book had chapters reporting then well-known social psychological experiments very much in the vein of current experimental studies—such as the Bruner and Goodman paper "Value and Need as Organizing Factors in Perception" and the article by Levine and Murphy titled "The Learning and Forgetting of Controversial Material," as well as the classic study of leadership by Lewin, Lippitt, and White—it also had substantial sections dealing with cultural influences on individual behavior and intelligence, children's socialization, industrial morale, prejudice, and social class. The second edition of the *Readings*, edited by Swanson, Newcomb, and Hartley (1952) and published in 1952, had much the same wide scope of topics and, like its predecessor, included articles by sociologists, anthropologists, and even a psychoanalyst, as well as by psychologists. The coverage in these two editions of the *Readings* was not unrepresentative of social psychology's interests in that period. If you look at the contents of the predecessor of the *Journal of Personality and Social Psychology (JPSP)*, the *Journal of Abnormal and Social Psychology,* in those years, you will see that the papers take up a similarly impressive range of topics.

I haven't queried a broad sample of other social psychologists to determine what they believe are the major changes that have occurred over the past few generations. All I can do is offer my impressions of these developments, as well as some speculations about a few of the conditions that could have helped produce the changes I see. Since these changes can be described along a variety of dimensions, my remarks undoubtedly oversimplify what is in truth a highly complex picture. I should also say that I am not necessarily opposed to many of these developments and in fact am favorably disposed to some of them. More important, it seems to me that a number (but not all) of them were inevitable as social psychology has matured.

Finally, let me hasten to add that my comments have to do primarily with social psychology as it is conducted in the United States. Many of our counterparts in other countries do not see the social world exactly as we do and have pursued somewhat different interests. Indeed one scholar's comparison of U.S. and European social psychology highlights points I make in this chapter:

> [In] North America the field of social psychology as a whole is moving much closer to mainstream psychology, and in particular towards cognitive psychology, embracing many of the same paradigms and models for research. Europeans, except for

those exclusively trained in the U.S., remain strongly interested in some of the traditional concerns of social psychology as a discipline wedged between psychology and
sociology. Whereas the individual and its functioning is becoming the paramount
object of study in North American social psychology (with the "social" being part of
the information to be processed), much of European social psychology, while studying individuals, is more interested in the social and cultural determinants of cognition and behaviour. (Scherer, 1993, p. 520)

This observation is a good starting point.

When many of us who contributed to this book began our careers in social
psychology, some of the most influential social psychologists (such as but not
only Theodore Newcomb) believed social psychology should integrate psychology with sociology and anthropology. In their writings and teachings and in
books such as the *Readings in Social Psychology,* they sought to bring about this
integration. This was the heyday of a number of attempts to establish social psychology as a bridge between psychology and sociology. Newcomb's social psychology program at Michigan is perhaps the best-known example, but there was
also Harvard's Department of Social Relations and, earlier, the Institute of Human Relations at Yale. Less well known today, the pioneering Maxwell School of
Public Affairs at Syracuse University, founded in 1924 with Floyd Allport as the
first professor of social and political psychology, and Columbia University's Bureau of Applied Sociology, led by Paul Lazarsfeld and Herman Hyman, could also
be included in this list of social psychologically oriented interdisciplinary endeavors.[2] Mention might perhaps also be made of the later interdisciplinary program at the University of California at Irvine.

All of these attempts to bring psychological social psychology formally together with sociology have failed, probably for a number of reasons. One undoubtedly has to do with the traditional departmental structure in our universities: Graduates of these interdisciplinary programs had to declare themselves to
be *either* psychologists *or* sociologists when they sought academic positions; they
had to be psychologists in psychology departments or sociologists in sociology
departments. More than this, though, I suspect that these interdisciplinary programs had difficulty bridging the different cultures of psychology and sociology.
These fields not only do not have the same theoretical interests but also have
somewhat different assumptions about the influences governing human thought,
feeling, and action. Even if the sociological social psychologists focus on the individual, by and large they are much more likely to adopt a social construction perspective and place a much greater emphasis on the role of the group and the culture in shaping thoughts, emotions, and behaviors. They are also much less likely
than their psychological cousins to conduct laboratory experiments and generally collect their data in the "field" by employing survey methodology and self-re-
ports. With their reliance on these latter procedures, sociologists as a group have
taken up econometric-like statistical analyses to a greater extent than have psy-

chological social psychologists. And also, I think it is fair to say, sociological analyses of human conduct are more apt to be largely rationalistic in nature; few sociologists are concerned with the nonrationalistic cognitive biases of the kind identified by Amos Tversky, Daniel Kahneman, Herbert Simon, and others that might affect human decisionmaking. Very few of them, I believe, would agree with this statement made by John Bargh (1997, p. 2) contending that a great deal of social behavior is controlled by automatic, nonconscious processes: "I argue that much of everyday life—thinking, feeling, and doing—is automatic in that it is driven by current features of the environment (i.e., people, objects, behaviors of others, settings, roles, norms, etc.) as mediated by automatic cognitive processing of those features, without any mediation by conscious choice or reflection."

Turning away from their cousins in the adjoining social sciences, U.S. psychological social psychologists have become ever more strongly identified with psychology as a whole. They are psychologists first and members of the social science fraternity second. It is not surprising, then, that in their study of social cognition, probably the most prestigious research area in contemporary psychological social psychology, "they increasingly use concepts, paradigms, and methods developed in cognitive psychology, applying them to social content with respect to perception, memory, and inference" (Scherer, 1992, p. 184). Scherer has pointed out that interest in social cognition need not be this individualistic in focus. Although growing numbers of European social psychologists are employing the same "concepts, paradigms, and methods" as their U.S. counterparts, it is worth noting, as Scherer (1992, p. 184) put it, that "when [most] European social psychologists talk about social cognition, they are often more concerned with the effects of the social environment, in particular the culture, social group, or institution the individual is part of, on cognitive processes that provide social meaning for the individual".

One consequence of U.S. social psychologists' identification with psychology is that very few psychological social psychologists in this country today are interested in concepts and theories that have a sociological flavor or are largely sociological in origin. As a result, they have deprived themselves of literature that, unknown to them, is pertinent to some of their theoretical problems. The concept of reference groups is a good illustration. This term was once of considerable importance in social psychology, and four papers on this topic were included in the Swanson, Newcomb, and Hartley *Readings,* one by Harold Kelley. These days, however, most contemporary social psychologists probably are totally unaware of how the reference group concept was employed forty or so years ago by Hyman and Merton, as well as Newcomb and Kelley. They probably also would tell you that the notion that people evaluate themselves by comparing themselves with others was first introduced by Festinger, when this idea actually originated with Herbert Hyman.

Yet another consequence of U.S. social psychology's increasing identification with psychology is that we have cast large areas of study out of our domain.

There are social psychologists, of course, who are interested in the various aspects of interpersonal relations, but even a casual perusal of the major journals in the field reveals that our discipline as a whole is now much more concerned with "within-the-skin" than "between-skins" matters than ever before. Aggression and helpfulness were never central areas of study, but except for a very few investigators, what interest there was in these topics in the 1960s has today dwindled even further. More revealing, studies of factors influencing the development of interpersonal attraction, once a major research topic, have now virtually disappeared from mainstream U.S. social psychology, and there are also relatively few papers in the related areas of friendship and love, areas that had once attracted considerable attention. Some years ago Harold Kelley, Ellen Berscheid, and several other eminent social psychologists were active in the affairs of a professional society devoted to the study of interpersonal relations. I do not know if they still are, but I have been told that for all intents and purposes, this particular field is now almost entirely dominated by people in departments of communication rather than by social psychologists in psychology departments.

Even more striking to me is the way mainstream psychological social psychology has lost interest in problems of group behavior. I started graduate work at Michigan shortly after the Research Center for Group Dynamics had moved to that university, and the study of people in groups was very much a growth industry at Michigan at that time. Among other things, Festinger was engaged in the experiments growing out of his theory of social communication in groups, and French as well as Cartwright and Zander would soon begin to develop their ideas about social power and influence. Social psychologists at other universities, such as Carter at Rochester, Bales at Harvard, and soon afterward Hemphill at Ohio State and Fiedler at Illinois, were also drawing considerable attention with their studies of group behavior and leadership. Group behavior is no longer a flourishing field of study. To my knowledge, there aren't even any studies of the interactions among group members being carried out today at Michigan's Research Center for Group Dynamics.

Contemporary U.S. social psychology's relative lack of interest in between-skin matters can also be seen, I believe, in the paucity of research on social facilitation we are celebrating in this book. A quick computer search of *PsychLit* revealed that 239 journal articles were published between 1990 and 1996 whose abstracts contained the words "social facilitation." However, of these 239 only three were in the most widely read social psychological journals, two in *JPSP* and one in the *Journal of Experimental Social Psychology (JESP)*. (Most of the other articles were in journals concerned with animal behavior or eating and addictions or sports psychology.)

Besides this increasing "psychologizing" of contemporary social psychology, we can say the field has changed in at least two other ways as well. Both have to do with a reduced concern with problems and issues in the surrounding world. When I was in graduate school, discussions of the relationship between naturalistic studies in field settings and laboratory experiments frequently held that social psychology's hypotheses grew out of observations in the real world and were tested under the controlled conditions of the laboratory. My impression is that this field-then-laboratory sequence was followed far more often in the 1950s than it is nowadays. Although I haven't checked this out, my guess is that the overwhelming preponderance of studies published in *JPSP* and *JESP* in the past decade or so were stimulated by other laboratory experiments rather than by naturalistic observations. Scherer (1992, p. 198) has the same impression, saying it is "rarely" the case in contemporary social psychology (he presumably is referring to the U.S. variety) that phenomena first "closely observed in the field" are "then carried into the laboratory."

At the risk of digressing too far from the main line of my essay, I think it's worth looking at one of the points raised by Scherer in this connection because it is a common criticism of contemporary social psychological research. For Scherer (1992, p. 199), a major reason relatively few social psychologists today derive their hypotheses principally from naturalistic observations is that the field in general is too bound to "'standard research paradigms' handed down from generation to generation in particular research 'traditions.'" As a consequence, he says, there is a danger of losing "sight of the real phenomenon to be explained." Social psychological studies of person perception are illustrative in his view:

> Although often methodologically refined, their problem is that they treat the perception of other people almost exclusively from the angle of impression formation on the basis of adjective lists describing a person's characteristics. We do base impressions on what other people tell us about a person, often in the form of adjectives. But more important, we judge others on the basis of a multitude of verbal and nonverbal cues—looking at photographs, talking to people on the telephone, and most often, interacting face to face. (p. 187)

Scherer's criticism here is reminiscent of how Harré and Secord (1972) faulted a large part of contemporary social psychological experimentation, such as Zajonc's investigation of the mere exposure effect. All of these writers maintain that the experiments ignore important aspects of the real-world phenomenon—person perception in Scherer's case and, for Harré and Secord, the development of interpersonal liking—and that the findings too often lack ecological validity. This type of criticism has been answered by a number of psychologists, including Kruglanski (1976) and Donnerstein and myself (Berkowitz & Donnerstein, 1982). In his rebuttal Kruglanski (1976, p. 105) observed that many of the objections to laboratory experiments do not distinguish between two types of research: (1) "particularistic" inquiries seeking to learn the accuracy of statements about specific instances and (2) "universalistic" (or theory-oriented) investigations testing the "causal relations among general constructs." Experiments are the procedure par excellence for these latter studies. In much the same vein, Donnerstein and I argued that ecologically validity is necessary if an investigation's findings are to be used in arriving at population estimates (e.g., how many American people will obey an authority figure's command to punish another person severely), but it is much less necessary for the testing of causal hypotheses (such as whether the sight of an object having an aggression-related meaning will prime aggression-related ideas).

These writers also addressed the complaint that experiments unduly simplify the rich complexity of the phenomena of interest. Along with Kruglanski, Donnerstein and I stressed that clear tests of causality require experiments to be highly "artificial"; they must abstract out for study only a few of those influences that might operate in a given situation and cannot allow to operate freely all of the other factors that might exist in the natural setting. It is this control over possibly confounding factors that makes experiments the best way to determine the validity of a causal hypothesis. In sum, experiments are not only narrowly focused and unrepresentative of the complexity of naturalistic situations but have to be so if they are adequately to fulfill their true purpose. And furthermore, one cannot say out of hand that the findings of tightly controlled laboratory experiments cannot be generalized to other settings (Berkowitz & Donnerstein, 1982).

Having said this, however, I agree with one of the implications of Scherer's comment. There can be little doubt that social psychology's dominant research methodology has had a major influence on what questions are defined as central to the field. Because of their focus on the testing of postulated "causal relations among general constructs," experimental procedures have concentrated on the development of abstract theoretical formulations rather than particularistic questions. Partly (but not only) because of this, as anyone reading our leading journals will acknowledge, the concepts and theorizing in contemporary social psychology have generally become not only more narrowly focused but also somewhat more formalized. A good example, I believe, can be found in the way much of the recent research on prejudice first narrowed to the study of stereotypes and now highlights the categorization process and the relatively precise specification of the nature, causes, and consequences of categorization. An outsider can't help but wonder if important aspects of prejudice aren't somehow being neglected.

Whatever one might think about this increasing emphasis on the development and use of ever more sharply focused abstract theoretical concepts, such a trend is inevitable as sciences mature. We can see this in economics. In the words of the eminent economist David Kreps (1997, p. 62),

> There is no question that economics underwent a revolutionary change around a half-century ago; mathematical modeling, a small piece of the subject until the 1940s and 1950s, became the all-encompassing (some would say suffocating) language of the discipline. Mathematical modeling and formal deductive logic have been a part of economic theory for much longer than that, but their embrace by the mainstream of the profession came in this period.

As you may know, there has been a recent spate of criticism directed against this increased attention to formal mathematical models in economics. Similar misgivings have been expressed about the same kind of trend toward formalization in the world of academic political science. A writer for the *Wall Street Journal* who visited the 1997 convention of the American Political Science Association talked to some of the attendees who "fear[ed] the field [political science] has strayed from the practical sensibilities it displayed early in this century, when one former APSA president, Woodrow Wilson, even became president of the United States. Some lament[ed] the impenetrable mathematical jargon and abstract theoretical musings that stump even the cognoscenti, much less the average candidate for city council or Congress" (Harwood, 1997, p. 1).

In my view, anyone trying to halt the trend toward the development of abstract theoretical formulations would be like King Canute attempting to stop the incoming tide. I am willing to bet that the critics, many (but not all) of whom are primarily concerned with their disciplines' relatively concrete, more or less practical issues, will have as little influence on their more academically oriented brethren in the most prestigious universities as King Canute had on the ocean.

In general, then, many of the leading academic social scientists, as well as a good proportion of eminent American social psychologists, have reduced their interest in everyday social phenomena because of their increasing involvement with abstract concepts and highly theoretical analyses. Although a variety of influences have contributed to this change, as I indicated earlier, it also reflects an alteration in these academics' primary reference group. More and more of the people in these disciplines seem to be concerned mainly with gaining the approbation of their disciplinary colleagues, to such an extent that they think relatively little of those in other fields or the public at large. The problems they select for study and the concepts they employ in their teachings and writings are increasingly designed to appeal to others in their field rather than other possible audiences.

This phenomenon may not be limited to the United States. According to the Carnegie Foundation for the Advancement of Teaching, which published a survey of university faculties in a number of technologically advanced countries in 1996 (cited in the *Economist* of October 4, 1997), the majority of the academics in many of these nations reported being more interested in research than in teaching. (In contrast, over 60 percent of the U.S. professors sampled indicated they were more interested in teaching than in research. The sample undoubtedly had only a relatively small proportion of faculty members from the more illustrious, research-oriented institutions. Undergraduates at these more elite institutions often complain that many of their classes are taught by graduate students while the professors focus their attention on research and publication.) This motivation to do research would of course promote a concern with the views of one's scientific peers in other institutions. And moreover, the desire to gain the approval of these other researchers throughout the nation and in other countries may be contributing to a decreased attachment to one's own university, at least in the United States. Many of my colleagues at Wisconsin, especially those of my cohort or older, have noted how younger faculty members do not seem to share their identification with the university. Instead, the newcomers appear to be more strongly and more exclusively career-oriented, much more concerned with getting ahead in their discipline than with joining with members of other departments in collegial activities. I've been told that similar trends can be seen in other American universities, and that this trend is manifested in, among other things, the demise of faculty clubs in many universities.

My observations to this point have not been particularly controversial even though I cannot back them up with hard data. However, I would like to add another impression that is even more speculative. One might think that this mounting concern with relative standing in one's discipline, to the extent that this has indeed been happening, has come about because of scarce resources. I suggest, though, that the changes I've described are largely due to the plenitude rather than the scarcity of financial support for research, especially from the government. Even though the federal government's budget for university research is now somewhat tighter than it was a generation ago, the amount of this research support is still far greater than it was in the 1950s, and many universities have come to rely increasingly on governmental funds. Federal grants comprised only about 10 percent of the research expenditures at U.S. universities before World War II, whereas this contribution had grown to over 60 percent by the mid-1980s (*Economist*, October 4, 1997, p. 12). A number of academic traditionalists have decried this flow of governmental funds for research, maintaining that it not only undermines the universities' independence but also heightens the dominant status of research over teaching. Be this as it may, the comparatively ready availability of this extramural money since the 1960s has meant that academics at research-oriented universities are frequently expected to seek governmental grants and, correspondingly, have to gain the approval of their peers at other institutions if their applications are to be successful. Grant-getting and academic status also require publication of the research findings, and here, too, academic researchers have to win the approbation of peers.

But there is a good chance they will not be altogether successful. Consider the extremely high rate at which manuscripts submitted to psychological journals are rejected. According to a report of the American Psychological Association (Eichorn & VandenBos, 1985), only about 2 percent of the manuscripts received by APA journals are accepted on their initial submission, and even when the papers are revised only about a quarter of all of the submitted manuscripts are eventually approved. The acceptance rate for the APA's most prestigious social psychological journal is even lower than this. In 1998 only about 15 percent of the papers sent in to the attitudes and social cognition section of the *Journal of Personality and Social Psychology* were eventually published there. Applications for federal research grants probably do not do any better. I have no idea what proportion of grant applications in social psychology are successful, but it is clear that exceedingly high research panel ratings are required for an application to be funded. Given this state of affairs, in being highly aware of others in their discipline academics must also realize, implicitly or explicitly, that they are competing for publication space and research grants.

The use of one's disciplinary peers as a reference group and the competitiveness that can arise in these social comparisons may be more pronounced in some branches of U.S. psychology, including social psychology, than in others. Especially high rejection rates in the journals serving these fields probably lead to a heightened awareness of one's disciplinary peers as both competitors for journal space and as manuscript reviewers. The summary report of the APA's journal operations[3] shows that, generally speaking, submitted papers are most likely to be rejected by those journals that cover mainly social behavior, such as *Developmental Psychology, Journal of Clinical and Consulting Psychology,* and *Journal of Personality and Social Psychology,* whereas journals that serve the fields related to the natural sciences, such as *Behavioral Neuroscience* and *Journal of Comparative Psychology,* tend to have the lowest rejection rates.

Undoubtedly, there are a number of reasons for these differences. The most obvious has to do with the volume of submitted papers; journals that receive the greatest number of submissions are obviously under the greatest pressure to be highly selective and have the highest rejection rates. I suspect, though, that other factors may also affect a journal's overall readiness to reject papers. For one, my impression from a series of informal discussions with several scientists in fields linked to biology, in and outside of psychology, is that the journals that tend toward the natural sciences are more willing to publish "mere facts" than are the social-science-oriented APA journals. The "facts" have to be regarded as theoretically sound and significant, of course, but the papers can be accepted without themselves presenting new, well-worked-out, and reasonably general theoretical formulations. Maybe this is because the theoretical conceptions underlying the reported findings are already fairly well substantiated in the areas related to natural science. By contrast, the social sciences do not have integrative theoretical schemes that are as well developed, and as a consequence (1) the manuscripts submitted in these fields are expected to offer new theoretical ideas or at least novel extrapolations from existing theoretical models, and (2) there is apt to be greater disagreement about the importance or validity of the presented theoretical ideas.

But in addition, the various academic disciplines might be different cultures, with each of them possessing a somewhat unique, widely shared set of assumptions as to what is significant research and what kinds of theoretical ideas are desirable. Some of these cultures may urge a relative tolerance of the members' research efforts, whereas other cultures might favor having a skeptical or even critical attitude toward other persons' endeavors. One of my nonpsychological informants suggests, as an example, that philosophers of science as a group are prone to be more critical of their disciplinary colleagues than are historians of science. These cultural differences may exist to some degree within psychology, with the people in some fields being less likely than the members of other fields to believe that a manuscript is "guilty" unless clearly proven "innocent." Social psychology might be in the latter camp. There is a widespread but not well-substantiated belief that the social psychological culture has a pervasive norm toward finding fault. We hear anecdotes about how the social psychological members of grant review panels are often more critical of the submitted grants in their area than are the panelists from other scientific disciplines. This attitude, if it exists, conceivably could contribute to the relatively high rejection rate in the most prestigious social psychological journals.

Of course we have no clear evidence whether U.S. social psychology does indeed have the pervasive critical attitude that has just been suggested, and further, if such a "cultural norm" does exist, why it has come about. If we can extrapolate from findings reported by Amabile,[4] it could be that many of our reviewers are engaged in a self-presentational strategy. Amabile (1983, p. 146) demonstrated that highly critical reviewers are often regarded as "more intelligent, competent, and expert than positive reviewers," regardless of the actual quality of their assessments. Social psychological grant review panelists and manuscript reviewers might be especially hard on the grant applications and manuscripts they see partly because of a strong desire to show how smart they are (perhaps because they are especially concerned about their relative standing in the field).

To continue with my conjectures, I wonder if the relatively great use of other social psychologists as the primary reference group and the professional comparisons and competitiveness that may occur with this heightened awareness of one's disciplinary peers have not led to a certain amount of anxiety in contemporary social psychology about one's work and worth. More than ever before, social psychology seems to be afraid of making mistakes, of accepting theoretical generalizations that may not stand up under further research. Paradoxically, though, I suspect that this anxiety has also led to a greater adherence to established concepts and ways of thinking and a greater reluctance to question these ideas. I believe I can provide some examples of this, but not being free of anxiety myself, I think it's better for me just to raise this last possibility and stop here.

Notes

1. I thank Aroldo Rodrigues and Robert Levine for organizing the Yosemite conference and prompting me to think about the changes in U.S. social psychology from the time I first began my graduate career at the University of Michigan in 1948. I thank Daniel Katz, my primary mentor at Michigan, for his comments on an initial draft of this essay. Klaus Scherer's observations on contemporary social psychology in the United States and Europe further enriched this chapter. I also thank Craig Berridge and Elliot Sober for their insight regarding research and publication practices in fields other than social psychology and, above all, for the interesting conversations I had with them.

2. Dan Katz recommended the inclusion of the Maxwell School and the Bureau of Applied Sociology in this list of interdisciplinary social psychological endeavors that are no longer functioning.

3. See "Summary Report of Journal Operations, 1966" in *American Psychologist, 52,* 908–909.

4. Amabile's (1983) study was kindly recommended to me by Arie Kruglanski in a personal communication.

References

Amabile, T. M. (1983). Brilliant but cruel: Perceptions of negative evaluators. *Journal of Experimental Social Psychology, 19,* 146–156.

Bargh, J. A. (1997). The automaticity of everyday life. In R. S. Wyer Jr. (Ed.), *Advances in social cognition* (Vol. 10, pp. 1–61). Mahwah, NJ: Erlbaum.

Berkowitz, L., & Donnerstein, E. (1982). External validity is more than skin deep: Some answers to criticisms of laboratory experiments. *American Psychologist, 37,* 245–257.

Eichorn, D. H., & VandenBos, G. R. (1985). Dissemination of scientific and professional knowledge: Journal publication within the APA. *American Psychologist, 40,* 1309–1316.

Harré, R., & Secord, P. F. (1972). *The explanation of social behaviour.* Oxford: Blackwell.

Harwood, J. (1997, August 29). Find out how many politicians can fit on the head of a pin. *Wall Street Journal,* p. 1.

Kreps, D. M. (1997). Economics: The current position. *Daedalus, 126*(Winter), 59–86.

Kruglanski, A. W. (1976). On the paradigmatic objections to experimental psychology. *American Psychologist, 31,* 655–663.

Newcomb, T. M., & Hartley, E. L. (1947). *Readings in social psychology.* New York: Henry Holt.

Scherer, K. R. (1992). Social psychology evolving: A progress report. In M. Dierkes & B. Biervert (Eds.), *European social science in transition: Assessment and outlook* (pp. 178–243). Boulder, CO: Westview Press.

_____. (1993). Two faces of social psychology: European and North American perspectives. *Social Science Information, 32,* 515–552.

Swanson, G. E., Newcomb, T. M., & Hartley, E. L. (1952). *Readings in social psychology* (rev. ed.). New York: Henry Holt.

8 Historical Sketches and Critical Commentary About Social Psychology in the Golden Age

Albert Pepitone

Albert Pepitone describes the wide range of subjects studied by social psychologists in the field's early years (a point Leonard Berkowitz has made earlier in this volume). After reviewing the most influential books published in the field before World War II, Pepitone concludes that the range and diversity of the subject matter in those early days, with special emphasis on "macrosocial phenomena at the level of society and culture," extended well beyond what is covered in contemporary texts. He next considers the wartime period, during which there was particular reference to social influence, judgments, reference groups, and group membership. Most of the chapter covers what Pepitone calls the "golden age," the postwar period up to approximately the late 1980s. Pepitone offers a critical analysis of some of the most significant research programs during this period. Pepitone is critical of the excess of experimentalism in testing hypotheses derived from narrow theories rather than suggested by field observations. He is also concerned with the disappearance of theoretical systems that synthesize a wide diversity of social phenomena. Finally, although he acknowledges advances in the specification of fundamental cognitive processes, he believes a more comprehensive understanding of social human beings requires that the discipline address theoretically and methodologically a broader range of phenomena, particularly through real-life observations of cultural and mass behavior.

If one were to make an end-of-century assessment of social psychology—a sort of state-of-the-field report—the most relevant desiderata would certainly be the findings of the major experimental research programs, the theories used to interpret them, and the contributions made to enduring bodies of knowledge. But without looking at the historical development of the field, especially the philosophical and methodological ideas that have driven it, even a detailed review of research would not provide a full understanding of what we social psychologists are, what essentially we have done, and where the field is going. For what is defined as the "official" subject matter of social psychology as well as what is excluded, the preferred methods of collecting and analyzing data, and the kinds of concepts that are introduced and avoided for the construction of theories are largely based on the metatheories, paradigms, and perspectives that prevail in any historical period.

In this chapter I examine a portion of the history of social psychology with the purpose of etching out some of the metatheoretical perspectives that defined the subject matter of the discipline and the research methodology that shaped the kind of data collected for theory development. The overall plan is to bring into relief the prescriptive conceptual frameworks within which most social psychologists have worked. Second, on the empirical level, I look at several major substantive areas or programs of theory and research that recruited large numbers of investigators and made voluminous contributions to the research literature. I take a special interest in the theoretical issues that were *not* investigated, the longevity of these programs, and the achievement of general social psychological theories. Two early "would-be" areas of social psychology begin my discussion.

Societal and Mass Psychology

Even a casual awareness of history suggests that what social psychology is about, the issues that are investigated, the research methods, and the dominant theoretical perspectives have changed and continue to change since the formation of the discipline roughly in the last quarter of the nineteenth century. One is also struck by the irony that the subject matter widely considered at the beginning to be the domain of social psychology and represented as such in one of the pair of first textbooks (Ross, 1908) never evolved into a major area of theory and research within the field. Societal and mass phenomena, including crowd behavior, social movements, the dynamics of social class, national character, marital and sexual practices, institutionally organized behavior such as religion, and other behavior at the collective level, were incorporated into sociology and have remained there ever since. In social psychology, sociologically coded phenomena are discussed in handbook chapters in which the vast majority of references come from sociology and political science (see, for example, Brown, 1954; Milgram & Toch, 1969). Textbook coverage is rare, as are research articles published in social psychology journals. But there are some exceptions. One of the most famous of all experiments in social psychology—the Milgram study on obedience to authority (Milgram, 1964)—is in fact interpreted as an analogue of the mass obedience of the German people to Hitler and Nazi ideology. In another example, LeBon's theory about the major dynamic responsible for the disinhibition observed in mobs and other forms of crowds received support in an experiment with small groups made up of strangers (LeBon, 1903). Festinger, Newcomb, and I (Festinger, Pepitone, & Newcomb, 1952) showed that "deindividuation," a state of a group in which members do not pay attention to each other (theoretically to achieve a temporary mutual suspension of personal identity) is correlated with the expression of normally inhibited hostility.[1] It is fair to say that at the collective level only small-group psychology, organizational psychology, and most recently, personal relationships have been admitted to the field as fully accredited areas of study.

Instinct Theory

If mass and societal psychology were nonstarters in social psychology, instinct theory was a later dropout. Whatever hardiness the concept of instinct had in theoretical discussions owed to the authoritative and erudite case developed in McDougall's textbook (1908). Although considered the "other" pioneer textbook in social psychology, one that went through thirty editions, there is today little discernible influence of McDougall's instinctualism or similar theories originating in psychology. In the 1950s and 1960s, as part of animal ethology, instincts did become a subject of considerable interest, particularly focused on the Lorenz thesis that there is an instinctual source of aggression in humans. A still later revival of interest in the biological basis of social behavior occurred in the late 1970s and early 1980s stimulated by sociobiology (Wilson, 1975). Indeed the issue of the selection of social traits in the evolutionary process still resurfaces from time to time (see, for instance, Brewer, 1997). But what made McDougall's instinctualism hard to swallow was the absence of a research program designed to specify how instincts work, how they interact with each other, their effects on cognition, and so on. After reading McDougall, it is difficult to see what issues remain to be investigated; he would have instincts "explain" everything without providing the details about when and in what form they function. In fairness, it must be recalled that McDougall considered his text as an introduction to social psychology, its foundations. His later *Group Mind* (McDougall, 1920) was the first of two books that would complete his coverage of the field. Although different from the group mind of the crowd (LeBon, 1903) in that it applied to organized groups, McDougall's conceptualization suffered the same fate: It never became part of mainstream social psychology.

Thus even in the infancy of social psychology, the philosophical and metatheoretical orientations that would determine the boundaries and character of the field until the present day were already in place. Much of what social psychology is, what it investigates, and how it interprets the data it collects was grounded in psychology founded about a half century earlier. How social psychology defines itself was and is strongly determined by its disciplinary identity and by being organizationally part of psychology departments. To a large degree, major shifts in paradigm and perspective in social psychology are reverberations of the same changes earlier in nonsocial or "general" psychology. Primarily, social psychology was to be an objective, empirical science about how the human individual is affected by the social environment (Pepitone, 1981). During the first two decades of the twentieth century, objectivity increasingly stood for observable and measurable behavior; subjective experience and what was called phenomenology were widely disregarded as scientific data. For those in the behaviorist movement, the causes of overt social "responses" were conceived to be internal (physiological) or environmental (physical) stimuli. Perhaps most important in its long-term consequences, the method of choice for a scientific social psychology was the controlled experiment.

Although the analysis of society and mass phenomena were largely left for sociology, some concepts of the earlier period were carried over into the social psychology of the 1920s, including particularly imitation and suggestion. The latter was the central concept in the analysis of social influence. One of the earliest studies in this country on the "susceptibility to suggestion" was prototypic. H. T. Moore (1921) had subjects make judgments of the seriousness of grammatical errors, moral wrongs, and the aesthetic value of musical themes. Later the subjects were given the judgments of a purported majority of the sample or the judgments of "experts" in the three domains. Shifts toward the majority were many times more than would be expected from random variation. The effect of suggestion by experts was only slightly less, the subjects changing almost half their previous judgments.

By the early 1920s, research-oriented social psychology was embracing the pure science perspective systematized in behaviorism, and its most articulate advocate was Floyd Allport. As his textbook makes clear, Allport (1924) was an uncompromising advocate of a scientific social psychology focused on the relation between the individual and the social "portion" of the environment. In his research the latter referred to the overt physical presence and responses of other people, the conditioning effects of speech, gestures, sights, sounds, and movements. Allport's experimental program on social facilitation, carried out from 1916 to 1919, dealt with what was already a classic problem of the influence on performance of the presence of others (Triplett, 1898; Mayer, 1903). Although the data were not analyzed by high-power statistical inference tests in common use today, the frequency counts in categories representing levels and quality of work sustain the proposition that on a variety of tasks individuals work at higher speed when stimulated by co-workers but that the co-worker effect on quality of work is more particularly dependent on the kind of task involved. Emblematic of his behavioristic "peripheralism" was Allport's separation of social facilitation based on sights and sounds of others from the effects of rivalry (wanting to do better than the others or not to do worse). He tried every way to eliminate rivalry—by holding constant the time for each test and measuring the amount of work completed, by prohibiting discussion of results, and by telling the participants that their scores would not be compared. But any rivalry that did enter was, he said, explained by emotional and physiological responses: "The visceral reaction in rivalry as in other emotions probably liberates internal secretions, and involves other responses characteristic of the sympathetic system" (Allport, 1924, p. 283).[2] Today one would see comparison processes at work in the co-worker situation and the perceived attributes of the co-workers as crucial variables affecting performance. One would also distinguish the case where two people work on identical tasks in each other's presence from the case where two people are members of a group working together on a task.

Allport was an early S-R behaviorist, but his views were never as extreme as those of Watson, the father of behaviorism. For one thing, Allport believed that introspection has a place in social psychology and indeed is necessary for a full account of social behavior. He also assumed that there were instinctual roots to learned social behavior, that humans were not a tabula rasa. Neither his experimentalism nor his individualism was set in stone.

In the early 1930s Allport actually changed course away from controlled experimentation. The J-curve studies in fact were decidedly uncontrolled behavioral observations—for example, of ritualistic acts while attending church services and the behavior of motorists at stop signs (Allport, 1933). The research focused on common everyday behavior that reflected prescriptive institutional norms such as those of the church and the law. Quite apart from the utility of the J-curve to represent the composite influences of conforming tendencies, chance, and biological dispositions, one is struck by the commonality and concrete authenticity of the behavior under investigation. There is no doubt about what is being studied or about the objective status of the norm or law applicable to the situation.

As early as the 1940s, Allport began to relax his individualistic stance. Whereas in the 1924 text he strenuously objected to the group unit of analysis—"there is no psychology of groups that is not essentially and entirely a psychology of individuals" (1924, p. 4)—in his later years he moved toward acknowledging the reality of the group, that group effects are not reducible to the sum of individual responses (Allport, 1962; see also Allport, 1940). If one were to define Allport's position, one would place it closer to Lewin in seeing the group as a reality based on its measurable, systematic effects.

But it was Allport's earlier experimental behaviorism that was to shape the field well after he softened a bit on it. Social psychologists who did their doctoral studies in the 1980s or even earlier may be surprised by the extent and duration of behavioristic influence in social psychology. In its day S-R behavior analysis and experiment dealt with aggression (Dollard, et al., 1939), imitation (Miller & Dollard, 1941), attitude change (Hovland et al., 1953), and socialization (Whiting & Child, 1953).

Looking back, it is easy to identify contributions of behaviorism, particularly experimental findings that have implications for practical behavior control, for example, research on attitude change (Hovland, Janis, & Kelley, 1953). Furthermore, behaviorism in social psychology was continuously improving theoretical analysis, adapting itself to deal with human social behavior. Thus the frustration-aggression hypothesis was clarified and modified to represent human phenomena more accurately (Berkowitz, 1962). But at the end of the day, the conceptualizations were limited by metatheoretical canon concerning the nature of psychological data. Physicalistic S-R theory left out crucial determiners of human social behavior—culture and cognition. In aggression, for example, there was no role for honor and shame in the provocation of aggression, nor for the perception of intent, responsibility, and justifiability as decisive variables in anger and assault.

Social Psychology of the 1930s

Although it was the most systematic and rigorous, the behavioristic, S-R perspective that descended from Floyd Allport was not the only one of the period. In fact social psychology in the 1930s covered a great range and variety of subject matter that went beyond the scope of learning theory. This observation can be documented by the textbooks of the period. I briefly review three that convey something of the rich diversity of the field. All, of course, were written at a time when ominous war clouds were gathering in Europe, which may account for the inclusion of topics that dropped out after World War II. But this in itself is an indication that the field was reflecting a larger social reality than individual responses to "social" stimuli.

J. F. Brown

Brown's (1936) book is the least research oriented, the most original in organization and content, and the most politically conscious. He defined social psychology as a discipline located "between sociology and psychology" and thus concerned with the effects of sociological laws on psychology and vice versa. The book includes chapters on national character, religion, social class, minority group status, and the family. In a psychology section, there are chapters on personality, Freud, and leadership. In the final, political science section, there are chapters on the state, the liberal democracy, the fascist dictatorship , and the communist dictatorship.

Given the detailed coverage of sociological and political issues, Freud's theory of personality development, and Lewin's field theory, it is not surprising that Brown cited few controlled experiments. The low priority is more than a matter of space; Brown was systematically critical of contemporary theory and research. Thus regarding Gordon Allport's well-known assertion that the concept of attitude is the "keystone in the edifice of American social psychology," Brown opined that other than clarifying the methodology of attitude study, social psychology had accomplished little since 1920 (Brown, 1936, p. 97). He further observed: "On the whole, social psychology has gone from the broad but important generalities of the nineteenth century to the specific but sometimes meaningless experimental researches of the twentieth" (Brown, 1936, p. 101). Brown directed much of his criticism toward the failure to represent the total field situation. An appendix to the book is devoted to the mathematical and methodological background of psychological field theory, including topological representations of class, religious, and political groups and other sociological fields. His analyses of these representations, however, are informed more by political theory than by theories of group psychology. As a former student of Lewin in Berlin, Brown was knowledgeable about the field theory analysis of the famous experiments in individual psychology published in the journal *Psychologische Forschung* (Psychological research) but acknowledged that his topological representation of macro sociopolitical events was new for field theory and not necessarily endorsed by Lewin. (I think Lewin would have considered Brown's representations insufficiently connected with psychological theory).

Murphy, Murphy, and Newcomb

In 1937 Murphy, Murphy, and Newcomb revised the text of Murphy and Murphy published six years earlier. They defined social psychology broadly as the discipline concerned with social interaction and were (probably) the first to identify it as an *experimental* social psychology. Their book (Murphy, Murphy, & Newcomb, 1937) dated the beginning of the field to the French psychologist Braid's investigations of suggestion between 1841 and 1860, which were extended by Bernheim of the Nancy school. But although suggestion and imitation were social psychological concepts, the early investigators were probably not aware they were defining a new discipline. That awareness didn't come until the end of the century in the work of Tarde and to a lesser extent LeBon, who referred to the experimental work of others.

In commenting approvingly on the growth of experimentalism, however, the authors expressed an uneasiness that echoed somewhat the worries of Brown and presaged some of the concerns expressed during the "crisis" of social psychology in the 1970s (see, for example, Pepitone, 1976). In 1937 the authors said "It has become very evident in recent years that the social psychologist has thrust many of his problems into the laboratory without adequate consideration of the matrix in which his most certain and valuable data lie. He has simplified his phenomena in such a way as to exclude essential facts necessary to the understanding of social life, and has succeeded in experimental and quantitative control by leaving out most of the variables about which we really need to know" (Murphy, Murphy, & Newcomb, 1937, p. 10).

The coverage and organization of the book are anything but standard. Of the seven chapters on social behavior, six have to do with children and their socialization. (Few texts today contain such material, and in contemporary research there is very little crossover between developmental and social psychology.) The book is also atypical in having the character of a handbook; original research findings are summarized in numerous tables: In one, forty-seven studies of aggression in children; in another twelve studies of praise and reproof in children; and in another fifteen studies of competition in children and college students. The chapter on adult social interaction describes studies of social influence, including suggestion, rivalry, and social facilitation; laughter; street conversation; judgments of pleasantness of odors; and work. The chapter concludes with a discussion of the anthropological data on cooperation and competition, drawn principally from Mead's comparison of primitive societies (Mead, 1937). Although insightfully interpreted and often based on specific observations, the ethnological material does not easily connect with the experimental findings on the same subject. This difficulty raises a question for the authors, the classic question of whether there are discoverable laws that span and unify the individual and group levels of analysis. Clearly, from its baptism as an empirical science, social psychology has pursued the strategy of constructing theories that transcend sociocultural boundaries and have universal validity. To many believers in universal theory, observed cultural differences recorded by ethnographic studies are phenotypical, reflecting differences of method, language, and so on. Whatever the merits in this argument, the avoidance of sociocultural comparisons precludes the falsifiability of hypotheses and the possible discovery of culture-transcendent generalizations.

Although the book provides the detailed results of experiments, Murphy, Murphy, and Newcomb slight the hypotheses behind the research and offer little discussion of their theoretical significance. Yet they do include serious reflections on "big" issues such as the role of culture in theory. The book is in fact a curious admixture of handbook and broad discourse about the nature of social psychology that altogether fills more than 1,000 pages, with 1,000 references in the bibliography. Though difficult to assess, the book probably had a mixed effect on the field; it reinforced the importance of experimental research in social psychology but contributed little to the conceptualization that guides experiments and organizes its findings.

Katz and Schanck

Katz and Schanck (1938) defined social psychology differently than did the authors of the other two texts. They contrasted social with individual psychology. The latter is the study of the world of raw materials on which the body depends; the former is the study of the social world on which helpless humans depend, the study of "the relation of man to his fellows" (p. 1). The book presents a social psychology that includes folkways, institutional norms, social interaction, the physiological basis of social behavior, and the development of language. In the fourth and last part of the book, there are chapters on society and culture, rural communities, and social classes; it includes discussions of the basic features of capitalistic society, such as surplus value of labor, moneymaking, the national state, fascism, political parties, the committee system of legislation, war, social classes, and class consciousness. In Katz and Schanck's scheme of things, one may conclude that experimental social psychology is no more than a part of the discipline. Many nonexperimental issues—the way society is organized, the way

resources are distributed, the relations between people of different socioeconomic status, and national wars and other group conflicts—are the grist for social psychology's mill.

Summing Up

What do these textbooks of the 1930s tell us? If they are taken as at least rough
markers of the boundaries of the field, the range and diversity of subject matter
extend well beyond what is covered by contemporary texts. All of the 1930s texts
have in common discussions of macrosocial phenomena at the level of society
and culture; all bring in the findings of other disciplines—sociology, anthropology, and political science. The picture, of course, is sharply different from the
narrower behavioral frame of Floyd Allport. And the concern with society and
culture contrasts with the inattention to these domains in contemporary social
psychology.

The War Period

Although not the dominant perspective, the broad view of social psychology of
the 1930s continued into the 1940s and is illustrated by the textbook of Klineberg
(1940). In the preface Klineberg stated that because of rapid changes in the concepts and data of social psychology and particularly the "increased concern of
psychologists with other cultures," it was fitting to include some of the findings of
ethnology and comparative sociology. "There might be some interest in an attempt at integration between psychology and ethnology," he wrote, and including
this new material had meant somewhat of a reduction in the coverage of the "traditional" content of social psychology (p. vii). In this connection Klineberg's
book has a whole chapter on the social behavior of animals and extensive reviews
of findings on ethnic, racial, and class differences in intelligence. There is also a
remarkable chapter on "emotional expression" that contains a comprehensive
analysis of wit and humor, presumably a universal feature of interpersonal relations.[3] It is in Klineberg's treatment of the research on prestige suggestion that we
see the roots of cognitive social psychology, which was to become the dominant
perspective decades later.

Social Influence

Social psychology was cognitively oriented in many ways even before the postwar
cognitive revolution in psychology. Social perception and the formation and
change in attitudes and judgments—hallmark research areas in social psychology—were being investigated by German psychologists at the turn of the century.
From that origin, we can trace a fairly direct line to the research in this country
from the 1920s to the 1950s. In one program, for example, the interest was in see-

ing how an individual's instructional set (*Aufgabe*) influences attention to various stimuli. Gestalt psychology's emphasis on the structure of the stimulus was a direct inspiration for social perception and influence (Koffka, 1922). In particular, the effect of the ground on the perception of the focal figure was especially seminal in conceiving social influence as the perception of social stimuli within referential frames such as categories, anchors, scales, and the judgments of others. Thus the influence of the group on individual judgments was seen as a (needed) structuring effect of the social situation. One of the best-known and influential Gestalt-oriented experimental programs was that undertaken by Sherif (1936), who observed conformity in the judgments of illusory light movement. The autokinetic effect, as it is called, is a universal perceptual (visual) response: The subject perceives movement in a pinpoint source of light in a dark surround. When briefly fixated, the light is seen as moving at speeds, in patterns, and distances that differ across individuals and from trial to trial in the same individual. When individuals hear the vocalized distance estimates of others in the room fixating (they believe) the same light source, their subsequent judgments tend to converge toward the group distribution. Sherif's penetrating insight was that the judgments of autokinetic movement made in a group represent the essential cognitive process in the formation of social norms. Conformity is an accommodation to the social behavior of others in order to establish a stable judgmental frame of reference. Presumably, there is an underlying need to create such a frame of reference or at least an induced need to make accurate estimates or to organize stimulus fields. Sherif further alluded to the importance of a sense of "incompetence" when discrepancies occur between the individual's and others' estimates. Just over a decade later, Festinger (1950) postulated a cognitive need to feel confident of the reality of opinions and judgments of ability as a major source of pressure toward uniformity in small groups.

The interpretation of conformity along such Gestalt lines began to dominate in the 1930s. Asch, Block, and Hertzman (1938), for example, investigated conformity in the judgments of photographs of faces as to their honesty, and intelligence and in judgments of professions as to their social usefulness, idealism, and so on. As in the autokinetic situation, when subjects were given no information, they made judgments within a framework created by their own previous judgments. But when in a later series the student subjects were given the judgments purportedly made by a peer group of college students, their judgments shifted in the direction of the group. However, when the group was "noncongenial"—for example, Nazis—the subjects' judgments shifted in the *opposite* direction. These studies are easily recognized as forerunners of reference group theory elaborated by Hyman (1942) and of Festinger's (1954) theory of social comparison.[4] The frame-of-reference interpretation was applicable not only to conforming behavior but to goal setting as well. The standards of groups served as reference frames that affected both the valence of goals and the probability of reaching them (Lewin, Dembo, Festinger & Sears, 1944).

Though perceptual structuring and the need for one's opinions to be right were the basic interpretive concepts in such experiments, it is easy to detect a more direct role of social variables. The latter is most apparent in the study of conformity in real-life settings, like the famous Bennington study, which showed that changes in political attitudes of students over their undergraduate years are a function of their shifting group memberships (Newcomb, 1943). At each stage individuals acquire the attitudes of the majority of their comatriculants and class leaders, to the extent that they regard those peers as a positive reference group.

Even this brief overview shows an evolution from the influence of the responses of others in situations where people are motivated to make organized and accurate judgments to the more general idea of reference and membership groups. In the latter conception, the influence depends upon the group's authority vis-à-vis the stimulus being judged or issue being discussed, the attractiveness of the group, the number of members with like judgments, and the position of the acknowledged leadership. In the evolution one clearly detects a change from the purely cognitive, informational basis of conformity to a more direct social basis where social approval and loyalty become central. The interplay of cognitive and social roles is seen in the famous Asch experiment on independence. A pioneer of the (Gestalt) cognitive conformity perspective, Asch (1952) asked the question about limits of social influence. Would you get the individual to conform to the majority of strangers, even when the physical stimulus on which judgments are made is not unstructured and hence when there is no cognitive need for structuring or reality confirmation? The results of his independence studies show that, yes, some of the sample do sometimes conform to the majority under such conditions, suggesting that social motives such as not wanting to be considered odd, isolated, or simply different are dominant, even when subjects know that the judgments of the majority are incorrect. But most subjects on most trials make independent, "nonsocial" judgments according to the information conveyed through direct perception.

The Golden Age

The war experience of psychologists who returned to the universities; the well-financed expansion of university enrollments, graduate programs, and faculty appointments; and generous research grants combined to bring about an explosive postwar growth in social psychology. The massive expansion can be quantified in terms of number of books published, specialized journals launched, and social psychology societies formed. From that initial postwar boom—and here I am somewhat arbitrary—into the late 1980s, marks a golden age. Social psychology of the 1990s is another chapter; given its diffuse and theoretically eclectic character, it would be a much more difficult story to tell.

The golden age was quintessentially the age of experimentalism and the passing of metatheories like field theory or systems like S-R learning theory and psychoanalytic theory. Textbooks and conference programs would also show a flowering of applied social psychology in social-problem areas such as war and peace, health, aging, human relations training, racism, gender discrimination, sexual orientation, law, conflict resolution, advertising, management, public opinion polling, worker morale and productivity, and environmental research, to name some. Some of the applied work—survey research, for example—was a carryover from the war. Much of it was a response to the demand for relevance made in the 1970s "crisis" of social psychology. In fact, since that time, for experimental social psychologists to crossover and help address important social issues has had a certain cachet. No doubt some of the thinking behind applied research derives from experimental findings, but taken as a whole, applied social psychology is driven by the practical strategies of amelioration rather than theory and is largely independent of lab research. Clearly, the canonical interdependence between field and lab research—according to which one takes a finding from a survey, observation, or other kind of study in the real world; conceptualizes it; and formulates hypotheses testable by a lab experiment and, in the other direction, takes experimental hypotheses and checks them out in the field situation where the raw phenomena is observed to assure their "ecological validity"—does *not* describe the typical relationship between experimental and applied social psychology. There are, of course, systematic reasons for this. To open a theme I play often, as experiments become driven by theoretical hypotheses, the separation becomes inevitable.

But the most striking development over some four decades is a narrowing of the range of subject matter. Compared with what was encompassed by the textbooks of the 1930s reviewed above, the issues that fall within the purview of experimental research cover a smaller range of social science subject matter. In part the relative narrowing is a by-product of what has become a principal feature of the lab experiment—the testing of hypotheses by *creating* the independent variable. That is, the reduction of subject matter range reflects the fact that not all subjects of interest to social psychology can be represented by manipulable variables.

Not inconsistently, however, within the smaller range of subject matter there has been increasing specialization, with greater differentiation of the issues under investigation, which are organized into programs of theory-research. As most textbooks from the 1950s document, social psychology has been made up of twenty to thirty such experimental programs. These would have to include interpersonal attraction, aggression, affiliation, achievement, attitude change, altruism, attribution, conformity, group conflict, competition and cooperation, decisionmaking, consistency theories (such as cognitive dissonance and balance), leadership, person perception, prejudice and stereotypes, risky shift, and social comparison. A salient fact about these programs is their independence; hypotheses in any one do not typically generalize over other theory-research programs. It is this state of affairs that frequently led to (and still leads to) the characterization of the field as fragmented. It is also clear that along with increased differentiation into distinct programs of research and theory, social psychology has become more isolated from sociology, economics, and anthropology.[5]

A thorough critical review of these programs would require considerably more space and energy than is available for this chapter. I can, however, examine a few of them, focusing on how phenomena have been conceptualized, the key issues that drove the research, and the present state of the program. From this exercise, I would hope to discern characteristics of most programs and draw some conclusions about the field as a whole. There is no ordering implied in the sequence of programs we are examining.

Group Dynamics

In 1946 the Research Center for Group Dynamics at MIT was recognized as an organization for developing a new area of research in social psychology. Although comparisons between individual and group performance, as in the social facilitation studies, were well known, theoretically driven programs of research on the dynamics of small groups did not appear until the late 1930s. It was Lewin's conceptualization of the group as a scientifically legitimate unit of analysis and the strikingly original and real-life-oriented group experiments by his graduate students and colleagues at the University of Iowa (e.g., Lippitt, 1940; French, 1944) that opened up the field of group dynamics and led Lewin to establish the MIT center. At the end of World War II, the center organized several programs of research and theory around social influence pressures, group cohesiveness, cooperation and competition, deindividuation, communication in social hierarchies, individual motivation for the group, and social perception. Some of these theory-research programs were continued at Michigan, where the center was relocated following Lewin's death. The research literature on group dynamics grew rapidly from the mid-1940s to the 1960s (cf. Cartwright & Zander, 1953, 1960). However, the theory-research programs of the original Lewinian group were never fully realized and one by one passed from the scene.[6] Besides being theory-driven, research in the group dynamics programs developed the state-of-the-art experiment in which the theoretical variables were created through artful manipulations of how subjects should interpret the situation. Although such stagings often involved fantastic scenarios and "cover stories" that stretched credulity, they were designed to focus sharply on a theoretical point permitting incisive tests of hypotheses. By the same token, however, theories based on the results of such experiments were inevitably incomplete. By definition, sharply focused experiments cannot themselves acquire comprehensive knowledge of a program or area of research. Thus the social influence experiments addressed not the large question of what accounts for observed uniformities but the narrow question of the sources of uniformity pressures in newly formed experimental groups. Moreover, the research program concentrated on one source of pressure: a hypothesized cognitive need to establish the social reality of opinions (Festinger, 1950). The body of evidence supported the hypothesis that when people who don't know each other first get together and are required to state an opinion on a subject they haven't thought much about before, they will influence and be influenced by others in the group. What drives the influence pressure is a need to be confident that one's opinion is right; social uniformity serves as a substitute for individually assessed physical reality. It will be recalled that the convergence of the estimates of light movement (the autokinetic effect) can be interpreted along the same cognitive lines. Subjects assume that objectively the light moves a measurable distance, and they see the distribution of estimates as approximating reality. Although valid under limited experimental conditions, the social reality hypothesis, as strictly interpreted, is probably not the explanation of many commonly observed uniformities that are due to social influence.[7] If one looks at people on the streets of Atlanta, Chicago, Los Angeles, New York, or Philadelphia, one observes uniformities everywhere: people holding coffee containers while walking, men and women wearing blue jeans for all occasions, sports utility wagons (driven by young women holding cellular phones), and so on. Is the motivation to certify the "rightness" of the behavior in the absence of a physical test of reality the most valid theoretical interpretation of such uniformities? I don't think so. For one thing, most of those behaving uniformly have already decided that their way—blue jeans, cell phones, and so on—is right; what they want to show others, or some others, is where they stand. More intuitively appealing than the cognitively based social reality hypothesis is the culturally based interpretation that in becoming uniform people unconsciously or consciously are affirming their identity with a cultural value orientation. It should be noted that although typically identity affirmation leads to disaffiliation from those who express no values or identify with opposing values, under certain conditions standing out as a lone deviate—wearing blue jeans among pressed-trouser or pleated-skirt types—can provide a delicious taste of one's (superior) identity. (It is interesting to note that the concept of identity did not come to be recognized as central in social psychology, and particularly in the analysis of intergroup conflict, until the 1970s [Tajfel, 1981]).

How theory-research programs, movements, schools, and so on become deactivated and fade into history is itself a social psychological question. In the case of group dynamics, there are certainly obvious factors, including the death of the leader (Lewin), changing interests of the leader of experimental research (Festinger), and dispersal of the young Ph.D.'s into different academic contexts and their need to build independent careers. Further, theories of group dynamics became infertile; they were not elaborated enough to sustain productive research programs (cf. Steiner, 1974). Given that the human intellect is ultimately responsible for fertilization, it is difficult to diagnose the potential of theories at any given time, but (as I argue below) theories that are built exclusively on experimental findings and not fed by real-life observation and experience tend to go dry.

Aspiration and Achievement

As already noted, theory and research on the level of aspiration was an active enterprise of the early 1940s (Lewin et al., 1944). The resultant valence theory is essentially a decision theory that predicts the aspiration level the individual will choose in a goal-setting situation. Although the sources of the valences associated with the levels of difficulty are assumed to be institutional and cultural norms, the latter were never specified and brought into the theory in any formal way. How norms affected the valences and probabilities that combine to predict aspiration and under what conditions remain uninvestigated questions. In the 1950s, research on level of aspiration began to decline, but as the program disappeared from the literature, there appeared a new line of theory and research on achievement.

In the early 1950s, McClelland and Atkinson (1953) published a book on the "achievement motive" that inspired a large theory and research program. According to these authors, Nach is a motive to achieve relative to a standard of excellence and is implanted in the individual's early socialization primarily by way of independence training. By the late 1960s there appeared a worldwide summary and analysis of Nach theory and research (Heckhausen, 1967). In the 1970s research on Nach had dramatically declined.

Other than the rhetoric used by educators and university presidents, especially new ones, the idea of "excellence" is not what most observers of everyday life would consider central to aspiration and achievement. In the first place, not all people in society have articulated career, economic, or even educational aspirations that can be described in terms of excellence. Second, if one scans the world of doctors, lawyers, and other professionals; the world of sports; the world of CEOs and business owners; the world of most well-to-do suburbanites; and even the world of art, "achievement" refers to "success" and, concretely, to money, celebrity, prestige, status, power, and competitive victory, singly or in combination. This is not to say that wanting to perform most excellently, to make an excellent product, to achieve the highest grades for excellence, indeed to be perfect by some standard is absent in achievement. When you hear Alfred Brendel playing a Beethoven sonata, you know that perfection is what he has in mind. But to judge by what we observe around us, excellence is certainly not the only motive, not the major motive, and not often an end in itself. Furthermore, although independence training may give individuals the freedom to excel or to achieve anything beyond what is prescribed by socializers, one has to look into culture to discover the root sources of what and how much families allow their young members to achieve.

There is another feature to human achievement that is not captured by either level of aspiration theory or Nach—insatiability. In this period of unabashed, unfettered American capitalism, many have made millions. It is astonishing to hear so often that people who have achieved what was beyond imagination, have the ability to acquire all they can conceivably want, and have enough to more than merely survive any economic downturn or costly life event want more. In his classic analysis of suicide, Durkheim (1897/1951) identified insatiability as the key distinction between animal and human motivation. Celebrity, fame, and power, as well as the acquisition of wealth, seem to be insatiable goals of achievement. Insatiability may be one consequence of being "spoiled" as a child, but if we note where in the social structure it is most concentrated, we would assume insatiability is more likely a characteristic spin-off of the economic system.

The theory of achievement motivation, however, did not neglect culture altogether. One of the most creative ideas of the Nach program, in fact, had to do with the cultural origins of the achievement motive. Taking off from Weber's thesis that there is a causal link between Protestantism of the sixteenth century—Calvinism in particular—and the rise of capitalism, McClelland (1961) ingeniously showed significant correlation between measures of Nach (based on the frequency of references to achievement imagery in children's readers in a wide sample of countries) and the increase in the kilowatt hours of energy consumed by those countries over a twenty-five-year period (when the children would have been adults participating in the economic system). The relationship presupposes the influence of a Calvinist belief that the acquisition of wealth is a God-prescribed "calling." Societies in which this belief is stronger tend to socialize children to become more acquisitive adults.

Bold ideas like this raise challenging questions that ultimately can lead to a big advance. First, there is an issue about the causal nexus implicit in the Calvinist hypothesis. Assuming that Calvinist values and beliefs induced an achievement motive, there is the issue of cultural diffusion, that is, how achievement values spread into other categories of persons, especially those who constitute the entrepreneurial cadres that directly create industrial growth. Calvinists (and other ethnoreligious groups independently) may be the source of capitalist values, but over time such values influence a large secular class of society. The influence of the capitalist "spirit," moreover, is selective; after all, there are religious sects and whole religions that deplore materialism and proscribe acquisitiveness. Indeed believers should shun wealth, celebrity, power, and the rest; a religious life should celebrate modesty and humility and reject the greed inherent in capitalism. The first step toward a general theory of achievement, then, requires the specification of the diverse and contradictory links between culture and achievement motives, followed by the construction of general theoretical statements that account most parsimoniously for them.

Game Theory and Choice Behavior

Essentially, game theory was about rational decisionmaking where "players" are in some way and degree related by the fact that their decisions affect one another's outcomes. The normative theory prescribes the optimal choice strategy, decisions that maximize rewards or minimize costs in economic, military, or other strategic domains (Luce & Raiffa, 1957). Game theory is also a method of presenting strategic problems to the players via a payoff matrix that specifies the outcomes contingent upon given patterns of their joint choices. In social psychology this payoff matrix became the basis of descriptive hypotheses about choice. Of particular historical importance was the Prisoner's Dilemma, a not purely competitive, so-called mixed-motive game that has the ambivalent characteristics of some significant interpersonal and intergroup relationships. PD experiments were designed primarily to observe the strategy or outcome preferred by the players as inferred by the pattern of their choices. In general terms, players in the PD game have both conflicting and common interests. In one of several variants, each player can try to maximize the gain but could take a loss if the other player makes same maximizing choice or go for a modest gain but take a big loss if the other player chooses the same alternative. Which alternative players choose thus depends on the balance each player estimates between the magnitude of the outcome desired and the choice he or she expects the other player to make. When the game is repeated in a series of trials, the alternative strategies can be described in various psychologically meaningful ways. In some PD game experiments, the maximizing alternative that can yield widely divergent, zero-sum outcomes is the "competitive" choice, whereas the alternative that can lead to similar modest outcomes for both is the "cooperative" choice.

PD research in social psychology was not only prolific but highly diversified. For example, the game can be considered a bargaining situation in which each of the parties may choose to go for the best, most profitable deal but risk considerable loss or go for a bargain that yields both parties modest losses or gains. The important issue investigated by Deutsch and Krauss (1960) is how the ability to threaten the other party affects a player's bargaining strategies—does threat enhance the cooperative or competitive tendencies of the players? In another approach the PD game was considered to be a relationship in which the "default" maximizing strategy would be offset by the motivation to distribute outcomes justly. The question was how the players' relative resources at the beginning of their interaction and the calculation of what just outcomes would be on the basis of that knowledge affect the frequency of maximizing choices (Pepitone, 1971).

By the end of the 1970s, it would have been safe to assume that multiple motives determine choices in non-zero-sum games, a conclusion reached a decade earlier (Messick & McClintock, 1968); among those potentially involved, we would include the desire to gain more than the other, to gain the maximum possible, to share gains and losses, to allocate rewards equitably, even to sacrifice gains for the other, to befog the other player, to make a random sequence of choices, to encode secret messages in the choices, and so on. General formulations like "maximizing utility" that fail to consider decision contexts are hopelessly tautological.

Although the decline of game theory research seemed as sudden as its beginning proliferation, the program never died. In fact, two vigorous theory-research programs descended from it at least indirectly. First, the investigation of decisions as games was reincarnated under the name of "social dilemma" research (see, for instance, Dawes, 1980; Messick & Brewer, 1983; Messick & Liebrand, 1997). Social dilemma research represents a major advance over PD-based research in that it deals with decisions that are common in real-world contexts. The "commons dilemma" represents the kind of controversy we often hear or read about in which the freedom for everyone in the group to maximize consumption of resources conflicts with severe, sometimes irrecoverable, long-term losses equally or unequally shared. How people deal with such dilemmas obviously depends on political views concerning freedom, regulation, and other cultural values.

The second and perhaps more fruitful contribution of game research is in the use of the outcome matrix to specify the basic structure of interpersonal relationships (Thibaut & Kelley, 1959; Kelley & Thibaut, 1978). Dedicated to the elucidation of group structure, the work continues with ever increasing conceptual refinement (Kelley, 1997). One problem addressed by these theorists is described as the "transformation" of the objective to the "effective" matrix definition of the structure. Although the goal structure defined by social norms, authority, or ecology can itself induce motivation—a "contrient" goal structure per se tends to make people competitive (Deutsch, 1949)—what adds complexity is that other motivations, values, and beliefs can modify the objective structure or even override and nullify its influence. For example, among the determinants of the operative matrix are normative values about interdependence itself. Thus in the same objective structure there can be those who value competitiveness in all things and others for whom human equality and cooperation are paramount. There is also the issue of when structures should be in place and respected and when informality, the setting aside of structures, is appropriate. Generalizations have to take account of cultural differences. In many modern societies much social life is by definition informal. What needs to be discovered and articulated are the cultures and the occasions when human relations structures are in or out. Finally, we humans are simultaneously imbedded in many structures, hierarchical as well as horizontal. Beyond describing the complex patterns, we need to know how the structures psychologically interact. Are there discoverable social psychological heuristics that govern the order of their dominance? And of course, are the structural determinants of behavior the same regardless of the content of the structures?

Altruism, Helping, and Prosocial Behavior

Although popular at first, the term "altruism" declined in use as the standard designation of a major theory-research program in social psychology; "helping" and then "prosocial behavior" came to designate the area. Prosocial behavior achieves maximum generalization, with only a "pro" to distinguish it from all social behavior (or at least from antisocial behavior). I venture to guess that "altruism" lost favor because of its religious and moral connotations, as much as because of its operational indefiniteness. If so, one can argue that the most essential compo-nent—moral pressure—may have been eliminated from the theoretical analysis.

Helping, or prosocial, research inspired ingenious designs, and I suspect at-tracted many experimentalists because the research issue was simple and straightforward: Under what conditions does an individual act to assist (typi-cally) a stranger who is manifestly in need? For the most part, experiments varied the need, the kind or appearance of the person in need, and the actions that rep-resented the appropriate helping. With the exception of a cost-benefit analysis, which did little to deepen understanding of the phenomenon, there are few con-ceptualizations that can represent any large portion of the diversity of experi-mental findings. An interesting subset of research on helping, inspired by a real-life event, focused on the question of bystander intervention in emergencies, and particularly the effect of one bystander or several (Latane & Darley, 1970). The results confirmed the hypothesis that when multiple persons perceive an emer-gency, there are lower rates of individual intervention, owing to a diffusion of re-sponsibility.

During the early years of research on prosocial behavior, scholars frequently debated one question that goes to the nature of the motivation to help: Is the helping observed in experiments motivated by truly "altruistic" motives, or is the behavior, however disguised, a reflection of self-interest? The sociobiology of the late 1970s may have had the last word in that debate, holding that animal proso-cial behavior reflects only the workings of the "selfish gene." Perhaps in part be-cause of the ambiguity concerning the authenticity of helping, the productive program sharply declined in the 1980s.

What seems in retrospect to have been gravely underplayed in the theoretical analysis of prosocial behavior is the role of moral pressure in the helping act. That moral motivation plays a role in helping does not imply that it is always pre-sent or that, when present, it necessarily dominates. But with few exceptions, helping because it is the morally right and good thing to do was left out of most theoretical accounts. The moral should not be interpreted narrowly in terms of any religious doctrine or commandment. Yes, people do perform noble deeds at great sacrifice under pressure of religious beliefs based on scripture or the direct word of God. But moral pressure works less directly through the individual's per-sonal identity, particularly the ideals about self. Thus when that man walking across the Washington, D.C., bridge a few years back saw the victim of a plane crash struggling to stay afloat in the icy Potomac, took his jacket off, and jumped in to save her, it is quite possible that the impulse behind that heroic act was his answer to the moral question, "What kind of a person am I?"

In passing, it should be noted that moral motivation and cognition have been slighted not only in the prosocial program but perhaps more conspicuously in the two major theory-research programs on justice—equity and "just world." Yet it is a matter of common observation that the perception of justice in life events and the world is linked to the belief in God or in a universal moral law (Pepitone

& L'Armand, 1996). It is also puzzling to note that although in developmental psychology moral judgment is a priority theory-research area, social psychology has preferred to theorize about cognitive-motivational dynamics that are independent of culture and biology. Even the diffusion-of-responsibility hypothesis of bystander unhelpfulness is not meant to imply that observers of a person in distress are wanting to relieve themselves of moral responsibility as opposed to not wanting to be bothered; the authors, in fact, explicitly downgrade the importance of norms (Latane & Darley, 1970).

Moral values and beliefs are not the only cultural variables given short shrift in the prosocial behavior theory and research program. A visit to India gave me at least a hint of another cultural source of helping acts. There I had frequently observed people giving coins to beggars and saw that many such donors were visibly nervous. Later I read about the widespread belief in the evil eye and that one of the classic casters of the eye is the beggar (Maloney, 1976). In South Asia, then, dropping a coin into the outstretched hand of a beggar is for many the direct way to avoid being zapped by the eye. The behavior serves the same function as placing a side wager in a crap game to please and importune Lady Luck. One has to conclude that there are multiple, distinct motivations underlying helping behavior, including those that may be culture specific, and that before general, content-free theories can be constructed, the phenomena have to be conceptually ordered according to the underlying dynamics. "Helping," or "prosocial," behavior is not a pure phenomenon and thus cannot be represented by a single theory.

Attribution

As dissonance declined as a major theory-research program in the 1970s, attribution theory and research were in ascendance and by the late 1970s became the dominant program in the country. As most social psychologists are aware, Heider's elucidation of the process of causal attribution was the seminal source of the major theoretical work less than a decade later (Heider, 1958). The way Heider framed the question of attribution derived from his earlier interest in perceptual constancy or, more precisely, in the tendency to perceive the invariances of things across varying and transient contextual media (Heider, 1926). The extension of the idea to social psychology was that there is perceptual constancy in stimulus persons: The dispositions that underlie a person's behavior remain constant across changeable situational determinants. The most influential attribution theories were thus focused on the locus of attribution: What are the conditions for "dispositional," "personal," or "internal" causal attributions as against "situational," "external," or "environmental" causal attributions (Jones & Davis, 1965; Kelley, 1967)?

Logically, the division of the universe of attributions into categories like internal and external covers exhaustively all causal loci. But even if it is assumed that all attributions in one or the other of the two categories are functionally the same, the locus is not the only important attribution issue. The more fundamental questions are, *What* is the attribution, and what determines it? If we look beyond the interpersonal context and want to know how life events or conditions of the world are interpreted—for example, how people interpret an earthquake—the behavior of an actor may not be a relevant variable. Moreover, besides the exclusionary narrowness of the locus question, there are multiple meanings of "causality." In the discourse on attribution, a number of distinctions emerged—cause, responsibility, blame, fault, explanation, and so on (see, for example, Buss, 1979). But although there are clear psychological distinctions here, they are by no means standard; the terms are often used interchangeably. Although extraordinarily productive, then, the attribution program was limited in its concentration on the locus of the behavior of another (actor) or oneself (observer).

Cognitive Social Psychology

In the 1970s, phenomena such as impressions of persons, stereotyping, the self-concept, as well as attribution were beginning to be placed in the framework of cognitive social psychology. The task of cognitive social psychology was explicitly modeled on the perspective of Heider and Gestalt psychology generally: to understand the "common-sense" ways in which individuals make sense of the self and the world (Fiske & Taylor, 1984). The unit of analysis was cognition, and the theoretical aim to specify the *processes* involved in how cognitions are formed, stored, and changed. As I see it, the establishment of cognitive social psychology as the dominant perspective marks the end of the golden age. By the mid-1980s a large portion of experimental social psychology was affiliated with the perspective; what remained outside the cognitive fold was diffuse and fragmented, with few overarching theoretical structures. In cognitive social psychology we have more than just a reorganization and relabeling of what had been packaged in separate theory-research programs; the cognitive movement has contributed original theoretical ideas of its own—heuristics and illusory correlations, for example—that can lead to deeper understanding of how people generally think about the social world and themselves. But such paradigmatic movements also have their limitations and risks. In concentrating the interests of social psychology on phenomena conceptualized as *cognition* and cognitive *processes*, scholars ignore important theoretical distinctions, and the field tends to become more isolated from the other social sciences. "Cognition" is an abstract category that lacks clear correspondence with psychological experience. Does it refer to what individuals know about themselves and the world? Does it refer to what persons believe about self and the world? Does cognition include attitudes, values, ideologies, as well as judgments, inferences, and deductions? In the comprehensive, and one might say defining, book on cognitive social psychology, the authors take up attitudes in a chapter titled "Attitudes: Cognition and Persuasion" (Fiske & Taylor,

1984). If attitudes thus have some relation to cognitions, there is no reference at all to values and beliefs; neither is listed in the index. One may argue that organizing social psychology under cognition can be heuristically useful; theories about cognition without any designation of kind would indeed be the most general. The emphasis on "process" serves the same purpose; theories based on process are more general than those based on phenomena defined by content. The problem is that when theories consider knowledge, beliefs, and values as cognitions, they gloss over the fact that the latter are experienced differently and have different behavioral effects. Believing that angels exist and knowing one's telephone number and believing that the world is unjust and the moral value of justice are different states of mind imbedded in different mental and action complexes. Thus the indiscriminate treatment of beliefs, values, and so on as "cognitions" creates a spurious conceptual generality.

Even considering one kind of cognition, there are important distinctions in content. Experiments have shown that common-sense explanations of life events that just happen to a person frequently include beliefs in a personal God, a predestined impersonal fate, good or bad luck, or moral laws (Saffiotti, 1990; Pepitone & Saffiotti, 1997). Although all such nonmaterial agents and powers may be considered "external," to code them as such would conceal their selective attributional function. The evidence is clear that which nonmaterial attribution is made depends in a systematic way on the kind of life event that needs to be explained.

There is another worry about cognitive social psychology. To draw the boundary of the field around individual cognitions and cognitive processes is to deemphasize or ignore the sociocultural context. The focus on endogenous processes involved in the formation and change of cognitions, such as information gathering, categorization, storage, and retrieval, lends itself to the conception of individuals as isolated psychological units. If the task is to understand what makes humans the social animals they are, their relationships to and imbeddedness in multiple social structures will have to be taken into account. The elemental fact is that beliefs, values, and knowledge, including linguistic grammars, are partly or entirely *shared*. What's in a person's head and how and in what circumstances it is used are to some degree dependent on the person's social relationships and the communication channels to which the person is tuned.

The Big Picture

The history of social psychology in the century or so of its existence has been one of impressive growth. Indeed if we take as indices of productivity the number of journals that have been created, the number of articles published in them, the number of books written, the number of Ph.D.'s engaged, the number of scientific meetings convened, the dollar amount of research grants spent, and the number of courses taught, the record is spectacular, especially in the decades I have labeled the golden age. There is little doubt that the conception and practice of social psychology as an empirical science are chiefly responsible for this record.

Yet, remarkably, throughout this period of growth there has been uncertainty as to what social psychology is and what it should be doing. The uncertainty is reflected in the shifts in perspective and paradigm discussed in this chapter and, more explicitly, in the "crisis" literature of the 1970s. Three concerns about the field's accomplishments relative to its aspirations have often been part of the informal talk at meetings. First, most social psychologists would agree that although there is a vast body of findings that bear on experimental hypotheses, the theory-research programs have produced few absolutely general, context-free, and universally valid principles or laws. The state of knowledge is certainly not like that in physics, even the physics of the seventeenth century. Now let it quickly be said that this state of affairs is not all that serious if we consider two arguments: (1) Social psychology has not had enough time to develop great principles representing solid, enduring knowledge; after all, before Galileo there were centuries of observation of natural phenomena, and on that time scale we are not much beyond the earth, water, and fire stage in physics. And anyhow (2) principles of social psychology are not going to be like those in physics; it is by no means decided that social psychology can develop absolutely general knowledge based on dynamics and structures that are invariant across all humankind. In any case, posing the question—Why the absence of general knowledge, given so many findings and confirmed hypotheses?—could produce useful insights about the science of social psychology.

Second, my abbreviated analysis of some major theory-research programs in social psychology suggests that not only did many of them not open up new areas of inquiry and create higher-order theoretical integrations, but after a period of high productivity involving large numbers of researchers across the country they declined to low levels of research activity, some virtually disappearing from the screen. The question is, Why did important areas of theory and research fade? Does the lack of staying power indicate inadequate or unfruitful conceptualization of the research issues or failure of experiments to yield incisive results, or are there other extraneous reasons for the decline of interest?

Third and not unrelated, the theory-research programs that constituted social psychology were incompletely covered; the conceptualization and experiments dealt with selective portions of the phenomena. Bear in mind, of course, that like other sciences in this country social psychology is a voluntary organization of scientists who pursue lines of inquiry according to their interests and payoff strategies; there is no obligation systematically to investigate all the issues in an area of research. Nevertheless, when looked at as a discipline engaged in the pursuit of knowledge in a segment of social science, social psychology shows large gaps in conceptualization and research. My analysis suggests that what was not investigated is as theoretically pregnant as what was. What accounts for the incomplete conceptual analysis and research?

Experimentalism

Paradoxically, at least partly behind the three shortfalls of social psychology is the highly *successful* development of the lab experiment as the principal method of testing hypotheses and the principle source of hypotheses. In the golden age (and now), the verification of hypotheses derived from experimental findings became the primary mission of social psychology; the construction of hypotheses that derived directly from "field" observations of social behavior in commonly identified real-world contexts became less typical. As experimentalism evolved, the major theoretical interest served was less in the experimental variables as such and more in the conceptual changes they represented. Thus when a subject is paid $20 for telling another subject that a boring task is interesting, the magnitude of cognitive dissonance, not the effect on attitudes of selling the task to someone else for a given reward, is being manipulated. As hypothesis-testing procedures, experiments became progressively removed from directly observed phenomena, and hypotheses became increasingly abstract. Of course to begin with, because of the primary role of manipulation, experimental social psychology is limited to the investigation of variables that *can be* experimentally manipulated. The manipulation requirement systematically constrains the field to leave out of theory and research much of what is observed about the influence of culture and social structure.

An overall summary of experimental research would show that findings infrequently lead to an outright rejection of the hypotheses being tested; sometimes findings suggest a correction or more general form of the hypothesis, but in the vast majority of published research articles findings confirm hypotheses. Ultimately, except for serendipitous findings, experiments that confirm hypotheses in a program area become less able to give birth to new, more general theoretical ideas. The limited generativity of experimentation would explain the lack of grand theoretical principles representing enduring knowledge in social psychology, as well as the demise of many theory-research programs. Although there is no doubt that theories can be decisively tested only by experiments, general theoretical ideas are more likely to come from observing or accessing data on people in real life, as inextricable parts of sociocultural groups and categories.

As for the patchy, incomplete analysis of the domains represented by theory-research programs, this deficiency is also due to the exclusive use of experiments. Quite simply, as the method of choice for testing hypotheses, experiments must be selective and focused; it is precisely because of their focus that they cannot contribute comprehensive knowledge about the program domain.

Gratuitous Generalization

The lab experiment, however, is not the only source of the problems under discussion; the philosophy behind experimentalism is also implicated. Most experimental social psychologists consider the field to be an empirical science; they share the view that scientific social psychology is in the business of producing propositions about social human beings that are not only unbiased and reliable but general. As alluded to earlier, hypotheses and theories aim to be general in two ways: over content domains and over samples (Pepitone & Triandis, 1987).

Content generality means that predicted theoretical effects will hold for all empirical instantiations or operational definitions of the independent and dependent variables. As I pointed out earlier, generality is at least implicitly claimed because the hypotheses refer to processes (Fiske & Taylor, 1984). The research literature of the golden age, however, contains few examples where processes represented or expressed by different content are compared. (Is the process of stereotyping the same for racial as for ethnic groups?) Yet at least in the long term, without some estimate of the invariance of hypotheses over variables of different content, the claim of generality must remain gratuitous or a "working assumption."

As to sample generality or universality, the avoidance of comparative studies has tended to preclude the discovery of disconfirming evidence. But since the mid-1980s, toward the end of the golden age, cross-cultural experiments have begun to contribute to discourse about the cultural universality of theories. And as might be expected, the data support both sides of the issue. For example, a south Indian sample tends to attribute responsibility for deviant behavior to situational (cultural) sources more than to personal dispositions, whereas a U.S. sample shows the reverse tendency, in line with the fundamental attribution error hypothesis (Miller, 1984). Evidence also points to an absence of dissonance in cultures where the self is perceived as interdependent (Heine, 1997). In contrast, selectivity in the use of nonmaterial beliefs to explain life events shown by a U.S. sample—the same ordered relationship between six beliefs and a set of standard life events—is also observed in European and Asian samples (Pepitone & Saffiotti, 1997; DeRidder et al., in press). If we interpret such findings correctly, universality has to be estimated empirically by comparative research on a theory-by-theory basis.

It is important to note, however, that if the a priori assumption of universality implicit in most hypotheses in the research literature can be gratuitous, the carrying out of cross-cultural research merely to show that cultural differences exist or to seek support for an ethnopsychology that rejects universals is equally without scientific rationale. When comparative experiments reveal differences between societies, socioeconomic classes, and ethnoreligious and other kinds of groups, investigators have the opportunity to isolate the sociocultural sources of those differences and theoretically account for them.[8]

Social Psychology in the 2000s

Toward the end of its century, social psychology has become a vibrant research discipline organized and conducted by a large number of highly talented, dedicated, and superbly productive people. In my view, it is the dominant vision of experimental social psychology as evolved in the golden age that requires some course corrections that will make it a science of real and whole social human beings. I have pointed to some core problems: the exclusive identification with the discipline of psychology and its concentration on the individual as the unit of analysis, the reductionism once in behaviorism now no less in cognitive social psychology, and the formulation of hypotheses based only on experimental findings along with a corresponding neglect of real-life observations of people in their natural sociocultural settings. The more broad-gauged social psychology of the future will include many heretofore neglected areas of theory and research. For example, as Marx and other social scientists have argued and as ordinary observation confirms, social cognition, intergroup relations, and a variety of other social behavior are profoundly affected by the economic system of a society, especially through the roles and socioeconomic categories the system creates and in consequence of the control over the informational environment exercised by economic interests.

Social psychology cannot continue to ignore the nonmaterial culture either. It does not take a visitor from Mars to notice that people throughout the world create and respond to agents, powers, forces, rays, magical numbers, charms, and so on that do not exist in any objective, physical frame of reference.[9] Ethnographic evidence has long since indicated that such mystical and magical beliefs are the common denominators across world cultures, and sociological research as well as clinically based observation persuasively suggest they serve functions deep in the human psyche (Murdock, 1945; Frazer, 1911; Durkheim, 1915; Freud, 1913/1953). Despite or perhaps because of their special nonmaterial reality, beliefs in gods, fate, stars, moral laws, witches, reincarnation, ESP, Lady Luck, and the like powerfully determine the organized and informal groups that people affiliate with, their helping behavior, their moral judgments, their political attitudes, their inspiration to aggression, their achievement motives, and their explanations of life events (Pepitone, 1997).

It would not be overly optimistic to predict that in the next century social psychology will be engaged with other social scientists in specifying how people in different sociocultural settings affect and are affected by the conflicts brewing among three fundamental determinants of human social cognition and behavior—science and technology, market "forces," and the powerful calls of nonmaterial realities.[10]

Notes

1. This basic finding was replicated using the same experimental procedure and measurements (Cannavale, Scarr, & Pepitone, 1970).

2. In animal and human experiments, Zajonc (1963) proposed a Hullian reinforcement interpretation of the enhancing effects of others' presence on performance.

3. Theory and research on humor is discussed by Allport (1924) but rarely in textbooks from the 1970s to the present.

4. They also foreshadow the concept of "relative deprivation."

5. An exception is the increasingly active relation with political science facilitated by the International Society of Political Psychology.

6. The Research Center for Group Dynamics at the University of Michigan continues theory-research programs on group processes and more recently has initiated a program on cultural social psychology. It should also be noted that there are widely circulated journals that specialize in group and organizational psychology.

7. Of course not all uniformities are the result of social influence. Thus when most pedestrians carry umbrellas during a downpour, it is individual utility that underlies the uniform behavior.

8. The implicit assumption in most of the social psychology research literature that confirmed hypotheses are universal may in part arise from a misinterpretation of the meaning of statistical significance: the confusion that reliability based on repeated random sampling from a hypothetical population means that a finding is valid across the human population.

9. To be sure, the boundary between the material and the nonmaterial is not always clear. The believer in a cherry tree twig's ability to locate underground springs is convinced there is a physical process involved.

10. A general approach to the understanding of how objective science, economics, and institutionalized systems of beliefs are transformed into psychological concepts can be seen in the original work on social representations (Moscovici, 1984). The importance of role behavior in authority structures was illuminated by the ingenious, *verissimo* prison experiment of Zimbardo (1973).

References

Allport, F. (1924). *Social psychology*. Boston: Houghton Mifflin.

_____. (1933). *Institutional behavior*. Chapel Hill: University of North Carolina Press.

_____. (1940). An event system theory of collective action: With illustrations from economic and political phenomena and the production of war. *Journal of Social Psychology, 11*, 417–445.

_____. (1962). A structuronomic conception of behavior. *Journal of Abnormal and Social Psychology, 1*, 3–30.

Asch, S. (1952). *Social psychology*. Englewood Cliffs, NJ: Prentice-Hall.

Asch, S., Block, H., & Hertzman, M. (1938). Studies in the principles of judgments and attitudes. *Journal of Psychology, 5*, 219–251.

Berkowitz, L. (1962). *Aggression—a social psychological analysis*. New York: McGraw-Hill.

Brewer, M. (1997). On the origins of human nature. In C. McGarty & A. Haslam (Eds.), *The message of social psychology*. Cambridge, MA: Blackwell.

Brown, J. F. (1936). *Psychology and the social order*. New York: McGraw-Hill.

Brown, R. (1954). Mass phenomena. In G. Lindzey (Ed.), *Handbook of social psychology*. Cambridge, MA: Addison-Wesley.

Buss, A. (1979). On the relationship between causes and reasons. *Journal of Personality and Social Psychology, 37*, 1458–1461.

Cannavale, D., Scarr, H., & Pepitone, A. (1970). Deindividuation in the small group: Further evidence. *Journal of Personality and Social Psychology, 16,* 141–147.

Cartwright, D., & Zander, A. (Eds.). (1953, 1960). *Group dynamics* (1st & 2nd eds.). New York: Harper & Row.

Dawes, R. (1980). Social dilemmas. *Annual Review of Psychology, 31,* 169–193.

DeRidder, R., Hendricks, E., Zani, B., Pepitone, A., & Saffiotti, L. (in press). Additional cross-cultural evidence on the selective usage of nonmaterial beliefs in explaining life events. *European Journal of Social Psychology.*

Deutsch, M. (1949). A theory of cooperation and competition. *Human Relations, 2,* 129–151.

Deutsch, M., & Krauss, R. (1960). The effect of threat upon interpersonal bargaining. *Journal of Abnormal and Social Psychology, 61,* 181–189.

Dollard, J., Doob, L., Miller, N., Mowrer, O., & Sears, R. (1939). *Frustration and aggression.* New Haven, CT: Yale University Press.

Durkheim, E. (1915). *The elementary forms of religious life* (J. Swain, Trans.). London: Allen & Unwin.

_____. (1897/1951). *Suicide* (J. Spaulding & G. Simpson, Trans.). Glencoe, IL: Free Press.

Festinger, L. (1950). Informal social communication. *Psychological Review, 57,* 271–282.

_____. (1954). A theory of social comparison processes. *Human Relations, 2,* 117–140.

Festinger, L., Pepitone, A., & Newcomb, T. (1952). Some consequences of deindividuation in groups. *Journal of Abnormal and Social Psychology, 47*(Suppl.), 382–389.

Fiske, S., & Taylor, S. (1984). *Social cognition.* Reading, MA: Addison-Wesley.

Frazer, G. (1911). *The golden bough.* London: Macmillan.

French, J.R.P. (1944). Organized and unorganized groups under fear and frustration. *University of Iowa Studies in Child Welfare, 20*(409), 299–308.

Freud, S. (1913/1953). Totem and taboo. In J. Strachey (Ed. and Trans.), *The standard edition of the complete psychological works of Sigmund Freud* (Vol. 13). London: Hogarth Press.

Heckhausen, H. (1967). *The anatomy of achievement motivation.* New York: Academic Press.

Heider, F. (1926). Ding und Medium. *Symposium, 1,* 109–157.

_____. (1958). *The psychology of interpersonal relations.* New York: Wiley.

Heine, S. (1997). Culture, dissonance, and self-affirmation. *Personality and Social Psychology Bulletin, 23,* 389–400.

Hovland, C., Janis, I., & Kelley, H. (1953). *Communication and persuasion.* New Haven, CT: Yale University Press.

Hull, C. (1943). *Principles of behavior.* New York: Appleton-Century.

Hyman, H. (1942). The psychology of status. *Archives of Psychology, 38*(Whole No. 269).

Jones, E., & Davis, K. (1965). From acts to dispositions: The attribution process in person perception. In L. Berkowitz (Ed.), *Advances in experimental social psychology* (Vol. 2, pp. 220–266). New York: Academic Press.

Katz, D., & Schanck, R. (1938). *Social psychology.* New York: Wiley.

Kelley, H. (1967). Attribution theory in social psychology. In D. Levine (Ed.), *Nebraska Symposium on Motivation.* Lincoln: University of Nebraska Press.

_____. (1997). Expanding the analysis of social orientations by reference to the sequential-temporal structure of situations. *European Journal of Social Psychology, 27,* 373–404.

Kelley, H., & Thibaut, J. (1978). *Interpersonal relations: A theory of interdependence*. New York: Wiley.

Klineberg, O. (1940). *Social psychology*. New York: Henry Holt.

Koffka, K. (1922). Perception: An introduction to Gestalt-Theorie. *Psychological Bulletin, 19*, 570–582.

Latane, B., & Darley, J. (1970). *The unresponsive bystander*. New York: Appleton-Century-Crofts.

LeBon, G.(1903). *The crowd*. London: Unwin.

Lewin, K. (1951). Psychology ecology. In D. Cartwright (Ed.), *Field theory and social science*. New York: Harper.

Lewin, K., Dembo, T., Festinger, L., & Sears, P. (1944). Level of aspiration. In J. Hunt (Ed.), *Personality and the behavior disorders* (Vol. 1). New York: Ronald Press.

Lippitt, R. (1940). An experimental study of the effect of democratic and authoritarian group atmospheres. *University of Iowa Studies of Child Welfare, 3*(16), 45–195.

Luce, D., & Raiffa, H. (1957). *Games and decisions*. New York: Wiley.

Maloney, C. (1976). *The evil eye*. New York: Columbia University Press.

Mayer, A. (1903). Über Einzel- und Gesamtleistung des Schulkindes. *Archiv für die gesamte Psychologie, 1*, 276–416.

McClelland, D. (1961). *The achieving society*. Princeton, NJ: Van Nostrand.

McClelland, D., & Atkinson, J.(1953). *The achievement motive*. New York: Appleton-Century-Crofts.

McDougall, W. (1908). *An introduction to social psychology*. London: Methuen.

———. (1920). *The group mind*. New York: Putnam.

Mead, M. (1937). *Cooperation and competition among primitive peoples*. New York: McGraw-Hill.

Messick, D., & Brewer, M. (1983). Solving social dilemmas: A review. *Personality and Social Psychology Review, 4*, 11–44.

Messick, D., & Liebrand, W. (1997). Levels of analysis and explanation of the costs and benefits of cooperation. *Personality and Social Psychology Review, 1*, 129–139.

Messick, D., & McClintock, C. (1968). Motivational bases of choice in experimental games. *Journal of Experimental Psychology, 4*, 1–25.

Milgram, S. (1964). Group pressure and action against a person. *Journal of Abnormal and Social Psychology, 69*, 137–143.

Milgram, S., & Toch, H. (1969). Collective behavior: Crowds and social movements. In G. Lindzey & E. Aronson (Eds.), *Handbook of social psychology* (Vol. 4). Reading, MA: Addison-Wesley.

Miller, J. (1984). Culture and the development of everyday social explanations. *Journal of Personality and Social Psychology, 46*, 961–978.

Miller, N., & Dollard, J. (1941). *Social learning and imitation*. New Haven, CT: Yale University Press.

Moede, W. (1920). *Experimentelle Massenpsychologie*. Leipzig, Germany: Hirzel.

Moore, H. (1921). The comparative influence of majority and expert opinion. *American Journal of Psychology, 32*, 16–20.

Moscovici, S.(1984). The phenomenon of social representation. In R. Farr & S. Moscovici (Eds.), *Social representation*. Cambridge: Cambridge University Press.

Murdock, G. (1945). The common denominator of culture. In R. Linton (Ed.), *The science of man in world crisis*. New York: Columbia University Press.

Murphy, G., Murphy, L., & Newcomb, T. (1937). *Experimental social psychology*. New York: Harper.

Newcomb, T. (1943). *Personality and social change*. New York: Dryden.

Pepitone, A. (1971). The role of justice in interdependent decision-making. *Journal of Experimental Social Psychology, 7,* 144–156.

_____. (1976). Toward a normative and comparative bio-cultural social psychology. *Journal of Personality and Social Psychology, 34,* 641–653.

_____. (1981). Lessons from the history of social psychology. *American Psychologist, 9,* 972–985.

_____. (1997). Nonmaterial beliefs: Theory and research in cultural social psychology. In C. McGarty & A. Haslam (Eds.), *The message of social psychology*. Oxford: Blackwell.

Pepitone, A., & L'Armand, K. (1996). The justice and injustice of life events. *European Journal of Social Psychology, 26,* 581–597.

Pepitone, A., & Saffiotti, L. (1997). The selectivity of nonmaterial beliefs in interpreting life events. *European Journal of Social Psychology, 27,* 23–35.

Pepitone, A., & Triandis, H. (1987). On the universality of social psychological theories. *Journal of Cross Cultural Psychology, 4,* 471–498.

Ross, E. A. (1908). *Social psychology*. New York: Macmillan.

Saffiotti, L. (1990). The selective use of beliefs to interpret life events (Ph.D. dissertation, University of Pennsylvania, Philadelphia).

Sherif, M. (1936). *The psychology of social norms*. New York: Harper.

Steiner, I. (1974). Whatever happened to the group in social psychology? *Journal of Experimental Social Psychology, 10,* 94–108.

Tajfel, H. (1981). *Human groups and social categories*. Cambridge: Cambridge University Press.

Thibaut, J., & Kelley, H. (1959). *The social psychology of groups*. New York: Wiley.

Triplett, N. (1898). The dynamogenic factors in pace-making and competition. *American Journal of Psychology, 9,* 507–533.

Whiting, J., & Child, I. (1953). *Child training and personality*. New Haven, CT: Yale University Press.

Wilson, E. (1975). *Sociobiology*. Cambridge: Harvard University Press.

Zajonc, R. (1963). Social facilitation. *Science, 149,* 269–274.

Zimbardo, P. (1971). The prison experiment (Manuscript, Stanford University).

9 One Hundred Years of Rationality Assumptions in Social Psychology

Robert B. Zajonc

Robert Zajonc argues that social psychology, like psychology itself, is not a cumulative science. In physics, biology, geology, and other branches of the natural sciences, there is a consensus as to "the core subject matter of their inquiry"; in social psychology no such consensus exists. Zajonc believes that this lack of agreement derives from "a schism in our conceptions about the basic nature of the individual"—specifically, the assumption of the rationality of humans. The rationalists, he says, believe that behavior is under the control of voluntary and willful reason; the irrationalists do not. He illustrates this schism by reviewing and classifying some of the most significant social psychological researchers over the past century. These differing views of human nature underlie the noncumulative history of the first century of social psychology. Zajonc maintains that social psychology must come to understand the realms of rationality and irrationality in human nature if it is to proceed in a cumulative fashion.

Two features characterize most sciences. First, they are cumulative. Their progress is fairly linear, and there is a way of knowing what the *next* problems are. In most fields textbook chapters follow in very much the same order. But social psychology (like psychology itself) is not cumulative. You can take any text in social psychology and shuffle the chapters at random without losing coherence. There is no *compelling* order. Zimbardo could rearrange the chapters of his splendid textbook in many different ways without loss of sales or intellectual quality.

Second, the scientists of a given discipline agree about the core subject matter of their inquiry. Physicists agree that physics is mostly about matter and energy, biologists agree that they study life and its processes, demographers agree that they study populations, and geologists agree that they are committed to the study of minerals. This is not to say that in any of these fields scholars believe they have the final answer. Physicists do not believe that they fully understand the nature of matter, and biologists do not pretend fully to know the nature of life. But for the most part they agree that until there is new evidence and new theory, matter and life will be treated as we understand them now. They agree.

But psychologists and social psychologists do not. We have no consensus about the core of our field's subject matter. What does psychology study? In Greece it was the soul. At the break of the century it was psychophysics. Then came consciousness, and in the time of Hull, Skinner, and Spence it was behavior. Now it is the mind. Or is it? Not all psychologists would accept the mind as the central concept because for them it is not directly observable.

What happened to us? Now, it is true that we are young as a field. But not altogether that young. It is true that there were wonderful physics and mathematics in ancient Greece. But there was also some decent psychology and even social psychology. Aristotle (1991), for example, had good insights on social influence in his work on rhetoric and very modern views of recall, construction, and implicit memory. Note the following from his essay "Memory and Recollection" (Aristotle, 1973, pp. 102–103):

> The two phenomena [remembrance and recollection] are not identical, for it is not the same people who have good memories and who have good powers of recollection; as a rule those people remember well who are slow-witted, while on the other hand those excel in powers of recall who are clever and quick at learning. . . . When one actually remembers, he must recognize in consciousness that previously he had heard or perceived or thought of the thing remembered. Hence memory is neither perception nor conceptual thought, but some permanent modification. . . . Hence it is clear to what psychic faculty memory belongs; it belongs to that to which imagination must be assigned.

And his further insights into recollection seem quite up-to-date:

> Recollection is neither the recovery nor the acquirement of memory. . . . Recollection differs from remembering . . . in the fact that, while many of the other animals possess memory, we may say that none of those known, except man, share in recollection. The reason is that recollection is like a syllogism. One who recollects comes to the conclusion that he saw or heard or had some experience previously and . . . recollection accrues only to those that have the power of deliberation, for deliberation is a sort of syllogistic process. (Aristotle, 1973, p. 117)

We are prone to attribute the concept of construction in recall to Sir Frederic Bartlett (1932). But it is clear that he was preceded in all the essentials of remembering by some 2,200 years. And there is no citation of Aristotle in Bartlett's famous book.

I believe that we lack consensus because there is a schism in our conceptions about the basic nature of the individual. This schism may derive from the differing premises that clinical and nonclinical psychologists rely upon. The clinical psychologist necessarily sees the person as a vulnerable bundle of problems, difficulties, and inadequacies. Clinical psychology's task, then, is to work out diagnostic techniques and remedies. Its aim is perfectibility measured by some arbitrary norm. The general or experimental psychologist is more inclined to ask questions about basic processes, about their generality, about how they interrelate to produce some systematic and observable outcomes in the form of action, reaction, and disposition—not about anomalies but about behavioral uniformities.

In social psychology in particular, this schism appears to take the form of a major premise about rationality of behavior. This essay highlights some major exemplars on both sides of the rationality assumption. The difference between the one side and the other depends on how much control over behavior is accorded to voluntary and willful reason and how much to the forces of nature and biological dispositions, often unconscious and uncontrollable. In the extreme, the one persuasion of social psychologists views the person capable of adapting to and subduing the environment by the power of intellect, whereas the other represents the individual in terms of the interplay of elementary processes, such as conditioning, discrimination, generalization, drives, habits, and the more complex elaboration of these processes. Thus, for instance, Fishbein and Ajzen (1975) held that behavior can be predicted by assessing the potential impact of beliefs and attitudes, where "beliefs" were the person's perceptions of reality, operated upon by processes mostly obeying the rules of logic, whereas "attitudes" were mainly preferences based on the other, noncognitive factors. In contrast, the participation of cognitive factors is very much restricted in cases where an attitude or a preference can be and often is accessed instantaneously, outside of conscious awareness (e.g., Wegner & Bargh, 1997). These attitudes, because they are not consciously monitored, must fall into the realm of the irrational. Also irrational are attitudes tinged by wishful thinking, such a demonstrated by Kunda (1990). In her experiments, participants' estimates of probabilities of uncertain outcomes varied with the subjectively experienced utilities of those outcomes.

Mark Lepper suggested to me that there are four different sources of the irrationality assumption. There is strictly *cognitive* or *logical* irrationality. An example is the conjunction fallacy of Tversky and Kahneman (1983), whereby the person judges a conjoint probability of two independent events to be higher than the probability of either. Second, irrational behavior might derive from *biological* causes—instinct or reflex, for example. Freud's concept of the id is the prototypical instance of biologically based irrationality. Third, we have irrational behavior arising when the individual is under severe *social* pressures, such as in the Milgram (1963) experiments. Finally, *personal* values, emotions, and goals can contribute to irrational judgments and decisions. Kunda's (1990) research on motivated reasoning, whereby probabilities of events are inflated by one's own wishes, is a good example.

Gordon Allport (1954, pp. 15–18) devotes a substantial section of his historical essay on social psychology to the question of rationalism and irrationalism in social psychology. He traces our beginnings to the idea of John Locke, who proposed the notion of a "social contract," an arrangement that can protect members of a community from each other such that their passions would not lead to a mutual destruction. He singles out Thomas Jefferson, Alexander Hamilton, James Madison, and *The Federalist* papers for acknowledging the irrational passions yet affirming a possibility of optimal collective outcomes by a proper balancing of passions and reason.

The question of rationality lurks as an implicit assumption in social psychological theories and in the theories of our sibling disciplines, but it is also an explicit concern highlighted already in the nineteenth century by Max Weber (1947) in his theory of organizations. And rationality continues to be a research area that today enjoys a great deal of attention in psychology and economics, most representative in the work of Tversky and Kahneman (1974). In the problems they examined, these authors highlighted mainly biases, that is, deviations and departures from a normatively rational outcome. Gigerenzer and Goldstein (1996) presented data showing considerable reduction in the effects typically reported in the area of heuristics. Their view of the human decisionmaker is more charitable than that of Tversky and Kahneman. However, Camerer (1995) is close to dismissing the various criticisms leveled against these authors. For, he says, "*Destructive* tests, often motivated by skepticism, are designed to check whether apparent anomalies are replicable, robust across settings, or might be due to flaws in experimental design. My opinion is that *some* occasional tests of this sort are essential, but too much energy has been devoted to destructive tests with very little payoff. Not a single major recent (post-1970) anomaly has been 'destroyed' by hostile replication of this sort" (Camerer, 1995, p. 674).

The theory of rational choice has developed to describe both the ways decisions are made (descriptive mode) and the ways decisions should be made (normative mode). A person who is offered two otherwise absolutely equal opportunities, say, a six-hour job paying $1,000 a day and an eight-hour job paying $500 a day, would no doubt choose the former, and the theory of rational choice advises that he should in fact chose the former. The basic concepts of the theory of rational choice compare the costs (six vs. eight hours of work) and benefits ($1,000 vs. $500) of each alternative.

Of course, we do not need an elaborate formal theory to make predictions about decisions as trivial as the above. It goes almost without saying that we confront much more complex and difficult decisions on a daily basis. It is for these complex situations that an extensive body of knowledge has developed (e.g., Dawes, 1988; Raiffa, 1961; Tversky & Kahneman, 1986; VonNeumann & Morgenstern, 1947).

There are countless examples of seeming departure from normative prescriptions of rational choice theory (Green & Shapiro, 1994; Herrnstein, 1990; Tversky & Kahneman, 1974). For example, when subjects in a series of hundreds of trials are asked to guess whether a light that is programmed to go on 70 percent of the time will go on, and they are paid a dime for each correct guess, they do not guess yes 100 percent of the time but, curiously, come fairly close to saying yes 70 percent of the time. That, according to rational choice theory, does not seem optimal because saying yes 100 percent of the time would give them $70 on 1,000 trials, but saying yes 70 percent of the time only $58 (a total of $49 for all correct yesses, i.e., $.7 \times .7 = .49$; plus $9 for all correct nos, i.e., $.3 \times .3 = .09$; e.g., Humphreys, 1939). When rats are confronted with a similar set of probabilities in a maze, they chose the more frequent alternative 100 percent of the time (Brunswick, 1939).

But there are circumstances for which rational choice results in an inferior decision. Suppose there are two candidates A or B, or two products or two courses of action to chose between. Assume that A is preferred to B 60 percent of the time. Now, by a strange set of circumstances, there materializes A', a third candidate (or product or a course of action). A and A' are "twins," identical in every respect. If they are identical, the preferences for them would split: 30 percent, 30 percent, and 40 percent for A, A', and B, respectively. B, the inferior and originally nonpreferred choice, would be selected.

I believe that the rationalist-irrationalist schism in social psychology persists today. In Figure 9.1 I list some major contributors to social psychology over the past 100 years.[1] The time line divides the scholars according to the degree of rationality they accord to humankind. On the left are those who view humans as minimally rational; on the right are those who view human action as the outcome of a more rational and deliberate proce

We begin by celebrating the work of Triplett (1898) on pacemaking and competition, the first experiment in social psychology. Triplett accords important roles to both behavioral and autochthonous factors, as Bruner (1951) termed them. The former depends on cognitive and attitudinal processes, whereas the latter derives from unconscious and deep-seated forces: "The bodily presence of another contestant participating simultaneously in the race serves to liberate latent energy not ordinarily available . . . the sight of the movements of the pacemakers or leading competitors, and the idea of higher speed furnished by this or other means, are probably in themselves dynamogenic factors of some consequence" (Triplett, 1898, p. 533).

"Dynamogenesis" was not a term original with Triplett but one developed in the context of the ideomotor theory of action. Instead of asking how ideas can produce action, scientists simply accepted that they can. In fact, by an appeal to the ideomotor theory of action, Michael Faraday (1853) explained the seemingly magical movement of a small table by spiritualists. It was nothing more, according to his account, than the effect of suggestibility, where the idea of the table's moving occasioned pressure on the hands held on the table without the participants' conscious knowledge. Thus Triplett recognizes the influence of autochthonous effects that derive from some form of mimicry or imitation, but he acknowledges the important motivational role of possible selves (Markus & Nurius, 1986), a concept relying heavily on cognitive representations of the individual's assessment of his or her own potentialities.

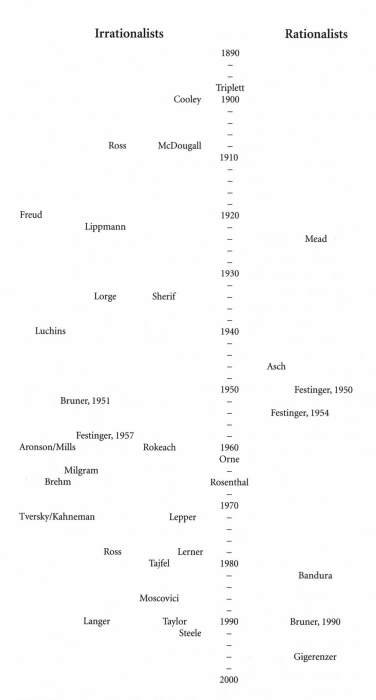

FIGURE 9.1   Some Examples of Rationalists and Irrationalists over the Past Century

The early years of the nineteenth century extended the Platonic concepts of faculty psychology, affect, cognition, and conation to apply to social psychology. At the social and collective level, cognition became sympathy (*feeling* like another person or under another person's influence), suggestion (*thinking* like another person or under another person's influence), and imitation (*acting* like another person or under another person's influence). Cooley's (1902) explanation of imitation relied on a spontaneous instigation to behave in a manner similar to one we observe. Allport (1985, p. 15) describes it very effectively: "The ideomotor theory is no longer 'generally taught.' But its potential value as an explanation of imitation, if it were true, would be great. It says, simply, that all 'ideas' press toward expression. Since many of our ideas come while we are observing other people (or things), it follows that we tend to act out (imitate) our perception of the stimulus pattern."

In 1908 two books, one by McDougall and one by E. A. Ross, both intended as textbooks of social psychology, were published. Both were concerned with suggestion, sympathy, and imitation. McDougall concentrated on induction of emotion, that is, sympathy, whereas Ross emphasized imitation and suggestion. Both authors acknowledged a mixture of autochthonous and behavioral antecedents, and both relied on the idea of instincts. Especially for McDougall, imitation was driven by a nonspecific innate tendency, not completely instinctive because it lacked the urgency of an instinct, but hardwired nevertheless. He defined suggestion as "a process of communication resulting in the acceptance with conviction of the communicated proposition in the absence of logically adequate grounds for its acceptance" (p. 100). Since in suggestion a proposition is accepted without logical scrutiny, suggestion effects are the outcomes of essential irrationality. A derivative of the concept of suggestion conceived in the form of collective aspects of cognition is found today in the notions of intersubjectivity and situated cognition.

Ross (1908) extended notions of suggestion to suggestibility, the tendency of some individuals and "races" to accept the influence of others more readily. The French and the Slavs, according to Ross, were more suggestible, especially in crowds. And of course a suggestible person cannot be a rational person. Both these authors, therefore, must be placed somewhat to the left of the neutral line. And Ross's explanation of social uniformity as deriving from the basic instinct of imitation leaves little room for according rationality to either the individual or the society.

It can hardly be disputed that Freud (1953), more than anyone else, propagated the irrational aspects of the mind. Such defense mechanisms as projection, rationalization,[2] and sublimation are classical forms of irrational behavior driven blindly by the unruly forces of the id, which the ego seeks to modulate. Freud's (1921) social psychology, too, represents an irrational view, for it endows the group leader with father-figure aspects, his followers blindly accepting his authority.

Dewey's contributions to social psychology cannot be ignored. The title of the 1922 edition of *Human Nature and Conduct: An Introduction to Social Psychology* highlights the work's place in the field. After he softened his insistence on the instinctive origins of human and social action, he was one of the first to recognize the power of the situation and the sociality of conduct. "Conduct is always shared," he wrote (Dewey, 1922, p. 17); "this is the difference between it and the physiological process." The consistency of behavior from one instance to another is explained jointly by *habit,* with the individual constituting the unique source of effects, and *custom,* a sort of collective habit evolved by the society. Not only overt action but thinking and reflection are subject to influence by habit and custom, both of which are modulated by the efficiency with which they can assure successful adaptation to their environment. Dewey, then, must be counted among the rationalists.

The concept of stereotyping, forming "pictures in our heads," we owe to Walter Lippmann (1922). Lippmann argued that when experience contradicts the stereotype, the contradictory experience may often be discounted or rejected. The person "pooh-poohs the contradiction as an exception that proves the rule, discredits the witness, finds a flaw somewhere, and manages to forget it" (p. 100). We cannot regard Lippmann as an expositor of human rationality. On the contrary, he offers a view of the individual who oversimplifies reality. Even when the representation of reality is wrong, the person will persist in conserving the stereotype.

G. H. Mead (1934) argued against an instinct of blind imitation. Imitation has to occur in a "conversation of gestures" where each individual is attentive and sensitive to the other's behavior, intentions, motives, views, and so on. Mead, therefore, must be regarded as a rationalist because he views action as occurring in a context processed for its significant information that all the participants weigh, interpret, and respond to.

One of the classical demonstrations of intellectual frailty was that by Lorge (1936). Students were asked to rate sixteen writers. They then received sixteen excerpts ostensibly authored by the writers they had ranked and were asked to rank the excerpts. Lorge found a substantial correlation between the rankings of the segments and the previous ranking of their authors. However, all samples given to the students were written by Robert Louis Stevenson. This outcome is described as a process whereby the individual rates the items not on their own merits but falls prey to suggestibility deriving from prestige (in this case, of the previously ranked writers). This loss of objectivity, termed "prestige suggestion," is thus taken as a manifestation of irrationality.

Better known is Sherif's (1936) experiment on group judgments of the autokinetic movement. The convergence of judgments when they were made in groups is generally regarded as a demonstration of our intellectual vulnerability. A rational participant would ignore the judgments of others and follow the "objective" impression. If there were some objective reality to respond to, there should indeed have been group consensus. But not a different one in each group. One could argue, of course, whether it is altogether irrational to depend on the judgments of others when the items to be judged are quite ambiguous. That, of course, constituted the basis for Asch's (1952) experiments on group judgments of lengths of lines. And contrary to his expectations, there was a great deal of "irrational" conformity. But Asch (1948) always maintained an antagonist position toward the irrationalists. His writing always featured people as superbly humane, and he struggled to disprove claims of false judgments. His experiments on "cognitive restructuring" (Asch, 1948) were designed to demonstrate that acceptance of prestige suggestion is not a blind process; instead, he said, individuals find reasonable and quite logical explanations for contradictions between a target's assertion and what they know of the target's beliefs.

An embarrassing revelation of human (or perhaps only sophomore) weakness in simple computation was offered by Luchins (1942). Participants were asked to solve several of the well-known jar problems: They were given three containers of different capacities and asked to bring a specified amount of water using the three containers. The most complicated problem involves filling one jar, pouring the contents into another either larger or smaller, and so on, until the remainder is equal to the amount of water requested. But among the last problems was one in which participants who had before them jars, of 5-, 15-, and 20-quart capacity were asked to bring 5 quarts of water. To the surprise of the experimenter, some participants persevered in subtracting 15 quarts from the 20-quart jar instead of filling up the available 5-quart jar.

Because Bruner's (1951) important initiative that produced the "New Look" was couched in the context of Freudian defense mechanisms and personality dynamics, it must be categorized on the irrational side. The work on perceptual defense and the influence of values of perception and judgment rendered an image of the individual vulnerable to bias and easy distortion. Above I cited the distinction Bruner made between the autochthonous and the behavioral factors in perception, allowing the autochthonous factors a much closer psychophysical correspondence and assigning departures from this correspondence to behavioral, emotional, and motivational variables. These were instances of Bruner's irrationalist position. His more recent work, especially in his brilliant *Acts of Meaning* (1990), is quite on the rationalist side.

Early work of Festinger (1950) definitely accepts a rational view of the person. The research on social communication specifies hypotheses that show utter rationality. People will direct communication to the member of the group who is most deviant. If the deviant does not accept group consensus, there will be a tendency to reject him or her. Cohesive groups tend toward greater agreement than noncohesive groups. All this makes a lot of good sense. The same can be said of the theory of social comparison (Festinger, 1954), which involves the reasonable proposition that when physical evidence is accessible, individuals will use it. In ambiguous situations, however, especially when it comes to self-judgments, there will necessarily be a greater reliance on social sources of information—social reality. Little need be said about the irrationality of cognitive dissonance processes

(Festinger, 1957). It is not irrational, to be sure, for a person to wish to resolve inconsistencies. But the means whereby inconsistencies are often resolved are quite irrational; for example, an individual may find acceptance into a trivial club more desirable after undergoing a severe initiation ceremony (Aronson & Mills, 1959).

Attribution theory (Jones & Davis, 1965) begins with a clear assertion of rationality—in fact hyperrationality, if the analysis-of-variance logic is assumed to be the standard tool of interpreting the motives of others and oneself. Bandura's (1982) theory of the self and agency must also be placed within the rationalist domain, for his image of the person is of one who seeks to attain reasonable goals by reasonable means. Especially important in reflecting the rationalist position is Bandura's concept of self-efficacy, for efficacy must be judged against some criterion rather than evaluated arbitrarily. And hence it is a rationalist concept.

Rokeach's (1960) concept of open and closed minds, with greater emphasis on the latter than on the former, is an instance of human irrationality. So is Brehm's (1966) idea of psychological reactance, Milgram's (1963) study of obedience, Langer's idea of mindlessness, L. Ross's (1977) fundamental attribution error, and Taylor's notion of self-delusion (1989).

Some conceptions are somewhat difficult to classify. The best examples of such ambiguity are the studies on experimenter bias (Rosenthal, 1966) and demand characteristics (Orne, 1962), the former describing a tendency of subjects to try to confirm the experimental hypotheses to please the experimenter and the latter presenting the participants as behaving so as to accept all the constraints of the experimental situation by guessing what is required of them. In neither case is it clear which is to be considered for rationality: the participant or the experimenter. When they arrange experiments so as to encourage participants to behave in a manner that confirms their hypotheses, experimenters can be viewed as rational only if they are viewed as maximizing their own ends. Yet if we consider that it is at the same time quite unlikely that the false manipulation will remain undiscovered, then the actions that deliberately produce experimenter bias or demand characteristics are patently silly.

If a child who is not rewarded for his performance works harder on a task and persists in doing it for a longer period of time than a child who receives rewards for doing the task (Lepper, Greene, & Nisbett, 1973), can we view the phenomenon as an instance of irrationality? The explanation of the phenomenon rests on the overjustification hypothesis, which holds essentially that being rewarded for something one wants to do in any case must downgrade the attractiveness of doing the given task. Note that if the performance on the task under the unrewarded condition is inferior to that under the rewarded condition, it must mean that the positive effects of the reward are more than obliterated by the overjustification effects. If this is the case, one would conclude a lack of rational evaluation of the situation. For why not accept the reward gracefully as an extra bonus?

The concept of "just world" may seem to lean toward rationality, but if we mean by "rationality" the "command of reason," then regarding one's current suffering as a "pre-payment on a future benefit" (Lerner, Miller, & Holmes, 1976) is not what one would call rational. The same might be said of stereotype threat, the very insightful concept introduced by Steele (1992) and one of the outstanding advances in the study of prejudice. Stereotype threat is the apprehension a member of a minority feels that he or she will be viewed in terms of the negative characteristics stereotyping his or her group. It is certainly rational to be on guard against a derogation. And it is certainly perceptive and rational to expect such overt or covert derogation from members of a majority or a hostile group. But that one's performance should suffer may not be fully justifiable on reasonable grounds. One can understand the irritation and the indignity of the situation. And one can sympathize with the suffering. Yet an equally or even more reasonable response could be to try to contradict the stereotype and to try harder.

Irrationality is not a monopoly of American social psychology. Tajfel (1981) and Moscovici (1983) feature instances of everyday life that show the individual as submitted to his or her "group," "community," "class"—in short, collectivity—and relying in judgment, categorization, evaluation on these group standards. The in-group-outgroup experiments of the Tajfel school of thought show that minimal and trivial group distinctions, such as based on preference for Klee over Kandinsky, may result in an unequal distribution of scarce resources. Fairness, equality, and rationality would have us ignore these preferences in the division of unrelated spoils. Moscovici's (1985) recent revival of LeBon (1895/1995), who extolled rationality of the individual alone over the irrationality of individuals in crowds, places him in the irrationalist camp. His view of lack of individual independence in judgments, decisions, and beliefs and their powerful dependence on social representations (Moscovici, 1983) is also an instance of the irrationalist position.

Some Conclusions

Besides the contributors to this book, a vast number of social psychologists are omitted in this review of rationalists and irrationalists. The scope of this brief note does not allow an exhaustive and detailed account of all social psychology. Necessarily, those listed in Figure 1 are selected, arbitrarily perhaps, but mostly to illustrate some trends that characterize our 100 years of work. I was likelier to choose scholars I believe represent those trends more clearly and conspicuously. For example, I did not include Heider's (1958) work because I was not sure whether to consider it on the rationalist or the irrationalist side. The same for Lewin (1951). Thus those who do not find their names in Figure 1 are in distinguished company. Any other writer would have a different sample.

Second, each name in Figure 1 is presented as a point in a two-dimensional space of time and rationality. Yet in both cases this is an oversimplification. Clearly, the careers of the scholars in Figure 1 span decades—hence the longitude in each case is a range rather than a single point. For some authors, such as Bruner and Festinger, who could be categorized on both sides of the rationality divide, I indicated this by multiple entries. The same is true for the lateral displacement. It, too, could represent a range of rationalities that the given scholar would find acceptable as calibrating rationality. Hence Figure 1 is more a topic for discussion than an affirmation of a historical document.

The 100 years of social psychology as recorded in Figure 1 present in part a cyclical set of swings, some of them arising as criticisms and oppositions to previously affirmed assertions. For example, Asch's work on cognitive restructuring, a rationalist view, was a contrary position to the phenomenon of prestige suggestion, which rendered a picture of humanity vulnerable to trivial influences, incapable of independent judgment, and readily swayed by popular stereotypes. Asch's reaction offered the opposite picture, of a person forced to accept an ostensibly true premise (e.g., that Herbert Hoover found the slogan "Workers of the world unite! You have nothing to lose but your chains" effective and attractive) seeks to find reasonable interpretations of the seeming anomaly. Asch presented the participants' interpretation as keeping the participants' own beliefs intact while guessing about circumstances, conditions, and meanings that would allow the ostensibly true premise to stand. Asch's work on conformity was a reaction to what appears to be a blind tendency to a false consensus that was reflected in Sherif's work. Gigerenzer in turn reacted to the heuristics research that released an avalanche of findings cumulatively affirming virtually without dispute the irrationality of human judgment.

The sheer volume of findings in such area as heuristics, biases, decision theory, cognitive dissonance, prejudice, ingroup bias, nonconscious processes, and a host of others imposes on an intelligent outside observer the view that the gap between the ordinary person's everyday judgment and behavior and what a normative rational model would require is vast. Perhaps this is not terribly surprising. An irrationalist position presents social psychologists with an opportunity to offer paths toward improvement, making them helpful, useful, needed. The rationalist position has only a scholarly merit. It holds that our decisions and judgments are products of an evolutionary development that surpasses all other species by orders of magnitude. It celebrates our minds for their complexity and potential. What then remains to be done is only to discover how such admirable mental capacities have come about, how they work, and how they relate to other psychological functions. Unlike the irrationalist social psychologist, a rationalist social psychologist is not likely to have clients or patients queuing up and seeking help: No help is needed. The rationalist persuasion is a less interesting promise and one that has received much less attention from the press than the irrationalist position. Perhaps that is why the irrationalist side of Figure 1 is more densely populated than the rationalist side.

But of course Figure 1 is not an accurate reflection of what humans are really like. It is merely a reflection of what social psychologists took to be interesting features of humanity that could be subjects of study. Just because we social psychologists seem to pay more attention to mental vulnerability than to mental attainments does not mean that on the whole we humans are deficient in the rationality department. Perhaps the next 100 years will produce knowledge that specifies the circumstances and conditions under which we are irrational and those under which we are not. Perhaps then we will agree on the realms of rationality and irrationality of human nature and proceed in our research in a cumulative fashion. From all we now know, it must be fortunately the case that we humans are both rational and irrational, and that is what makes psychology fascinating.

Notes

1. For irrational reasons, I do not discuss the positions of this book's contributors and would not presume to qualify my own. And of course those whom I have listed are there only for illustrative purposes. Many others—all of us, in fact—could be considered for their rationalist or irrationalist views. But the scope of this chapter does not allow an exhaustive treatment.

2. "Rationalization" was a term first used by E. Jones (1908) to describe Freud's notion that irrational actions can be "justified by distorting the mental processes concerned and providing a false explanation that has a plausible ring of rationality."

References

Allport, G. W. (1954). The historical background of modern social psychology. In G. Lindzey (Ed.), *Handbook of social psychology.* Cambridge, MA: Addison-Wesley.

———. (1985). The historical background of social psychology. In G. Lindzey & E. Aronson (Eds.), *Handbook of social psychology* (3rd ed., pp. 1–46). New York: Random House.

Aristotle. (1973). *De sensu* and *De memoria* (G.R.T. Ross, Trans.). New York: Arno.

———. (1991). *The art of rhetoric* (H. C. Lawson-Tancred, Trans.). London: Penguin.

Aronson, E., & Mills, J. (1959). The effect of severity of initiation on liking for the group. *Journal of Abnormal and Social Psychology, 59,* 177–181.

Asch, S. E. (1948). The doctrine of suppression, prestige, and imitation in social psychology. *Psychological Review, 55,* 250–276.

———. (1952). *Social psychology.* New York: Prentice-Hall.

Bandura, A. (1982). The self and mechanisms of agency. In J. Suls (Ed.), *Psychological perspectives on the self* (Vol. 1). Hillsdale, NJ: Erlbaum.

Bartlett, F. C. (1932). *Remembering.* Cambridge: Cambridge University Press.

Brehm, J. (1966). *A theory of psychological reactance.* New York: Academic Press.

Bruner, J. S. (1951). Personality dynamics and the process of perceiving. In R. R. Blake & G. V. Ramsey (Eds.), *Perception: An approach to personality.* New York: Ronald Press.

———. (1990). *Acts of meaning.* Cambridge: Harvard University Press.

Brunswick, E. (1939). Probability as a determiner of rat behavior. *Journal of Experimental Psychology, 25,* 175–197.

Camerer, C. F. (1995). Individual decision making. In J. H. Kagel & A. E. Roth (Eds.), *The handbook of experimental economics* (pp. 587–703). Princeton, NJ: Princeton University Press.

Cooley, C. H. (1902). *Human nature and the social order.* New York: Scribner's.

Dawes, M. (1988). *Rational choice in an uncertain world*. San Diego, CA: Harcourt Brace Jovanovich.

Dewey, J. (1922). *Human nature and conduct: An introduction to social psychology*. New York: Henry Holt.

Faraday, M. (1853). Experimental investigation of table-moving. *Athenaeum, 1340*, 801–803.

Festinger, L. (1950). Informal social communication. *Psychological Review, 57*, 271–282.

_____. (1954). A theory of social comparison processes. *Human Relations, 7*, 117–140.

_____. (1957). *A theory of cognitive dissonance*. Evanston, IL: Row-Peterson.

Fishbein, M., & Ajzen, I. (1975). *Belief, attitude, intention and behavior: An introduction to theory and research*. Reading, MA: Addison-Wesley.

Freud, S. (1921/1953). Group psychology and the analysis of the ego. In J. Strachey (Ed. and Trans.), *The standard edition of the complete psychological works of Sigmund Freud* (Vol. XVIII). London: Hogarth Press.

_____. (1953). *A general introduction to psychoanalysis*. Garden City, NY: Permabooks.

Gibbard, A. (1990). *Wise choices, apt feelings*. Cambridge: Harvard University Press.

Gigerenzer, G., & Goldstein, D. G. (1996). Reasoning the fast and frugal way: Models of bounded rationality. *Psychological Review, 103*, 650–664.

Green, D. P., & Shapiro, I. (1994). *Pathologies of rational choice theory*. New Haven, CT: Yale University Press.

Heider, F. (1958). *The psychology of interpersonal relations*. New York: Wiley.

Herrnstein, R. J. (1990). Rational choice theory. *American Psychologist, 45*, 356–367.

Humphreys, L. G. (1939). Acquisition and extinction of verbal expectations in a situation analogous to conditioning. *Journal of Experimental Psychology, 25*, 141–158.

Jones, E. (1908). Rationalization in everyday life. *Journal of Abnormal Psychology, 3*, 161–169.

Jones, E., & Davis, K. (1965). From acts to dispositions: The attribution process in person perception. In L. Berkowitz (Ed.), *Advances in experimental social psychology* (Vol. 2, pp. 220–266). New York: Academic Press.

Kunda, Z. (1990). The case for motivated reasoning. *Psychological Bulletin, 108*, 480–498.

Langer, E. J. (1989). *Mindfulness*. Reading, MA: Addison-Wesley.

LeBon, G. (1895/1995). *The crowd*. New Brunswick, NJ: Transaction Publishers.

Lepper, M. R., Greene, D., & Nisbett, N. E. (1973). Undermining children's intrinsic interests with extrinsic reward: A test of the overjustification hypothesis. *Journal of Personality and Social Psychology, 28*, 129–137.

Lerner, M. J., Miller, D. T., & Holmes, J. G. (1976). Deserving and the emergence of forms of justice. In L. Berkowitz & E. Walster (Eds.), *Advances in experimental social psychology* (Vol. 9, pp. 134–162). New York: Academic Press.

Lewin, K. (1951). *Field theory in social science* (D. Cartwright, Ed.). New York: Harper.

Lippmann, W. (1922). *Public opinion*. New York: Harcourt, Brace.

Lorge, I. (1936). Prestige, suggestion, and attitudes. *Journal of Social Psychology, 7*, 386–402.

Luchins, A. S. (1942). Mechanization in problem solving. *Psychological Monographs, 54*(Whole No. 248).

Markus, H., & Nurius, P. (1986). Possible selves. *American Psychologist, 41*, 954–969.

McDougall, W. (1908). *An introduction to social psychology*. London: Methuen.

Mead, G. H. (1934). *Mind, self, and society* (C. M. Morris, Ed.). Chicago: University of Chicago Press.

Milgram, S. (1963). Behavioral study of obedience. *Journal of Abnormal and Social Psychology, 67,* 371–378.

Moscovici, S. (1983). Social representations and social explanations: From "naive" to the "amateur" scientist. In M. Hewstone (Ed.), *Attribution theory: Social and functional extensions.* Oxford: Blackwell.

———. (1985). *The age of the crowd.* Cambridge: Cambridge University Press.

Orne, M. T. (1962). On the social psychology of the psychological experiment: With particular reference to demand characteristics and their implications. *American Psychologist, 17,* 776–783.

Raiffa, H. (1961). *Decision analysis: Introductory lectures on choice under uncertainty.* Reading, MA: Addison-Wesley.

Rokeach, M. (1960). *The open and closed mind.* New York: Basic Books.

Rosenthal, R. (1966). *Experimenter effects in behavioral research.* New York: Appleton-Century-Crofts.

Ross, E. A. (1908). *Social Psychology.* New York: Macmillan.

Ross, L. (1977). The intuitive psychologist and his shortcomings: Distortions in the attribution process. In L. Berkowitz (Ed.), *Advances in experimental social psychology* (Vol. 19). New York: Academic Press.

Schmidtz, D. (1995). *Rational choice and moral agency.* Princeton, NJ: Princeton University Press.

Sherif, M. (1936). *The psychology of social norms.* New York: Harper.

Steele, C. (1992, April). Race and the schooling of black Americans. *Atlantic Monthly,* pp. 68–78.

Tajfel, H. (1981). *Human groups and social categories: Studies in social psychology.* Cambridge: Cambridge University Press.

Taylor, S. E. (1989). *Positive illusions: Creative self-deception and the healthy mind.* New York: Basic Books.

Triplett, N. (1898). The dynamogenic factors in pace-making and competition. *American Journal of Psychology, 9,* 507–533.

Tversky, A. (1969). Intransitivity of preferences. *Psychological Review, 76,* 31–48.

Tversky, A., & Kahneman, D. (1974). Judgment under uncertainty: Heuristics and biases. *Science, 185,* 1124–1130.

———. (1983). Extensional vs. intuitive reasoning: The conjunction fallacy in probability judgments. *Psychological Review, 91,* 293–315.

———. (1986). Rational choice and the framing of decisions. *Journal of Business, 59,* 251–278.

VonNeumann, J., & Morgenstern, O. (1947). *Theory of games and economic behavior.* Princeton, NJ: Princeton University Press.

Weber, M. (1947). *The theory of social and economic organization.* (A. M. Henderson and T. Parsons, Trans.). New York: Oxford University Press.

Wegner, D. M., & Bargh, J. A. (1997). Control and automaticity in social life. In D. T. Gilbert, S. T. Fiske, & G. Lindzey (Eds.), *Handbook of social psychology* (4th ed.). Boston: McGraw-Hill.

10   Afterword: Reflecting on Reflections

Robert V. Levine and Aroldo Rodrigues

In the previous chapters nine legends of experimental social psychology look back on the field they helped to create. The chapters do not fit neatly together. But what else should we expect? If we invite nine authorities to sit around a table, we should be prepared for a many-sided conversation. In fact, we hoped for such a conversation and the present authors did not disappoint us. But although the chapters diverge on many levels, there are several common themes worth noting.

Kurt Lewin

With the exception of Pepitone's detailed review of early social psychology textbooks, there is here little reference—and certainly little sense of intimate connection—to roots going back as far as 100 years or, for that matter, to very much before Kurt Lewin in the late 1930s. When Berkowitz goes back to early textbooks, for example, he begins with Newcomb and Hartley's 1947 *Readings in Social Psychology*. Partly, of course, this simply reflects Berkowitz's choice to focus on the times he lived through rather than those he just read about. But it also speaks to the perceptible roots of the field as it is practiced today. In textbooks much older than Newcomb and Hartley, the tables of contents are not just broader and more interdisciplinary than those of textbooks today, as Berkowitz points out, but seem almost unrelated to the topic areas as defined in current books.

If we look, for example, at a late edition of William McDougall's 1908 *Introduction to Social Psychology* (which Pepitone describes as the "other" pioneer social psychology textbook), we find an almost unrecognizable table of contents (McDougall, 1923). The first section ("The Mental Characters of Man of Primary Importance for His Life in Society") contains the following chapters:

"The Nature of Instincts and Their Place in the Constitution of the Human Mind"

"The Principal Instincts and the Primary Emotions of Man"
"Some General or Non-Specific Innate Tendencies"
"The Nature of the Sentiments and the Constitution of Some of the Complex Emotions"
"The Development of the Sentiments"
"The Growth of Self-Consciousness and of the Self-Regarding Sentiment"
"The Advance to the Higher Plane of Social Conduct"
"Volition"

Section 2 ("The operation of the Primary Tendencies of the Human Mind in the Life of Societies") includes the chapters:

"The Reproductive and the Parental Instinct"
"The Instinct of Pugnacity"
"The Gregarious Instinct"
"The Instincts Through Which Religious Conceptions Affect Social Life"
"The Instincts of Acquisition and Construction"
"Imitation, Play and Habit"
"Theories of Action"
"Derived Emotions"

Virtually none of these subjects appears in today's social psychology texts.

When we leap forward to the tail end of the pre-Lewinian era, 1935, the historical connectedness with today's books is no less equivocal. Examining, for instance, the table of contents to the first *Handbook of Social Psychology* (Murchison, 1935), we see the following chapters:

"Population Behavior of Bacteria"
"Social Origins and Processes Among Plants"
"Human Populations"
"Insect Societies"
"Bird Societies"
"The Behavior of Mammalian Herds and Packs"
"Social History of the Negro"
"Social History of the Red Man"
"Social History of the White Man"
"Social History of the Yellow Man"
"Language"
"Magic and Cognate Phenomena"
"Material Culture"
"The Physical Environment"
"Age in Human Society"
"Sex in Social Psychology"

"Attitudes" (by Gordon Allport)
"Social Maladjustments: Adaptive Regression"
"Relatively Simple Animal Aggregations"
"Social Behavior of Birds"
"Social Behavior in Infrahuman Primates"
"The Influence of Social Situations Upon the Behavior of Children" (by Lois Murphy and Gardner Murphy)
"Experimental Studies of the Influence of Social Situations on the Behavior of Individual Human Adults"

With the exception of Allport's chapter on attitudes and the Murphy and Murphy chapter on the influence of social situations on behavior (we refrain from commenting on the "cross-cultural" chapters), this material seems even less connected to the four editions of the modern *Handbook of Social Psychology* (e.g., Gilbert, Fiske, & Lindzey, 1998) than McDougall's text is to current social psychology textbooks. (It is also notable that the tables of contents in McDougall's text and the Murchison handbook also have very little in common with each other. There was little agreement over the proper subject of study for social psychology within the era between Triplett and Lewin.)

Today's practitioners of social psychology find it difficult to relate to the pre-Lewinian era because it was a such a different field. Echoing Allport (1985), Deutsch points out that early social psychology was mostly armchair theorizing. Turn-of-the-century theorists like Cooley (1902), Tarde (1899), and McDougall (1923) offered programs that, as Deutsch writes, were "grandly ambitious in scope but meager in detail." These are the roots from philosophy and sociology—not the empirical social psychology that defines the field today. The first group of social psychologists who rebelled against this armchair theorizing, turning to a more empirical approach, had an unfortunate tendency to ignore theorizing completely. Not until Lewin and his famous dictum, "There is nothing so practical as a good theory," do we see something of the familiar shape of modern social psychology.

Speaking of Lewin, there he is again. It is striking how often and for such a diversity of reasons—for example, his emphasis on a balance between theory and experimentation, between the pure and the applied, and his methods of teaching and training—the authors refer to Lewin. As Aronson points out, a remarkable number of this book's contributors were part of the first small group in Lewin's graduate program at MIT fifty-plus years ago. Raven recalls how his passion for social psychology was first aroused when he read articles by Lewin during his first social psychology course in 1947—almost precisely the field's midcentury mark. The course was taught by no less a force than Donald Campbell, yet it is Lewin's vision about what psychology could be that dominates Raven's recollection. Variations on Raven's Lewin story run through many of the chapters of this book.

It is noteworthy that this focus on Lewin is typically something of a curiosity to the younger generations of social psychologists. After all, very little of his work is mentioned in today's textbooks; even less is read as original source material. Yet if any single figure should be identified as the founder of modern social psychology, Lewin certainly appears to be that person. More than anything, it seems, it is Lewin's way of thinking about social psychology that has survived. When Aronson's student Shelley Patnoe (1988) interviewed Lewin's students and their students, she found that virtually all of these individuals shared similar attitudes toward graduate student training and had often re-created the very techniques Lewin used at MIT. Few of them, however, realized they were emulating Lewin; his method just seemed natural to them. As we see in Zimbardo's wonderful endnote story, even Alan Funt was quietly influenced (in, of all places, the Home Economics Department at Cornell) by Lewin's way of thinking.

Aronson likes to tell a story about when he once umpired a baseball game. The day after the game he met an acquaintance who had been in the stands watching the entire game. When Aronson asked the man what he thought of his umpiring, the man seemed surprised. He said he had not noticed that Aronson was the umpire or noticed much about the umpiring at all. To Aronson this was the ultimate compliment of a job well done. He had successfully moved the game along without getting in the way. It might be said that in the game of contemporary social psychology Kurt Lewin is Aronson's perfect, invisible umpire.

The other figure who takes a central role in most of the chapters is Leon Festinger. Festinger's research and teachings left an indelible mark on the field. As Gerard points out in his chapter, Festinger's profound impact is all the more stunning in that his work in social psychology, at least the work we remember him for, took place over a period of only about twenty years. But although it may be argued that Festinger's bearing on the course of the field was in its time as profound as Lewin's was in his, Festinger's legacy is met with more mixed feelings. On the one hand, his work—most notably that on cognitive dissonance—endowed a dynamism to social psychology that has come to represent the field at its best. On the other hand, Festinger's rigid emphasis on pure science is now seen as only one possible approach to the study of social psychology. Many of the current criticisms of the field today—for example, an overemphasis on experimentation, a lack of humanism, an unwillingness to focus on the applied—are part of Festinger's legacy. His passionate message represents one aspect of Lewin's grand design, but not all of it. In a sense Festinger may have done his job too well. He captured so many of the best minds of his generation that his brand of social psychology has advanced grandly since his time, but as a result other pieces of Lewin's message may have been left behind. We turn to some of these themes below.

Two Faces: The Tough-Minded and the Tenderhearted

Aside from the depth and direction of our historical roots, several other types of common themes appear in the chapters. One is the balance between the pure and the applied. Related to this is the question of social relevance. Festinger (1980), in his earlier *Retrospections,* addressed these questions, mostly with great pessimism. Festinger was particularly critical of the legacy of the social turmoil of the 1960s on social psychology, which he believed had resulted in a demand for instant solutions to difficult social problems. Festinger believed that these events led researchers to move in either of two directions, both of which were detrimental to the field: Some laboratory experimentalists, he argued, defended against being attacked for being insufficiently socially relevant by working on issues as far enough away from real-life social problems as they could. Others plunged into the real world without a sufficient backlog of scientific knowledge to develop adequate solutions.

The present authors, for the most part, are more sympathetic to the possibility of merging the pure with the applied, and several of them have defined their careers in this way. Raven, for example, recalls how it was the very blend of socially relevant issues and good science that he observed in Lewin (yes, there he is again) and his students that led him to dedicate his career to social psychology. In the Lewinian work on democratic leadership, for example, Raven saw "that it was possible to study in a scientific laboratory a phenomenon that was so complex and socially significant." He also observes how religious ideology, or certainly the sense of social purpose in religion, had a powerful influence in those midcentury years. A number of important figures, including Theodore Newcomb, Rensis Likert, Dorwin Cartwright, and Angus Campbell, had come from a background of liberal religious training. The first two issues of the *Journal of Social Issues,* in fact, were about religious themes: "Racial and Religious Prejudice in Everyday Life." Included, as Raven points out, was a commentary by a Jewish leader, Rabbi Mordechai Kaplan. Many other midcentury social psychologists may not have shared this religious commitment but were nonetheless driven to the field by a parallel devotion to liberal, socially active causes. Raven points out, for example, how before the war many of these pioneer researchers were actively concerned with issues like poverty and the depression and had worked in the labor movement. This theme of liberal, social activism was a common thread in much of the early work in social psychology.

Deutsch describes his career-long attempt to forge a bond between the ways of thinking of Leon Festinger and Ronald Lippitt—the tough-minded, pure science of Festinger and the commitment to applied, socially relevant research by Lippitt. Aronson offers a remarkably similar reflection when he describes how so much of his work has been an attempt to forge a marriage between the ways of thinking of his mentors Leon Festinger and Abraham Maslow: like Festinger, to do experiments as rigorously as possible and, like Maslow, to address issues that might be of benefit to humanity. In his depiction of social psychology as a story of sin and redemption, Aronson argues that social psychology has the unique tools to use the findings from rigid experimentation to better the human condition. Like Lewin, he believes that social psychology offers the possibility of being *both* tough-minded and tenderhearted—a possibility that social psychologists like Deutsch and Aronson have so masterfully achieved in their own work.

Giving Social Psychology Away

A related issue concerns the proper audience for social psychological research. At the Yosemite conference one presenter recalled a story that Milton Rosenberg used to tell: A man goes to a friend and tells him he has a great deal for him—a whole carload of sardines, and, "I can sell it to you for $1,000." The man jumps at the bargain and buys the sardines. He then goes to a third man and tells him he has a great deal for him—a whole carload of sardines, and, "I can sell it to you for $1,500." That buyer turns around and sells the same carload of sardines to yet another man for $2,000. A few hours later, the most recent buyer comes back to his seller and complains: "I went to the railroad yard, unloaded the sardines, opened a can, took a bite and, whew, they were the worst sardines I ever tasted." The seller asks the man how he could be so stupid: "Those aren't eating sardines. They're selling sardines."

Few would question that experimental social psychology has become an increasingly prolific enterprise. There is more research, more publications, more journals, and as we saw in the introduction, even more studies per article. We need not look far to identify the forces that have produced this spiraling flow of publications. The systems of university tenure and promotion press social psychologists, like their colleagues in other fields, to publish as many studies as they can. But what happens to these publications? Do they serve as building blocks for more sophisticated research? How many are ever even read again? In other words, are we just selling each other sardines?

In his famous 1969 address as president of the American Psychological Association, George Miller called on psychologists to "give psychology away" (Miller, 1969). He concluded his speech with these words: "For myself . . . I can imagine nothing we could do that would be more relevant to human welfare, and nothing that could pose a greater challenge to the next generation of psychologists, than to discover how best to give psychology away" (p. 1074). This admonition applies to social psychology as much or more than to any subfield of psychology. How much if any progress has been made in giving psychology away? Berkowitz asks whether the problems we select for study show an overconcern with appealing to others in the field and too little concern with meeting the needs of the public at large.

This brings us back to the issue of the appropriate balance between pure science and applied information. In the best of cases, the pure and the applied feed off one another. They are mutually reinforcing. As already observed, many of the contributors to this book have shown great artistry in achieving this balance. In Deutsch's chapter, for instance, we see how his work—on racial prejudice and desegregation, the NTL, cooperation and competition, conflict resolution, distributive justice—always moved between theory, research, and social practice. Aronson's work on the jigsaw classroom, energy conservation, and AIDS prevention has done the same. Raven points out how one researcher's work on the pure is so often integrally connected with subsequent individuals' work on the applied. His own career project on social power can be seen in seminal research ranging from Milgram's obedience studies to Janis's work on groupthink, both of which have had important consequences for public policy. Much of Zimbardo's work also represents profound examples of controlled research that has had significant social applications: His studies on deindividuation have led to work on reducing urban vandalism, his research on shyness resulted in the establishment of the first shyness clinic, and the famous Stanford prison study has served as a vehicle for prison reform and judicial legislation. To many in the field, this merging of the pure and the applied is social psychology at its best—this science with a heart. We would argue that work like this is exactly what Miller had in mind about giving psychology away without comprising scientific standards. To paraphrase Zimbardo, "for social psychology, application matters."

A Narrowness in Research Strategies

Several authors highlight the need for balancing laboratory research with research in naturalistic settings, arguing that there has been an increasing overreliance on the former. Several chapters argue that this is part of a more general problem of a narrowness in research strategies.

These observations are to some extent verified by objective reviews of publication trends in the field. The current editors and our students recently reviewed trends in the form and content of articles (as demonstrated by impact/citation scores and quality ratings) in the premier journal in the field, the *Journal of Personality and Social Psychology*, between the years 1966 and 1996 (Williams et al., 1998). We found that today a smaller proportion of studies rely exclusively on experimental designs than they did in decades past. But we also found that although longitudinal studies and field research have increased since 1966, the use of both methodologies decreased between 1986 and 1996. A related and particularly troubling indicator that emerged in our review is the continued vast reliance on college students as experiment subjects. David Sears (1986) has observed that social psychology research was based on a wide variety of subjects and research sites prior to 1960 but began to rely predominately on college students as subjects after that. Our analyses show that a little more than 70 percent of studies were based on student subjects in 1966, and this percentage has remained virtually the same since then.

As the chapters in this book point out, there are a number of negative consequences of the narrowness in research strategies. Pepitone writes that sharply focused experiments provide incomplete information; they answer only the specific questions under study, leaving unanswered more comprehensive issues in the topic domain. He argues vehemently that this is one of the problems with relying exclusively on laboratory experiments. Berkowitz, as already mentioned, contends that social psychologists in the past decade are less inclined to move outside the controlled conditions of the laboratory. Aronson points to a certain conservativeness in today's approach to social psychology experiments. He would not be surprised that another finding in our review of *JPSP* trends was that paper-and-pencil questionnaires are far and away the most popular dependent measures in these studies. Their use has actually grown since the early years, and they are now included in nearly 90 percent of all studies.

Of course nearly all of *JPSP* and virtually every other social psychology journal is based on systematic empirical studies. This raises the question of the flow from theory to research. Berkowitz argues that forty years ago the hypotheses of laboratory experiments were more often generated by real-world observations than they are now; most of today's laboratory experiments are stimulated by other laboratory experiments. Raven questions several characteristics of today's massive flow of research—for example, how it often lacks grounding in theory or past research, continues to be overly based on college sophomore subjects, and too often ignores nonexperimental research. Aronson describes the need for "an elliptical flow" from theory to hypothesis, to laboratory experiment, to application, to evaluation, back to theory." Pepitone argues that "theories that are built exclusively on experimental findings and not fed by real-life observation and experience tend to go dry."

Zimbardo argues eloquently for a return to what he believes has become the lost art of people-watching in the process of generating social psychological research. Zimbardo observes that up through the years when cognitive dissonance theory dominated the field, there was a greater appreciation for the effects of meaningful situational manipulations on behavior, for the study of "real on-line behavior: what people do, how they act, what they report feeling or thinking, in response to the particular situation they have encountered. . . . It is not research that begins and ends with what people *say* they would do in a given situation; rather, it is about what they *do*, how they actually behave." Many of today's researchers, he argues, lack the "street smarts" of their predecessors. He points out the importance of social skills, above and beyond the knowledge learned from books, in creating research that makes a difference. It is a tradition, Zimbardo believes, that is now dead.

Aronson expresses related sentiments in his regrets about the decline of "high-impact" methodologies in experimental designs. He points out that high-impact experiments are often difficult and time consuming but have a history of making important contributions. Of course, as Zimbardo points out, not everyone in the field laments the passing of high-impact interventions or those that call upon the "social skills" of experimenters. Zimbardo's observations about the forces that are responsible for the demise of these type of studies—"a cabal of some cognitive social psychologists, human subjects research committees, Protestants, and female social psychologists"—is certain to create controversy. But whatever and whoever may be responsible for the decline of this approach to research, it would be difficult to find a social psychology instructor who does not appreciate the importance of the findings from the best of these high-impact studies of former years. One of the finest examples of such social psychology is perhaps Zimbardo's (1971) own Stanford prison study. Zimbardo would be the first to agree that the situational manipulations in that study exacted a cost in both methodological precision and experimental ethics. But more than twenty-five years after its publication the study not only remains a centerpiece of textbooks in the field but is among the most influential studies in our discipline in its impact on public policy and in the raising of social consciousness about the power of social psychological forces.

Robert Cialdini, well on his way to becoming one of the next generation of legends in social psychology, also argues compelling for more real-life observation in the research cycle (Cialdini, 1980). "If we accept that the task of social psychology is to study normal human behavior," Cialdini observes, "it is odd that so little of current mainstream social psychology *begins* with observation of such everyday behavior"(p. 24). Cialdini calls for a "full-cycle social psychology," in which naturalistic observation and controlled experimentation mutually reinforce one another in repeated cycles: The initial natural observation leads to controlled experimentation, the outcomes of which are tested for external validation in the real world, which then drives further controlled experimentation. Much of Cialdini's own work on social influence (e.g., Cialdini, 1993) demonstrates this possibility.

Several of the current authors express concern with the triviality of so much that is published in social psychology journals. This is, of course, a defensible argument. It is a criticism that has been leveled at the field for many years. It is equally arguable, however, that the triviality quotient in social psychology is not very different from that in other intellectual and artistic fields. It may be seen as a normal by-product of growth and progress. Robert Zajonc (1997) expressed this viewpoint eloquently at the Yosemite conference. Zajonc was responding to Bert Raven's observation, made earlier in the conference, about the exponential increase in research and publications by practitioners of the field and his questioning where it was all leading to. Raven asked whether too much of social psychology is wasted on trivial work. Zajonc remarked:

> In part this is true; but I think this is true in all fields. Think of literature. How many books are produced every year and how many become part of our literature? Think of composition. How many pieces of music are composed each year, and what remains as a worthwhile contribution to this art? Or think of pharmaceutical companies, in which thousand and thousands of experiments are carried out, most of it producing absolutely no results and no expectations, but once in a while they'll hit on something like Prozac and they'll make three billion dollars. So it may be worthwhile for social psychologists, too, to think that way and to hold that among all these

experiments which are produced, some value is obtained. And I do think that a great deal of value, perhaps greater than the Prozac that has been produced by the pharmaceutical companies, is obtained from social psychological experiments. Unfortunately, we are not always given the credit for the findings and for what has been accomplished. Because if we look to the Government, to business, to marketing, to advertising, to military, to education, to health behavior—a variety of areas have appropriated findings from social psychology and they simply become common lore without giving psychology the credit for the origin of these ideas.

The Individual, the Group, and the Social

Several chapters focus on the proper tension among the individual, the group, and the social. Kelley addresses a number of profound issues about the study of the individual and the group in presenting four categories of analysis: the individual or the group, the individual versus the group, the individual from the group, and the individual against the group. Kelley raises many important questions: Should social psychology focus on the individual or the group? In which— the individual or the group—does the image of behavior originate? When do group members stand up against the group? Kelley as well as Pepitone refers to Steiner's (1974) question, "Whatever happened to the group in social psychology?" as an indication of the neglect for the group by social psychologists. Another concern that we see in several chapters is increasing inattention to the "social" in social psychology, the "social" going beyond the group and encompassing society and culture.

Raven recalls how the social psychology program at the University of Michigan drew from both sociology and psychology. The intent of the program, under the direction of Theodore Newcomb, was to create hybrid social psychologists. Upon graduation, however, every student, Raven included, had to make what was to become a familiar choice, one with major consequences for one's career of study: whether to work in a sociology department or a psychology department. Berkowitz also discusses the division of "social" social psychologists into sociology departments and "psychology" social psychologists into psychology departments. The "psychology" social psychologists, he argues, are more closely identified with the field of psychology than with the fraternity of the social sciences. As a result, Berkowitz argues, the psychology version of social psychology focuses more on "within-the-skin" than "between-skins" matters than ever before. Deutsch describes his career-long emphasis on the effects of cooperation and competition as motivated in part by his belief that these issues are fundamental concerns to a "social" versus an "individual" social psychology. Gerard argues that researchers have forgotten the importance of intrapsychic dynamics in understanding social psychological phenomena. His own turn to psychoanalysis, he observes, is an attempt to reach out for this more complete approach to the field. Pepitone points out how little attention social psychology has paid to other cultures and cultural differences but how rewarding these findings have been when we have done so. Will social psychology in the twenty-first century reestablish its ties with the "fraternity of the social sciences"?

Fragmentation

There is the related issue of whether social psychologists have become overly insulated and narrowly focalized in their studies. Berkowitz observes that we are less interdisciplinary than we once were. He points out how Theodore Newcomb argued for an integration of psychology with anthropology and sociology. Pepitone, in his review of early textbooks, observes that not only has social psychology become increasingly isolated from other disciplines but the discrete experimental programs that define the field—such topics as interpersonal attraction, aggression, attitude change, person perception, and prejudice—are too often disconnected from one another. He believes that the current emphasis on cognitive social psychology has in many ways exacerbated this fragmentation.

This criticism could, of course, be made of most any traditional academic field of study today. But it is also true that social psychology may be particularly prone to the problem of fragmentation. We are reminded of a statement by the anthropologist Paul Bohannon (1990), who argued that the title "interdisciplinary social science" is a redundancy. All worthwhile social science, Bohannon believed, is by nature interdisciplinary. Given the broad territory covered by social psychology, one might expect our field to be a defining example of this statement. But although we do occasionally see an interdisciplinary emphasis in contemporary social psychology, it seems that the vast majority of researchers have their hands full simply trying to integrate the disciplines of social and personality psychology, let alone reach out to other disciplines—or, as Berkowitz and Pepitone point out, to different cultures.

A Field of Men from the United States?

A note on demographics: If the reader had not yet noticed, every member of our dream team is a Caucasian man, and with the exception of Aroldo Rodrigues, every author in this book has spent virtually all of his career in the United States. This sampling was not a casual oversight. Rather, we believe it very much reflects what was the demographics of the power structure of social psychology until perhaps the 1970s. Until the mid-1960s academic social psychology was with rare exceptions a field of white males. It may also be argued that the core of experimental social psychology as it is practiced today in most, although not all, of the world is an American phenomenon. This is not meant as an evaluative judgment but simply an objective observation. A survey of several books in social psychology written by Europeans and Latin Americans indicated that the percentage of references to authors who worked in the United States ranged from 71 to 94 percent (Rodrigues,

1979). Certainly, seminal work in experimental social psychology has been produced in other parts of the world, but the birth, the initial push, and the overwhelming proportion of experiments has come from American social psychologists and non-American social psychologists who did their work in the United
States. It seemed appropriate at this point in the history of the field, then, to focus
this book on experimental social psychology as it developed in the United States.

The omission of women in this volume raises other questions about the development of the field. Although it may be arguable whether one or more important
female social psychologists should have been included in this book, the fact is
that the field has been dominated by males. Ellen Berscheid (1992), for example,
recalls that after receiving her doctorate in 1965 she expected simply to retire
from academic life. She observes that this was the norm for female graduate students at the time, as women were rarely hired for tenure-track positions at universities. She was told, for example, that the University of Minnesota Psychology
Department, where she received her Ph.D., once had a woman faculty member,
"but it just didn't work out." (To the good fortune of social psychology, it did
work out for Berscheid.) Christina Maslach tells a similar story about her first
years in the Psychology Department at the University of California, Berkeley.
Maslach recalls how students would come into her office and ask her to give a
message to Dr. Maslach "because 'he' was apparently not in 'his' office." She describes how she "would see people watching me and hear whispers of, 'Look,
that's the woman'" (Patnoe, 1992, p. 7). At about the period between Berscheid
and Maslach's entries into the university system, the climate for women in academics began to change, and it has changed drastically since. Berscheid in fact argues that one of the most significant changes in social psychology since the mid-
1960s has been the exponential increase in the number of women social
psychologists.

Deutsch in his chapter observes that all of the key students and faculty members in Lewin's Research Center for Group Dynamics at MIT were men, though
most of his students in Berlin had been female. Deutsch raises the provocative
question of what the field of social psychology might look like today if the MIT
group had included a substantial number of women. As we look toward a future
in which women and non-Caucasian American males have begun to play a com-
manding role, answers to these sort of questions will come. It might be interesting in turn to speculate on who might be most likely to be invited to write chapters in a book like this one in fifteen years. How many of these people will be
women? How many will be white males? How many will come from outside the
United States?

History

Finally, in this book about history it is interesting to note the authors' multifac-
eted approaches to the importance and role accorded to historical developments

in the evolution of the field. As a whole, the authors are in general agreement about two aspects of the 100-year birthday of experimental social psychology: First, they perceive the conceptual and methodological roots of contemporary social psychology to be more closely bound to Lewin, who worked a little more than a half century ago, than to Triplett, whose work a century ago we are celebrating. And second, they share a sense that many contemporary social psychologists are relatively illiterate about the history of their field beyond the past two or three decades. It would be interesting to see how today's social psychologists score on a test about the long-term history of the field.

This inattention to early literature in social psychology may be interpreted on a number of levels. One is the cost of not attending to history. Aronson refers to Gerard's (1992) observation that many younger social psychologists seem ignorant of the bulk of research before the 1970s. Raven echoes this observation that many young investigators are not in touch with the older literature. He argues that a consequence of this lack of attention to history is a great deal of wasted time and energy. We hear echoes here of the classic warning from historians that those who do not remember the past are condemned to repeat it. In many ways this book is an attempt to avoid that fate.

In social psychology the problem of negligence of history is further complicated by the lack of attention and rewards for conducting replication research. This shortcoming has long characterized the field and according to objective reviews persists as much today as ever (Williams et al., 1998). Raven points out that ignorance of history leads to much reinventing of the wheel. Without replication, it is also difficult to know which wheels are worth remembering.

None of the authors refers to Kenneth Gergen's (1973) article "Social Psychology as History," and only Pepitone mentions the "crisis" in social psychology the article added to. Gergen, of course, argued that the subject matter of much of social psychology is in many ways more constructively approached through the methods of history than through those of classic science because as a whole that subject matter is primarily a reflection of contemporary history. For example, that the personality profile of social activists in one era does not correspond to the profile in another does not necessarily indicate a lack of reliability in research. Rather, these phenomena are most productively studied as indicators of social change, part of the historical cycle. Research in social psychology needs to draw from the traditions of history and other "nonscience" disciplines. A target of research could be the study of causal sequences across time (see Gergen, 1973 for a more complete description of his argument). If Gergen is correct that the subject matter of social psychology is primarily a historical inquiry, then the field should be held to even higher standards of historical awareness than might be the case for other "sciences."

Zajonc's chapter observes the flow of history in social psychology from a new and profound perspective. Zajonc, too, argues that new work does not build upon earlier work in social psychology as much as it does in many other fields. He believes the body of knowledge in social psychology, as in psychology itself, is not cumulative. But Zajonc's analysis is not concerned with whether researchers are willing to take the time to study historical material. He believes that the noncumulative nature of social psychology results from an important characteristic of the field itself: that social psychologists and other psychologists do not agree about the core subject matter of their discipline. This lack of agreement centers on "a schism in our conceptions about the basic nature of the individual," namely, the extent to which people are perceived to be rational beings. The "rationalists," he argues, believe that behavior is under the control of voluntary and willful reason; the "irrationalists" do not. In his chapter Zajonc reviews and classifies some of the most significant social psychological research of the past century based on this schism of rationality. He makes a strong case that these differing views of human nature underlie the noncumulative history of the first century of social psychology. In a sense Zajonc is suggesting a review of the history of experimental social psychology through a template of historical connectedness.

Concluding Comments

In his book *The Story of Psychology,* the scholar Morton Hunt begins his chapter on social psychology with the question, "What extremely busy and productive field of modern psychology has no clear-cut identity and not even a generally accepted definition?" His answer: "Social psychology. It is less a field than a no man's land between psychology and sociology, overlapping each and also impinging on several other social sciences" (Hunt, 1993, p. 396). As we have seen in the previous chapters of this book, there is more than a kernel of truth in this observation. This absence of a unifying theme as well as a clear boundary between the field and its related disciplines of sociology and anthropology and even a lack of consensus about basic issues of human nature remains a cause for concern for the discipline.

In many ways, however, this ambiguity and breadth have been responsible for the unusually wide range of profound contributions that practitioners in the field have made. One of the net results of our hybrid background is that social psychology casts a remarkably wide net. Unlike our colleagues in the fields of personality psychology and sociology—the first of whom tend to focus on the private, internal functioning of people, the latter on their social groups and institutions—social psychologists are concerned with the give-and-take between individuals *and* the groups that guide their behavior. We study—with no small arrogance—what Lewin called the "life space," the inextricable interchange between the person and the environment. A task of this scope certainly makes it difficult to develop a unifying theme. But if the contributions of the field are not easily ordered, they are no less impressive. Hunt, after reviewing many of these contributions, comes to the same conclusions: that social psychology's "jumbled mass of findings impressively add to humankind's understanding of its own nature and behavior" (1993, p. 433) and that the beneficial applications that have come out of the body of work in our field have been truly remarkable.

Gerard concludes his personal recollections by observing the prominent role that happenstance played at critical points in the course of his career. One wonders how applicable this statement is to the history of experimental social psychology. It has been said that if Newton and Einstein had not made their monumental discoveries in physics when they did, one of their successors eventually would have. In music, in contrast, without Bach it is unlikely the world would ever have heard the Brandenburg concertos. Where does social psychology fit between these extremes? If there were no Lewin or Festinger—or no Aronson, Berkowitz, Deutsch, Gerard, Kelley, Pepitone, Raven, Zajonc, or Zimbardo—how differently might the field have evolved?

Leon Festinger concluded his *Retrospections in Social Psychology* (1980) by describing a scene from the movie of Joyce Cary's (1944) novel *The Horse's Mouth*. The novel centers upon Gulley Jimson, an eccentric artist who has been holed up without permission in an apartment whose owners are away on vacation. Gulley has just completed, unauthorized, a huge mural on the living room wall. He has worked on the mural with a single-minded obsessiveness that has left most of the apartment in ruins. Besides leaving messes throughout, he has pawned everything pawnable in the apartment to finance his creation, buying paints and brushes and paying for models. As he walks out the door of the decimated apartment for the last time, Gulley looks back at the mural—which will later be considered a masterpiece—and comments: "It's not exactly what I had in mind." Festinger remarked that this was very much his own overall evaluation of both the *Retrospections* and the progress of the field of social psychology up to that time.

As we look back on this first century of experimental social psychology, almost two decades after Festinger wrote his words, we personally are less apprehensive. The discipline is certainly not without its problems. But the careers and accomplishments of the nine leaders who contributed to this book give us confidence that we are headed in the right direction. When we look back at these chapters and the work and vision that these nine individuals have brought to experimental social psychology, we can only conclude: "They are exactly what we had in mind."

References

Allport, G. W. (1985). The historical background of social psychology. In G. Lindzey & E. Aronson (Eds.), *Handbook of social psychology* (3rd ed., Vol. 1, pp. 1–46). New York: Random House.

Berscheid, E. (1992). A glance back at a quarter century of social psychology. *Journal of Personality and Social Psychology, 63*, 525–533.

Bohannon, P. (1990). Untitled lecture. California State University, Fresno.

Cary, J. (1944). *The horse's mouth.* New York: Harper.

Cialdini, R. (1980). Full-cycle social psychology. In L. Bickman (Ed.), *Applied social psychology* (Vol. 1, pp. 21–45). Beverly Hills, CA: Sage.

_____. (1993). *Influence: Science and practice* (3rd ed.). New York: HarperCollins.

Cooley, C. H. (1902). *Human nature and the social order.* New York: Scribner's.

Festinger, L. (1980). Looking backward. In L. Festinger (Ed.), *Retrospections in Social Psychology.* New York: Oxford University Press.

Gerard, H. (1992). Dissonance theory: Cognitive psychology with an engine. *Psychological Inquiry, 3,* 323–327.

Gergen, K. (1973). Social psychology as history. *Journal of Personality and Social Psychology, 26,* 309–320.

Gilbert, D., Fiske, S., & Lindzey, G. (Eds.). (1998). *Handbook of social psychology* (4th ed.). New York: Oxford University Press.

Hunt, M. (1993). *The story of psychology.* New York: Doubleday.

Miller, G. A. (1969). Psychology as a means of promoting human welfare. *American Psychologist, 24,* 1064–1075.

McDougall, W. (1923). *An introduction to social psychology* (15th ed.). Boston: John Luce.

Murchison, C. (Ed.). (1935). *A handbook of social psychology.* New York: Russell & Russell.

Newcomb, T. M., & Hartley, E. L. (1947). *Readings in social psychology.* New York: Henry Holt.

Patnoe, S. (1988). *A narrative history of experimental social psychology.* New York: Springer-Verlag.

_____. (1992). Interviews with past-presidents: Christina Maslach. *Western Psychologist, 5*(3), 3–8.

Rodrigues, A. (1979). *Estudos em psicologia social [Studies in social psychology].* Petrópolis, Brazil: Ed. Vozes.

Sears, D. (1986). College sophomores in the laboratory: Influences of a narrow data base on social psychology's view of human nature. *Journal of Personality and Social Psychology, 51,* 515–530.

Steiner, I. D. (1974). Whatever happened to the group in social psychology? *Journal of Experimental Social Psychology, 10,* 94–108.

Tarde, G. (1899). *The laws of imitation* (E. C. Parsons, Trans.). New York: Macmillan.

Williams, R. L., Chua, P., Rodriquez, A. J., Khoo, K. M., Levine, R., & Rodrigues, A. (1998, April). *Research trends spanning four decades of the* Journal of personality and social psychology. Paper presented at the annual meeting of the Western Psychological Association, Albuquerque, NM.

Zajonc, R. (1997, March). *One hundred years of rationality assumptions.* Paper presented at the conference "One hundred years of social psychology," Yosemite National Park, CA.

Zimbardo, P. (1971). *The psychological power and pathology of imprisonment.* A statement prepared for the U.S. House of Representatives Committee on the Judiciary, Subcommittee No. 3: Hearings on Prison Reform, San Francisco.

About the Editors and Contributors

Elliot Aronson was born in 1932 in Revere, Massachusetts. He received a B.A. in 1954 from Brandeis, where he worked with Abraham Maslow; an M.A. in 1956 from Wesleyan, where he worked with David McClelland; and a Ph.D. in 1959 from Stanford, where he worked with Leon Festinger. He is currently professor emeritus at the University of California at Santa Cruz. He has taught previously at Harvard, the University of Minnesota, and the University of Texas at Austin. He has written or edited over 120 research articles and seventeen books, among them *The Social Animal* (1973). His prizes include awards from the American Association for the Advancement of Science and the American Psychological Association, and the Gordon Allport Prize for contributions to prejudice reduction (1981). In 1992 he was inducted into the American Academy of Arts and Sciences. He was honored with the Distinguished Scientific Career Award by the Society of Experimental Social Psychology in 1995. He has served as president of the Western Psychological Association and president of the Society of Personality and Social Psychology.

Leonard Berkowitz, Vilas Research Professor Emeritus at the University of Wisconsin–Madison, grew up in New York City and attended New York schools. After serving in the U.S. Air Force, he received his Ph.D. from the University of Michigan in 1951 and has been on the faculty of the University of Wisconsin–Madison since 1955, although he has also held visiting positions at Stanford, Oxford, Cornell, Cambridge, the University of Western Australia, and the University of Mannheim. Berkowitz was one of the pioneers in the experimental study of altruism and helping but since 1957 has been engaged mainly in studying situational influences on aggressive behavior, using both laboratory experiments and field interviews with violent offenders in the United States and Britain. The author of about 170 articles and books, most of them concerned with aggression, he was also the editor of the well-known series "Advances in Experimental Social Psychology" (Academic Press) from its inception in 1964 to his retirement from that post in 1989. Berkowitz has been president of the APA's Division of Personality and Social Psychology and the International Society for Research on Aggression, was given Distinguished Scientist Awards by the American Psychological Association and the Society for Experimental Social Psychology, and was recently elected to the American Academy of Arts and Sciences.

Morton Deutsch is professor emeritus and director of the International Center for Cooperation and Conflict Resolution at Teachers College, Columbia University. He studied with Kurt Lewin at MIT's Research Center for Group Dynamics, where he obtained his Ph.D. in 1948. He has published extensively and is well known for his pioneering studies in intergroup relations, cooperation and competition, conflict resolution, social conformity, and the social psychology of justice. His work on conflict management, cooperative learning, peace psychology, and the application of psychology to social issues has been widely honored by such awards as the Kurt Lewin Memorial Award, the Gordon Allport Prize, the Carl Hovland Memorial Award, the AAAS Socio-psychological Prize, the Samuel Flowerman Award, the Distinguished Scientific Contribution Award, the Distinguished Research Scientist Award, and the Nevitt Sanford Award. A William James Fellow, he has received the Teachers College Medal for his contributions to education, the Helsinki University Medal for his contributions to psychology, and the doctorate of human letters from the City University of New York. He has been president of the Society for the Psychological Study of Social Issues, the International Society of Political Psychology, the Eastern Psychological Association, the New York State Psychological Association, as well as several divisions of the American Psychological Association.

Harold B. Gerard was born in Brooklyn, New York, in 1923. He had all his early schooling in Brooklyn, including undergraduate studies at Brooklyn College. He was briefly a junior high school teacher until returning to graduate school at Columbia University. He finished his graduate work in social psychology at the University of Michigan, where he was a research assistant and then research associate at the Research Center for Group Dynamics. Leon Festinger was his dissertation sponsor. His first job after graduate school was in the Research Center for Human Relations at the University of Michigan with Morton Deutsch. In 1954 he moved to the Psychology Department of the University of Buffalo. The following year he was in the Netherlands on a Fulbright Fellowship and in 1956 took a job at the Bell Telephone Laboratories. In 1962 he returned to academia in the Department of Psychology at the University of California, Riverside. Six years later he transferred to UCLA, where he has remained ever since. In 1982 he entered psychoanalytic training; he qualified as an analyst in 1992.

Harold H. Kelley was born in 1921 in Boise, Idaho, and at the age of ten moved with his family to California, where his father established a vineyard in Delano. Kelley obtained an M.A. in psychology from Berkeley in 1943, then served in the Aviation Psychology Program of the Army Air Corps until entering MIT in 1946. After completing his Ph.D. at the Center for Group Dynamics (under the direction of Dorwin Cartwright) in 1948, he moved with the center to Michigan and served successively on the psychology faculties there, at Yale, and at Minnesota. In 1961 he went to the University of California, Los Angeles, where he is now professor emeritus of psychology. His major contributions have been the establishment (with John W. Thibaut) of interdependence theory, the early integration of various lines of work into what has become known as "attribution theory," and the application of interdependence concepts to the phenomena of close relationships. His scientific contributions have been recognized by awards from the American Psychological Association, the Society of Experimental Social Psychology, and the Society for the Study of Personal Relationships. His memberships include the American Academy of Arts and Sciences and the National Academy of Sciences.

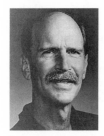 **Robert V. Levine** was born in Brooklyn, New York. He is currently a professor of psychology at California State University, Fresno. Levine received his B.A. from the University of California, Berkeley, and his Ph.D. from New York University. He has received awards for both his teaching and research, including being named the university's "outstanding professor." Levine has been a visiting professor at Universidade Federal Fluminense in Niteroi, Brazil, at Sapporo Medical University in Japan, and at Stockholm University in Sweden. His research has focused on cross-cultural differences in social behaviors and their consequences, particularly concerning the psychology of time, helping, and altruism. His book *A Geography of Time* received the 1998 Otto Klineberg Intercultural and International Relations Award from the Society for the Psychological Study of Social Issues.

 **Albert Pepitone** was born in Brooklyn, New York. During his high school and college years (at New York University), he was a musician and arranger. He switched to psychology after hearing Theodore Schneirla's lectures on the behavior of army ants and went on to Yale for a master's degree. There he worked under Donald Marquis developing a shadowgraphic method of measuring psychological expectancies. He served for thirty months in the U.S. Air Force Psychology Research Program at several posts in the United States and the Pacific theater, where he helped develop combat criteria for validating flight personnel selection tests. Following the war, he worked at the Commission on Community Interrelations in New York City on methods of investigating prejudice. It was at CCI that Pepitone met Kurt Lewin, who invited him to the MIT Research Center for Group Dynamics. After Lewin's death, Pepitone moved with the center to the University of Michigan, where he finished his Ph.D. dissertation project under the direction of Leon Festinger. After postdoctoral work with Theodore Newcomb and Dorwin Cartwright, Pepitone moved to the Department of Psychology at the University of Pennsylvania. His research interests and publications have ranged from social perception and cognitive processes to group dynamics and culture. He has been president of several divisions of the APA and vice-president of the Interamerican Society of Psychology. He has received several honors for contributions to social psychology, including the Lewin Prize by the New York State Psychological Association and election to the Indian National Academy of Psychology.

Bertram H. Raven is professor of psychology at the University of California, Los Angeles. He received his B.A. and M.A. degrees from Ohio State University and his Ph.D. in social psychology from the University of Michigan. While at Michigan, he was associated with the Research Center for Group Dynamics, where he worked closely first with Leon Festinger and later with John R. French Jr., with whom he developed the bases of power model. Though he has carried out research in various areas of social psychology, he has devoted most of his attention to theory and research on interpersonal influence and social power and has attempted to apply his power/interaction model to issues in health, education, school consultation, political behavior, and religion. Raven has a long association with the Society for the Psychological Study of Social Issues, where he has served as president, member of the council, and general editor of the *Journal of Social Issues*. SPSSI recently awarded him its Distinguished Contribution to SPSSI Award. In 1998 he was selected for the Kurt Lewin Award for contributions toward the integration of psychological research and social action.

Aroldo Rodrigues was born in Rio de Janeiro, Brazil. He did his undergraduate work in Brazil and obtained a master's degree at the University of Kansas. His contacts with Fritz Heider while he was in Kansas led him to switch from clinical to social psychology. He earned his Ph.D. at UCLA, where he worked under Harold Kelley and served as research assistant to Bertram Raven and Richard Centers. He returned to Brazil and taught in private as well as public universities until 1993, when he joined the Department of Psychology at California State University, Fresno. He currently serves as chair of the department. Since 1993 he has also been a visiting professor at Gama Filho University in Rio de Janeiro. He has been president of the Brazilian Association of Applied Psychology, the Latin American Association for Social Psychology, and the Interamerican Society of Psychology and has received the Interamerican Award, among others. He has published six books and more than 120 articles, monographs, and book chapters, most of them in the areas of balance theory, social power, attitudes, and attribution.

Robert B. Zajonc received his Ph.D. from the University of Michigan in 1955. He remained there until his retirement in 1994. During his tenure at the University of Michigan, he served as director of the Research Center for Group Dynamics and director of the Institute for Social Research. Zajonc's research spans a number of theoretical problems, such as the nature of the relationship between cognition and communication, emotional influences (including unconscious effects), the emergence of preferences, and the aggregate pattern of intellectual performance scores as they are influenced by changing family patterns. He is the recipient of the APA Distinguished Scientific Contribution Award, the Society for Experimental Social Psychology Distinguished Scientist Award, and honorary doctorates from the University of Louvain and the University of Warsaw. He is currently professor of psychology at Stanford University.

Philip G. Zimbardo, who received his Ph.D. from Yale in 1959, has been professor of psychology at Stanford University since 1968, having taught previously at Yale, New York University, and Columbia University. He is the author of more than 200 research articles and professional works and twenty books, including *The Cognitive Control of Motivation; Changing Attitudes and Influencing Behavior; The Psychology of Attitude Change and Social Influence; Shyness: What It Is, What to Do About It;* and *Psychology and Life,* now in its 15th. edition. Zimbardo is also the creator, writer, and narrator of the twenty-six-episode PBS series *Discovering Psychology.* His research has spanned his interests in persuasion, cults, mind control, violence and the psychology of evil, the social-cognitive bases of madness, and dissonance and affiliation. Zimbardo has won numerous honors for his teaching, research, writing, and media productions. His Stanford prison experiment has become a classic demonstration of the power of social situations.

Index